I0762790

# PRAISE FOR *NAVIGATING YOUR NEXT*

Like a Taylor Swift album, *Navigating Your Next* unfolds in a series of familiar moments leading you to realizations about yourself and your career, providing clarity about what you want and motivation to get it. A work of real craft and insight.

**—Nick Mehta,**
*President and CEO, Gainsight; Board Director, F5 and Pubmatic (Nasdaq)*

In a world obsessed with speed and achievement, *Navigating Your Next* reminds us that real success begins with self-awareness. Julian Lighton weaves together insight, strategy, and humanity to help people move from confusion to clarity—and from career success to personal fulfillment.

**—Debi Hemmeter,**
*Cofounder, LEAN IN; President, Inner Mountain Foundation*

At every stage of his own journey, Julian has taken the opportunity to successfully reinvent himself, setting new goals and accepting new challenges. And he has done this while remaining curious, direct, and open—and always brimming with positive energy. I can think of no better guide to navigate your next career move.

**—Paul McNabb,**
*Managing Partner, Episode One Ventures, UK*

This is the book I wish I'd read at twenty-five. To have Julian in my corner would have been invaluable, and I highly recommend his wise and entertaining words to anyone contemplating their next step.

**—Nicky Sargent,**
*Ex-CEO and Chairwoman, The Farm Group (WPP); BAFTA Award Winner*

A refreshingly smart, practical, and inspiring guide to career change. Packed with real-world exercises and tools, this book turns ambition into achievable action. Kudos to Julian for writing the best and most useful book on careers I have ever read.

**—David Kuizenga,**
*Chief Financial Officer, Common Sense Media*

I am lucky enough to have had Julian help me in understanding and getting what I want. You want to read this book.

**—Gimmy Chu,**
*CEO, Nanotech*

Seriously insightful. Julian Lighton has written the best book on understanding careers and navigating them I have ever read.

**—Sylvie Chanel,**
*Presidente Directrice Generale—CEO, Le Revenu, France*

Brimming with insights, guidance, anecdotes, frameworks, and tools, *Navigating Your Next* makes career success practical and achievable. Julian Lighton offers hope that career success isn't just luck or who you know. It's like having an executive coach in book form. I only wish I'd had it thirty years ago!

**—Laura Daley,**
*CEO, Goodstone Group*

A no-nonsense guide that challenges readers to broaden their definition of success, fostering a deeper and more meaningful perspective that can lead to a more fulfilling life. An excellent read for people who feel like there must be something more and just need a few tools to help them on their journey of self-discovery.

**—Charlotte Saulny,**
*CEO, Coaching.com*

I wish I had read this book when I was twenty-two years old! Julian has so many insights that take a lifetime to accumulate but are here for the taking.

**—Steven Fletcher,**
*Board Director, Lee Enterprises and LifeSignals Group; Former MD and Head of Software Banking, GCA*

Wise, clear, actionable, pragmatic advice for discovering and getting what you want out of your career. A must read.

**—Marc Singer,**
*Senior Partner Emeritus and Head of North American Marketing Practice, McKinsey & Company*

I can just see Julian standing in front of a whiteboard, designing concrete next steps with this new book. Clear, actionable, pragmatic advice for discovering and getting what you want out of your career. A must read.

**—Darren Ware,**
*Senior Vice President and Global Lead, Public Sector Partnerships, Mastercard*

*Navigating Your Next* is a book to keep on hand for wise counsel. I am often asked for career guidance, and I can highly recommend this book to gain the insights and clarity needed to energize and focus you in finding your best and brightest Next.

**—Vicky Sargent,**
*Senior Vice President, People and Organization, Siemens Software*

If you are looking for a pragmatic career guide designed to help you discover the best career path, this book is that plus a road map on how to find that fulfilling professional life.

**—Bryan Lamb,**
*Senior Vice President, Manufacturing and Supply Chain, Titleist (Acushnet)*

*Navigating Your Next* offers both a mirror and a map: it helped me reflect on the fulfillment and happiness of a long career and provides the frameworks and inspiration to support others as they navigate their own journeys.

As I look back on a long career and watch my children begin theirs, I'm reminded how essential it is to define success on your own terms. *Navigating Your Next* captures that beautifully. It teaches that happiness is not a finish line, but a habit of perspective.

*Navigating Your Next* reflects lessons I've lived: the measure of a life and career isn't the ladder you climb, but the meaning you make along the way. This is a rare book that helps professionals reconnect achievement with joy and guides seasoned executives to help others.

I've spent decades surrounded by high achievers and learned that accomplishment and contentment don't always arrive together. This book is a thoughtful reminder that success is internal before it is external. It's a guide for anyone ready to move from striving to savoring.

**—Simon Heap,**
*Advisory Senior Partner and Emeritus Head of Software Practice, Bain & Company*

Julian Lighton hits it out of the park.

**—Sasha Bratyshkin,**
*Founder and CTO, Housing.com*

*Navigating Your Next* is an extraordinary book for an extraordinary time. Julian Lighton has created a new *What Color is Your Parachute?* Clear, insightful, pragmatic, and full of practical examples, stories, and lessons. I wish I had had this in my thirties.

**—Heather Simonsen,**
*CEO, Boomerang Medical*

A highly relevant book. With the dramatic acceleration of volatility, uncertainty, and complexity in the workplace, it is increasingly important to keep asking questions about what career success looks like. *Navigating Your Next* provides a great framework and tools to work out the answers that are right for you.

**—Mark Nelson-Smith,**
*Chairman and Nonexecutive Director, Attento, Consolis, and PXGEO*

The best book on careers I have read in twenty-five years. A must read for anyone who wants to be successful.

**—Jeff Vockrodt,**
*CEO, Fair Labor*

Julian shows that navigating what's next isn't about chasing quick fixes but about meeting uncertainty with intention. His writing guides leaders to a more authentic path forward. A timely and wise guide for anyone at a crossroads.

**—Doug Randall,**
*Senior Partner, The Trium Group*

I love this book. It would have been so helpful to me at two or three times in my life as I faced big career transitions. Very clear, actionable, and a good read.

**—Brad Bell,**
*CIO, Qualys*

Everything you would expect from Julian Lighton. An insightful, intelligently written, and complete view of how to manage your career proactively and successfully. The detailed exercises, cases, and stories carry you along. Highly recommended.

**—Dr. Gary Pusateri,**
*CEO, Paradise Genomics*

An encyclopedic, insightful, and powerful view of pursuing success in your career. Bravo! A must for anyone trying to figure out what to do next.

**—Stephen Jones,**
*Chairman, Investment Banking at Panmure Liberum (Ex CEO UK Finance)*

# NAVIGATING YOUR NEXT

# NAVIGATING YOUR NEXT

DISCOVER THE CAREER **YOU WANT** AND THE PATH TO **GET THERE**

JULIAN LIGHTON

Advantage | Books

Copyright © 2026 by Julian Lighton.

All rights reserved. No part of this book may be used or reproduced in any manner whatsoever without prior written consent of the author, except as provided by the United States of America copyright law.

Published by Advantage Books, Charleston, South Carolina.
An imprint of Advantage Media.

ADVANTAGE is a registered trademark, and the Advantage colophon is a trademark of Advantage Media Group, Inc.

Printed in the United States of America.

10 9 8 7 6 5 4 3 2 1

ISBN: 979-8-89188-198-3 (Hardcover)
ISBN: 979-8-89188-199-0 (eBook)

Library of Congress Control Number: 2025925664.

Cover design by Lance Buckley.
Layout design by Ruthie Wood.

This publication is designed to provide accurate and authoritative information in regard to the subject matter covered. It is sold with the understanding that the publisher is not engaged in rendering legal, accounting, or other professional services. If legal advice or other expert assistance is required, the services of a competent professional person should be sought.

Advantage Books is an imprint of Advantage Media Group. Advantage Media helps busy entrepreneurs, CEOs, and leaders write and publish a book to grow their business and become the authority in their field. Advantage authors comprise an exclusive community of industry professionals, idea-makers, and thought leaders. For more information go to **advantagemedia.com**.

02-17-2026 4:26

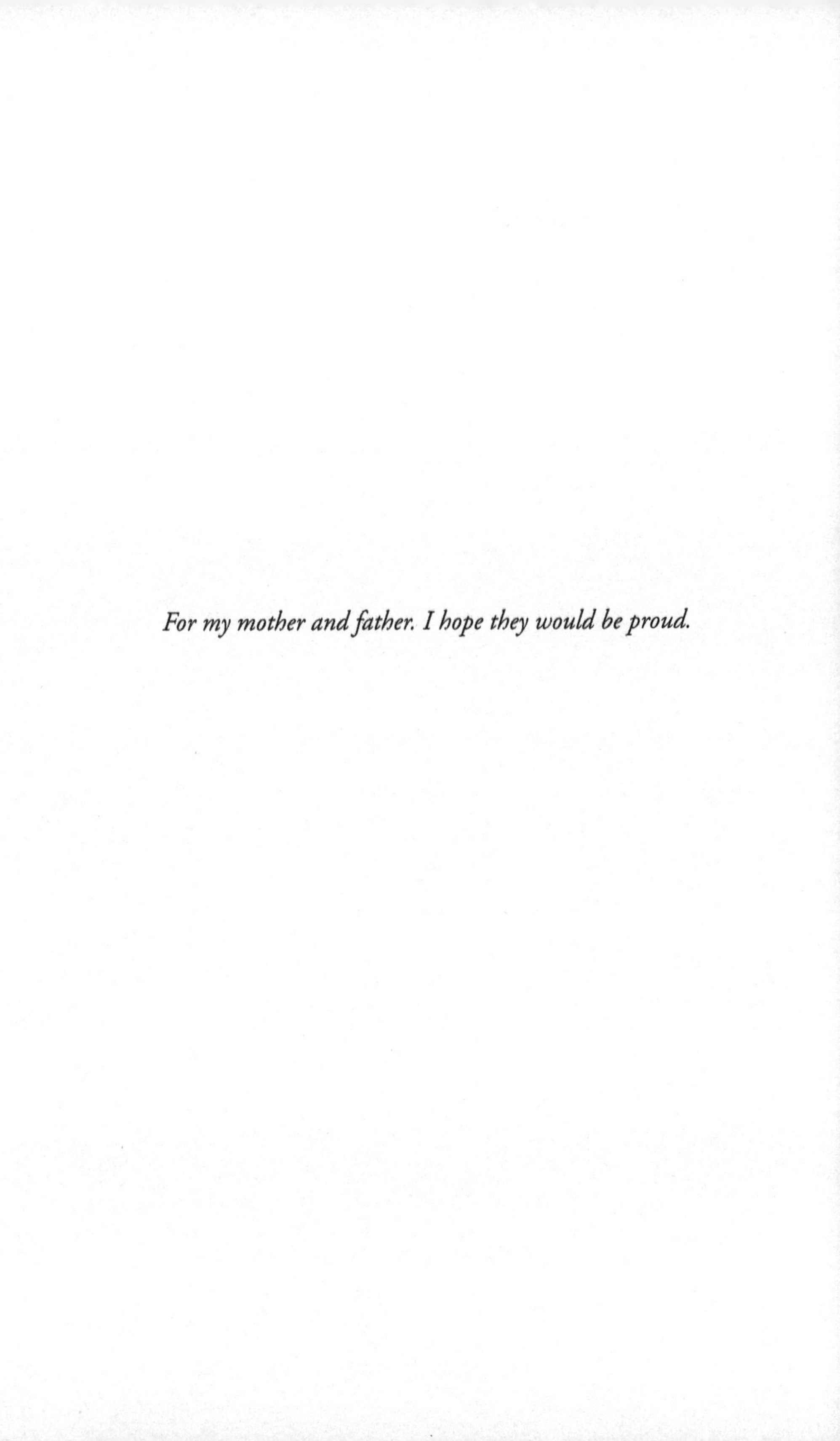

*For my mother and father. I hope they would be proud.*

# CONTENTS

# ACKNOWLEDGMENTS

This book has been a labor of love and would not exist without the insights, input, and support of many thoughtful and generous people I want to acknowledge here.

I am immensely grateful to the early readers and reviewers who gave their time and well-honed critical eyes to help me sharpen and strengthen the ideas within: John Bartol, Quentin Manley, Jazz Mack-Smith, Katrin Schuman, Simon Kelton, Nikki Sargent, Katie Barnfarther, Paul McNabb, Anna Norman, Rui Chen, David Kuizenga, and Chris Grimm. Your feedback made this a better book.

I'm especially grateful to my thought partner and editor, Michelle Tullier, for her questions, her research and experience, our wonderful free-flowing discussions, and her guidance and precision through every draft. I also wish to thank the Forbes editorial and publishing team—Elizabeth Kennedy, Lance Buckley, Kristin Hackler, Alison Morse, Katie Walter, Shandi Thompson, and Kari Johnson in particular—for their support in bringing this project to life.

My professional coaching path has been enriched by brilliant colleagues and collaborators whose ideas and partnership informed this book in ways both subtle and significant. Thank you to Tom Pollock, Michael Hudson, Terry Hackett, Fred Walkover, Lynn Thorsell, Karie

Brown, Quentin Manley, Parsa Naderi, Robby Swinnen, Alex Pascal, Charlotte Saulny, Chris Grimm, Allard de Jong, Georgina Woudstra, Laura Daley, Doug Randall, Monica Chi, and Michael Klein.

To those individuals who shaped my thinking, craft, and career, whether formally or informally, I give thanks: my school teachers Bob Stanley, John Woodward, "Noddy" Hymer, Bob Woolmer, Barry Williams, and George Griffiths; Professors Oliver Taplin, John Feltham, David Ibbotsen, and Roger Smith at Magdalen College; and my colleagues Geoffrey Moore, John Hagel, Marc Singer, Shyam Lal, Avery Lyford, Jonathan Ballon, Paul McNabb, Malcolm Frank, Elby Nash, Chase Nelson, Darren Ware, Darren May, Brad Bell, Enrique Rueda Sabater, Mohsen Moazami, Stefan Bewley, Paul Mountford, Jaime Valles, Peter Hajdu, Mike Evans, Jack Lynch, Jeff Hunter, Paul Weisskopf, Steve Fletcher, Jonathan Smare, Ahmed Shah, Jeff Russakow, Ron Ricci, Gary Moore, and John Chambers.

Deep appreciation goes to the organizations that helped shape both my professional development and my worldview, particularly McKinsey & Company; Cisco Inc; the Hudson Institute; the Team Coaching Studio; the Leadership Circle; Birkman; the Program on Negotiation at the Kennedy School, Harvard University; and Magdalen College at Oxford University.

My coaching clients at McKinsey & Company and my own company, Moo Pie Advisors, inspired and informed much of what's in here. Thank you for trusting me with your journeys.

Special thanks to the staff at Hotel Endsleigh in Milton Abbot, the Post Ranch Inn in Big Sur, The Randolph Hotel Oxford, the Old Parsonage in Oxford, and the Sheraton Grand London Park Lane. Without their kindness and constant fulfillment of my need for coffee, tea, and sandwiches, this book would not exist.

To my close friends Mike Simonsen and Leyl Black, Sylvie Chanel, Joel Pigeon, John Bartol, Quentin Manley, Jazz Mack-Smith, Katrin Schuman, Simon Kelton, Mike Grier, Brad Bell, Jonathan Ballon, Sabra Ballon, Lionel Neave, Tom Russell, Andrew Williams, Ian Atkins, Graham Atkins, Jeremy Atkins, Nigel Chadwick, Sean Carr, Patrick Palmer, Rupert Plumridge, Mick Spicer, Mark and Francesca Nelson-Smith, David Tusa, Stephen Jones and Katie Barnfarther, Susannah Frieze, David Kuizenga, Ron and Rie Collett, Susie and Rob Cornish, Carolyn King, Vicky Sargent, and Jeni Englander, thank you for the encouragement, perspective, and occasional distraction. You kept me grounded and moving forward.

To my dear sister, Bianca, thank you for all you have done to love, educate, support, and enable me over the years. Love always.

Finally, my deepest love and gratitude to Heather and Libbe Simonsen, my family. Your love, humor, emotional support, infinite patience, and practical help (including keeping me fed) carried me through this process.

Oh, and of course, to my furry friends Martha, Hamm, Ellie, and Mutley (Anika).

# INTRODUCTION

> Trevor Noah: Over the last thirty years you have talked to everyone in the world who's been successful in just about any walk of life. What would you say is the one common characteristic that you have found among those successful people?
>
> Oprah Winfrey: People get to where they want to go, because they know where they want to go. Most people don't know where they want to go ... The most important question you can ever ask yourself is: What do I really want?[1]

Most of us will spend approximately ninety thousand hours of our lives working. That equates to a third of the average lifespan. Your time spent working is likely to contribute heavily to your sense of identity, well-being, social circles, and legacy, and to create most, if not all, of your wealth. What do you want to do with this time? Who do you want to be?

---

1 The Daily Show, "Oprah's Advice for Success," YouTube video, October 6, 2023, https://www.youtube.com/shorts/v9NxSOwhOmM.

How you want to spend your ninety thousand working hours is one of the most relevant questions you can ask yourself. This book will help you answer that question.

## What Is This Book About?

If you are trying to discover what you want in your career and grappling with how to get it, this practical and pragmatic guide is for you. If you want to learn how to be successful, this book is here to guide you in building both the skills and the mindset to:

### DISCOVER WHAT YOU WANT IN YOUR CAREER

- Get clarity on what you want in your career.
- Identify skills, habits, and behaviors you need to develop.
- Articulate your credibility and relevance to employers.
- Understand your fit with potential companies or teams.

### GET WHAT YOU WANT

- Harness your motivation and turn your aspirations into goals.
- Focus and stay focused.
- Develop and execute your plan, including building your network to gain access, support, and acceleration toward your goals.
- Negotiate to shape the role and close the deal.
- Understand what success looks like for you and how to celebrate it.
- Shift from being an individual contributor to being a leader of teams.

## Whom This Book Is for

This book is written for professionals who are motivated and want to take a proactive role in shaping their careers and futures. This book is for you if you are on a trajectory where growth, learning, and advancement matter, whether you work—or want to work—in the corporate world, in nonprofit leadership, government, academia, or as an entrepreneur.

*Navigating Your Next* will resonate most with those who are university educated, to at least the undergraduate level or with MBAs or other advanced credentials, and who have already made a commitment to their careers. However, it is not limited to those with college or graduate degrees, as the common thread is a readiness to pause, reflect, and make intentional choices about what comes next.

*Navigating Your Next* is a process primarily focused on people in one of three career stages that are at the core of understanding what you want and getting it:

- **Mid- to late twenties:** forging your career identity, beginning to match your competencies with your desires
- **Early thirties to mid-forties:** shifting from following others' agendas to pursuing your own, discovering what truly motivates you
- **Mid-forties to mid-fifties:** reflecting on the journey you've been on and deciding whether to continue on the same path or repurpose your skills and experiences in new ways

This book and the process are also very useful if you are fresh out of school or in your very first job. You will find valuable insights here to get you started, particularly in steps 3, 4, and 5.

At the other end of the spectrum, those approaching retirement or contemplating entirely new goals in your fifties will also find resonance here. The reflections on success in chapter 6, for example, can inspire new ways of thinking about what your Next might look like in those later stages of life.

In short, this book is for anyone who wants to chart a course toward meaningful, sustainable career success.

## How This Book Is Different

This book is different from the many other career- and habit-focused books already available. I admire other books out there and have mentioned them in the Recommended Resources listings near the end of this book. But *Navigating Your Next* is distinguished in three ways.

First, the book is informed by and based on proven lessons learned from actual real-world experience in world-class institutions, rather than being written by theorists or academics who have not been operational practitioners as consultants, managers, executives, and board members. These insights come from my own thirty-five-year career and the many colleagues I have worked with, the successful executives and industry figures I have interviewed for this book, and the reflections and feedback of the hundreds of people I've successfully coached in career transitions over the last five years.

Second, it is practical and pragmatic, focused on actionable frameworks, exercises, and advice. This is the insight and advice I wish had been taught in school and university and that I would have wanted at three critical life-stage transitions as I grew in my career. I have tested this methodology, the exercises, and the lessons learned with hundreds of professionals and executives, and they work.

Third, this guide is descriptive but not prescriptive. I am not going to tell you—not going to prescribe—what to want. Many other books dictate a direction or a destination. They tell you how to be. I'm not going to name your destination. You own that decision. What I will do is describe how to decide and how to get there.

## Inescapable Life Transitions

We all go through at least four major, inescapable transitions in our lives that inform and shape what we want in our careers and that lead to shifts in our identities. The progression of stages and how they relate to career and identity are shown in figure 1. This is adapted from adult development expert Frederic Hudson, founder of the Hudson Institute and author of the seminal book *The Adult Years*. While our own internal maturity clock can cause some of us to pass through the stages at our own pace, outside the traditional chronological age bands shown (ever known a "late bloomer"?), the stages are inescapable. Three of these stages are addressed by this book and are of the most critical interest in terms of career.

### EARLY ADULTHOOD TRANSITION/CRISIS

In your twenties or thirties, you might find yourself forging your identity, asking, "Who am I? Who am I, separate from my parents and background? What am I good at? What do I enjoy? Which career shall I pursue? Do I want to be an entrepreneur? Do I want to be a manager or an individual contributor?" You are essentially experimenting by doing—trying out different ways of being and working. Luckily, you have time—the one unreplaceable asset—and a lot of it!

## ADULTHOOD TRANSITION/CRISIS

In your thirties or up to your mid-forties, you might ask, "What kind of life am I building, and is it the life I want? Whom am I responsible for, and what are our collective goals? Why am I doing the job I'm doing? Should I do something different? Do I have the work-life balance I want? Which skills do I want to develop? What does success look like for me? How do I succeed?" You have time, resources, and competency, so what now? You are renewing your identity as a result of the experiences you have had so far together with external factors that influence you (marriage, children, home ownership, travel, etc.), as well as internal growth you've experienced. Updating this identity for yourself and others is crucial, or else you and your reference group will get stuck in the image of you as an earlier version of your identity. It is hard to be an astronaut when you still think of yourself as an undergraduate or when others know you as that!

## MID-LIFE TRANSITION/CRISIS

In your forties to mid-fifties, the questions may shift to "Is this it? Is it time to let go of responsibility for others? Should I free up time for other interests? Am I ready for a transition of purpose? Am I doing the right thing? What is meaningful to me? Should I do something different—a second career? Can I do better?" You have experience, resources, and, hopefully, wisdom. What will you do? Once again, your identity is in flux, and you have the power to shape a new one for yourself. This time, it is for keeps. Time's arrow heads in one direction, and this opportunity to ask what you want in your career and to define yourself again is crucial.

## Figure 1: Typical Life Transition Stages

**The adult journey - We all go through the same four life transitions**

**Focus of This Book**

| | | | |
|---|---|---|---|
| • What am I good at?<br>• What do I enjoy?<br>• What is important to me?<br>• Who do I want to spend my time with?<br>• What can I get paid for?<br>• Which career shall I pursue?<br>• Do I want to be an individual contributor or a leader? | • How can I be more successful?<br>• Do I have the right skills?<br>• Should I do something different?<br>• What kind of life am I building, and is it the life I want?<br>• Who am I responsible for, and what are our collective goals?<br>• What does success look like? | • Can I do better?<br>• Am I successful?<br>• Am I doing the right thing?<br>• What is meaningful to me? Is this it?<br>• Should I do something different—a second career?<br>• Do I have the work-life balance I want?<br>• Should I free up time for other interests? | • What is my identity outside of work?<br>• Is it time to let go of responsibility for others?<br>• What does the world need?<br>• What makes me happy?<br>• Am I ready for a transition of purpose? |

First Act: ~Age 20 - 30

Second Act: ~Age 30 - 55

Third Act: ~Age 55+

Early Adulthood Transition "Forging Your Identity"

Adulthood Transition "From Their To My Agenda"

Mid-Life Transition "Reawaken All That Matters"

Recasting Life Transition "Free of Roles"

Source: Moo Pie Advisors/Hudson Institute

*Adult development expert Frederic Hudson identified these four challenges, or crises, most adults progress through during the three acts of our lives. If you have taken a more circuitous path in life, you might face these challenges outside of the age bands Hudson outlines, and that's OK. Source: Hudson Institute of Coaching, based on Frederic Hudson,* The Adult Years: Mastering the Art of Self-Renewal.

At each of these vital career and life transition points, we need to reassess what it is that we want based on our changing circumstances—family, relationships, financial means, social and professional status, motivations, competence, and more. Our social and physical contexts change to influence our wants and needs. For example, in my twenties, I had few responsibilities. I wanted my career to be fun and glamorous, I wanted to be listened to, and I wanted to have money and status. I had no clear plan but stumbled my way to opportunity. In my thirties, I suddenly felt I needed a career direction and that I wanted a path to progression with status and certain titles, to have control and authority, to get to the top, and, of course, to have money. In my forties, I changed again to want deeper insight and mastery: I wanted success and authority, and still more money.

These were my hopes. But hope is not a strategy. Hope is not a plan. That's where this book comes in.

**No matter your age or stage of life and career, this book is for you.**

No matter your age or stage of life and career, this book is for you.

## Ikigai and Finding Your Next

Your destination might be a career move to a new industry, occupation, or sector of the work world, such as a pivot from corporate to nonprofit. Or your destination could be a job with a different employer or a functional role shift. Your goal might be to advance and grow in your professional life, or perhaps you're looking for the opposite, such as retiring or scaling back your focus on work. Some goals are multifaceted—perhaps a mosaic of paid work with volunteer service, community leadership, and other productive pursuits that go beyond the narrow confines of job and career.

Understanding and being able to pursue what you really want is liberating and empowering. The Japanese have a concept for this called *ikigai*, which is the place where what you are good at, what you love, what the world needs, and what you can get paid for converge. Figure 2 illustrates this convergence. When you identify a path that fulfills all four elements, you've found your ikigai—a career or lifestyle that provides personal satisfaction, financial stability, and a sense of making a difference. Ikigai helps you align your career with your authentic self. It's a reminder that work can be more than a paycheck; it can be a source of purpose and joy.

The journey to finding your ikigai is deeply personal and rarely linear. It's about balancing self-discovery with practical action, remaining open to possibilities, and aligning your career with your values and purpose. While it may take time to pinpoint your ikigai, including lots of reflection, exploration, and even experimentation, the effort is worthwhile: A life guided by ikigai can be both fulfilling and impactful, helping you wake up each day with a sense of meaning and excitement for what lies ahead.

## Figure 2: Ikigai: A Japanese Concept Meaning "a Reason for Being"

*The Japanese concept of ikigai (pronounced "EE-key-guy") is a powerful framework for thinking about purpose and fulfillment. Ikigai refers to the intersection of what you love, what you are good at, what the world needs, and what you can be paid for. It's a way of aligning your skills, passions, and values with a sense of purpose that brings satisfaction and meaning to your life. When at a crossroads in your career, understanding ikigai can bring clarity and direction. Source: Moo Pie Advisors Inc., 2025.*

I did not find my own ikigai until I was fifty, embarking on my fourth career. Now, I "feel" my ikigai each time I experience the satisfaction and fulfillment that come when I sit down to have a conversation with someone I can help. I found my ikigai in service to others. Your ikigai will look and feel different; you might find you actually look forward to getting back to work after a holiday, or you find you would gladly do your work tasks even if they weren't for your job or business. We each carve out our own path that brings us to our own version of ikigai. In my case, the discovery of my ikigai led me to write this book.

## Why I've Written This Book

I have lived the confusion of figuring out what I really wanted in my career and have managed and coached hundreds of others working through their own questions.

I have personally dealt with the internal struggle. Should I be a consultant? A general manager? A functional leader? Mentor? Coach? A combination of those? Don't get me wrong—I've been very successful. And I'm grateful for and proud of that success. However, I realize I have been lucky and successful rather than planful and successful.

I have pursued and won fourteen jobs, from manager to C-level officer at some of the most prestigious public and private companies in the world, including McKinsey & Company, Hitachi, Cisco, TiVo, and CORSAIR, and I've been interviewed for four or five times as many. I've been appointed to seven board director roles—five with for-profits and two with educational charities. I have gained entry to and earned qualifications from the University of Oxford and Harvard University, as well as from two prestigious coaching academies and the Institute of Directors in the UK. I have also mentored and coached more than a thousand executives, seventy-five or more executive and business teams, and several university sports teams.

I spent the first ten years of my career advising clients as a consultant. This meant I always had to be one step ahead of my clients. I had to solve problems. So, my motivation and value were as an advisor. I did not make the decisions, but I wanted to see my advice implemented.

I spent the second ten years of my career as a general manager and functional leader. This meant I was responsible and accountable for outcomes. I had to make decisions. So, my motivation and value were as an operator. But I wanted to broaden my influence and affect the whole playing field.

The third ten years of my career were spent as a head of company strategy, corporate development, and new ventures for billion-dollar-revenue public and private technology companies. I had to coordinate boards of directors and C-suite executives to make decisions collectively. But something was missing.

I had achieved world-class levels of competence and was very well paid for the outcomes I delivered, but I was not fully satisfied. I eventually figured out that the key for me was combining my competency with being of service to others. I wanted to access meaning not just by advising or operating or coordinating, but by coaching. By becoming a coach, I could do what I do well, do something I could get paid for, and do what I love. Sound familiar? I found my ikigai. I took control of my career and started an independent consulting company, Moo Pie Advisors.

## About the Methodology

Beyond my own journey of the last thirty-five-plus years, I have been an observer, often in a hands-on way, as I have led and worked with some of the most talented individuals and teams on earth. I have sought to understand why some individuals and teams are successful in making things happen and reaching goals, while many are not. I can tell you that talent most definitely does not equate to success. Too often, individuals and teams have enormous talent but are unsuccessful. Why? Three core reasons: They either cannot get clear on what they really want, are not prepared to make the difficult decisions and to say no to other opportunities, or they fail in execution. I don't want this to happen to you.

I have therefore put together a steps-to-success methodology for how to get what you want. I have tested this methodology rigorously while coaching more than five hundred highly talented emerging leaders at McKinsey & Company and more than five hundred senior and first-time executives in my private practice. I have tested it while personally managing teams, leading group trainings and workshops, and consulting for organizations. Based on extensive feedback and seeing positive outcomes, coupled with my experiences seeing what works and what doesn't in my own life, I now share that methodology in this book, confident it will work for you as it has for so many others.

## How This Book Is Organized

In *The Hitchhiker's Guide to the Galaxy*, characters Arthur Dent, Ford Prefect, and Zaphod Beeblebrox are able to get from place to place in their adventures as they ponder the meaning of life, the vastness of the universe, and other big mysteries because *The Hitchhiker's Guide to the Galaxy* helps them to always find themselves on the map. This book you are now reading is designed to be a practical hitchhiker's guide for your career. While neuroscience, advanced studies of adult and career development, management science, and other research have informed my methodology and the writing of this book, my ultimate goal here is to give you pragmatic advice, practical tips, and insights based on success.

The seven chapters cover how to think about your reality, your current competencies and the context you have exercised them in, your values and what makes you a fit for certain organizations and teams, and your motivations and beliefs. We will look at how to uncover your aspirations and goals and how to prioritize and sequence them, always keeping watch to ensure your self-limiting beliefs don't get in the way. We will uncover your decision-making style and how to match your career to it. We will use this information to narrow your focus from the possible to the probable, and, further, to what you really want.

Based on this, you can derive a vision of where you want to be in three to four years' time and develop a prioritized, sequenced developmental road map to guide you there. You'll reach waypoints along the journey so that, in a matter of months, you will see real progress toward knowing what you want and getting it.

I share what hiring managers are looking for and how to build and articulate your value proposition on paper, digitally, and in person. I walk you through how to build your network and get support, insights, and opportunities to grow your career and enable you to get what you want.

This book is divided into three parts, covering seven steps to success (see figure 3).

Figure 3: Three Book Parts, Seven Steps to Success

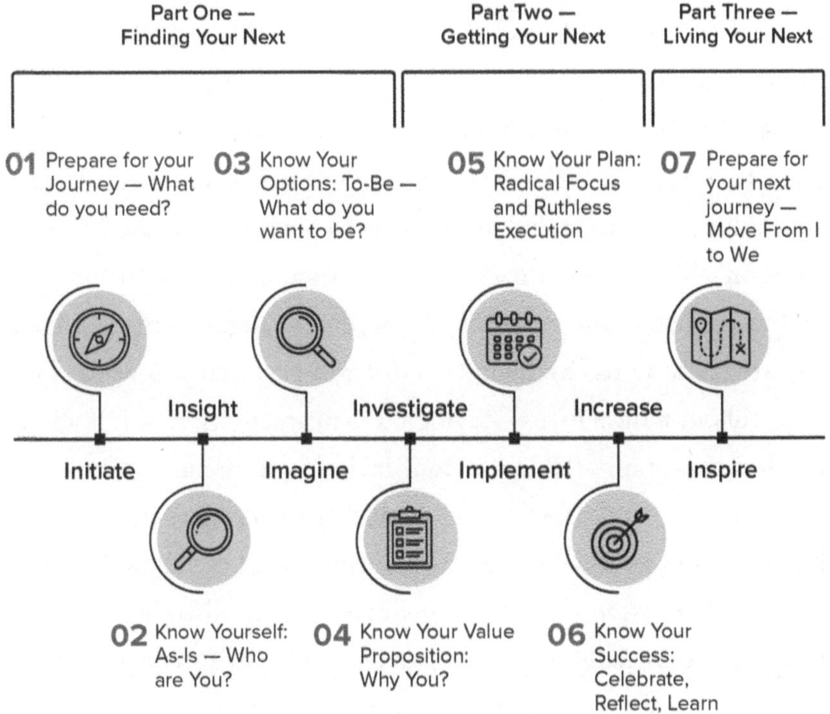


*Each step in this process corresponds with a chapter in the book, so as you read and complete the exercises in each chapter, you'll have the satisfaction of knowing you've completed one more step toward your Next! Source: Moo Pie Advisors Inc., 2025.*

In Part One: Finding Your Next, you will learn how to get to a place of clarity and avoid confusion. You'll do this by using a framework I have developed over the last decade called the Four Axis Framework. The Four Axis Framework is exceptionally useful in helping you understand what reality looks like for you today and starting to compare that reality to what you want in your career and life. It will allow you to determine your competence (what you are good at and in what context) and your fit (where and with whom you are most likely to succeed). This is incredibly important in articulating your value proposition (your credibility and relevance). We will also look at your mindset, the way you view the world, and what motivates you. This will allow you to move from what is possible to what is probable to what you really want.

In Part Two: Getting Your Next, you will continue to follow the Steps to Success model, now focusing on Steps 4 and 5 to identify your value proposition and make a plan to put it into action. You will focus on which competencies you need to acquire, in which contexts, and which habits and practices you need to change—some of which you are likely all too aware of—in order to get what you want. This step is about radical focus—saying no to distractions. And it is about ruthless execution—taking action, including rational experimentation with new things. And you'll look at networking as more than a buzzword and see how relationships, mentors, and even building your skill set will provide access to what you want next. Also covered is the role that six crucially important behaviors play in success—positive mental attitude, curiosity, flexibility, grit (which is made up of persistence and consistency), and kindness.

Finally, in Part Three: Living Your Next, you will focus on the sixth step, celebrating, making meaning out of and sharing your success, and reflecting on what you have learned along the journey to your next destination. And the final step encourages you to make a broader impact beyond yourself by iterating your process. You will be primed to take your learning and action to the next level, applying the principles of my seven-step process to teamwork, organizational goals, and leadership.

## How to Use This Book

To make the most of this book, I hope that you will do as much as you will read. Do complete the exercises, do reflect on the stories and case studies, and do use the recommended resources. This book will help you find yourself on a map, but the opportunities to name the destination and complete the journey are yours alone. So, take ownership of what is next for you, and take responsibility for getting there, knowing you have me (and this book) as your partner along the way.

**For more information about me and my qualifications for writing this book, check out my website and socials.**

This is the book I wish I had had years ago to guide me through the confusion of too much possibility, the blinders of only seeing the probable, and the lack of know-how that kept me from getting where I wanted to be. I am delighted to provide you with *Navigating Your Next* so that you may find clarity, confidence, and commitment when navigating to your next adventure.

# PART 1

# Finding Your Next

# STEP 1

## Initiate: You're About to Embark on a Journey

> **"The beginning is the most important part of the work."**
>
> **—Plato**

So, how do you prepare for the journey to your next career destination?

A highly successful management consultant in her mid-thirties was poised to become a partner in the firm where she had been working fourteen-hour days and traveling every week, in addition to being a recently divorced mother of three. She came to me for coaching in a terrible state—burned-out and frustrated. She hoped to figure out what she really wanted from her career. She had been metaphorically running as fast as she could since high school to be top of the class and to succeed in every role she took on for nearly twenty years. She was driven to continue on her current path by her own perfectionism, competition with colleagues and friends, the expectations of her parents, her own perceived needs for a high standard of living to provide for her children, and her desire for status from working for an elite institution. She knew something needed to change but didn't know what that would look like.

Another coachee came to me earlier in his career, equally frustrated and unclear about his next steps. He had found success in his twenties working for a major accounting firm straight out of his MBA, but he was miserable by the three-year mark. He was unsatisfied with his career choice as a whole and with the specifics of what he did on a daily basis. He couldn't imagine how he could make a change after investing so much in his education, feeling entrenched professionally, and with pressure put on him by his family to succeed. Working with me, he began to see his current reality more clearly and how it was not meeting his needs or wants.

Both of these clients needed to pause and take a closer look at their realities. You will be doing the same in Step 2. This will ensure you are clear about your starting point. I have coached many talented people whose expectations of their abilities or their comparative opportunities were out of kilter with reality, either under- or overestimated. Further, many friends and people I have managed or coached have no idea what recruiters or hiring managers are looking for and how they grade applicants. The same is true of entrepreneurs and their knowledge of what investors or clients are looking for. The result is confusion, frustration, and anxiety, making you less likely to perform at your optimal level.

Until my late twenties, I had no idea how to think about or articulate what I was really good at—what made me stand out. My father would often try to get me to talk about my career plans, but that just made me nervous and embarrassed. I now regret missing those opportunities to get his input and understand his point of view, especially after his recent passing. If I had had some clarity, if I could have talked about where I was, what I was good at, and what I wanted, that would have helped tremendously with my confidence and my relationships with family, friends, and colleagues. I also found myself tense, and even bad-tempered, too often during that period of my life, my underlying anxiety leading to frustration and anger. Confiding in others and opening myself up to their support would have served me well.

## Clarity Versus Confusion

People who are successful and know what they want have clarity. Clarity is a state of understanding and focused thought in which information is easily processed and perceived, while confusion represents a mental state of uncertainty, disorientation, and difficulty comprehending or making sense of something, often leading to difficulty concentrating or making decisions. Very often, because we are overloaded with information or too many wants, we feel disoriented and unable to think clearly, and we struggle to understand the information we're receiving. We have too many possibilities to be able to understand what is probable and what we really want.

Why do we want to avoid confusion? Human beings are very bad at dealing with being confused (see figure 4). A little piece of our brain, the amygdala, which is involved in the fight, flight, or freeze response, is hijacked and begins to reduce our rational capacity and dial up our emotional volatility. This can make us more likely to suffer from fear, anger, defensiveness, doubt, passivity, aggressiveness, or outbursts. All this can put us in a place opposite from excellence, opposite from focus. Confusion also often leads to prevarication or procrastination. We might not be able to prioritize and sequence when confused, so we struggle to focus our efforts and are likely to

**Confusion also often leads to prevarication or procrastination.**

find our energy scattered or dissipated. So, we want to avoid confusion as much as possible, especially when making life-changing decisions.

This was happening to the successful but burned-out management consultant I started telling you about earlier. She was frozen in her current lifestyle and unable to conceptualize taking time off to recover and relax, unable to envision doing something different in her career. She completed my Four Axis Framework (the same one you are going to work through in Step 2), which let her see her current reality and how it was not what she wanted or needed. She started to think about her options—her possibilities that would fulfill more of what she wanted from her career. She took leave from work and went on vacation for several weeks, sailing in the British Virgin Islands with her children. (She had spent a lot of her youth sailing at school and university, and although not a competitive sailor, she loved it.) She decompressed, thought about what she really wanted, and came to some conclusions.

She decided to utilize her competency in running and scaling service businesses. Her desired context was to be an entrepreneur in a small team, in a small organization, with no boss, and with a lifestyle that offered a great deal more time for herself and her children. Her desired work values and culture were to have integrity, health, and freedom. And she aligned her mindset, being motivated by making her family secure and being of service to others, with a goal of being an entrepreneur owning her own business. She also overcame her limiting beliefs in her own capabilities, her need for extrinsic rewards, and her competition with her colleagues for status. She decided to buy a sailboat charter business in the British Virgin Islands. Today, she is successful and happy. She got what she wanted.

My goal is to help you try to be at rest, to not have your amygdala triggered, and to not experience confusion, so that you can do your own conceptualizing of what you want as your next destination.

Figure 4: The Consequences of Confusion

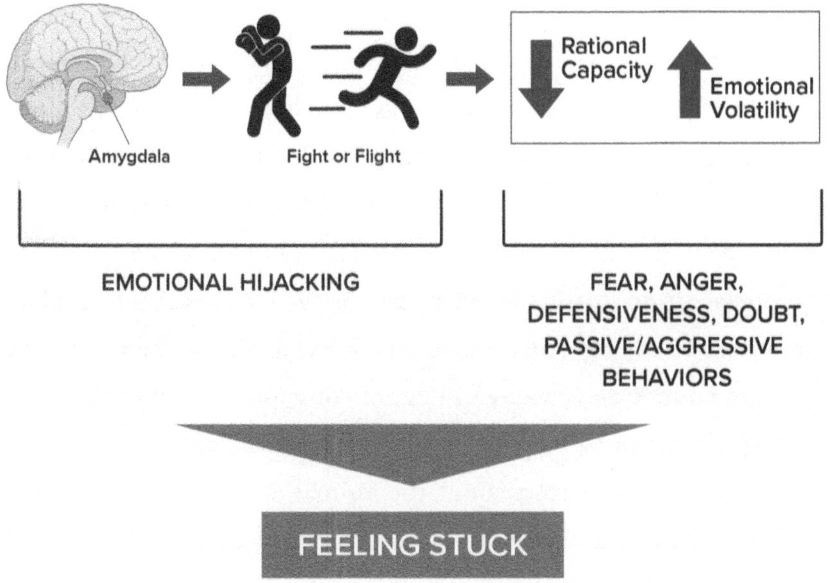


*Being in a confused state hijacks us emotionally, calling up the primitive part of our brains that gets us stuck in a cycle of unproductive behaviors. Source: Moo Pie Advisors Inc., 2025.*

## Reality Versus Expectation

One of the most frequent sources of confusion is the gap between our expectations and reality. Human beings are decision-making machines. We wander through space and time, encountering various stimuli, and we make decisions, mostly unconsciously, through pattern recognition based on our previous experiences.

Imagine you are wandering down a street when you encounter a four-legged animal with big teeth, a tail, and covered in spots. What would you do? Imagine if I told you that you do not experience confusion, you do not panic, and you do not start to fight, flee, or freeze.

Your experience of having met a Dalmatian dog before allows you to make sense of reality and not react as though this animal were a threat to your life—as if it were a leopard. This situation is subconsciously handled based on your existing patterns of learning. When we experience a new situation that we have not encountered before, we try to extrapolate from existing learned patterns. When these fail to explain or rationalize what is going on, we get confused. The gap between what we expect and what is reality causes our conscious mental processes to be hijacked by underlying anxiety, fear, frustration, or anger.

When you first read about the animal above, did you picture a friendly dog or a ferocious wild animal? If the latter, did you feel yourself tense up? I want to make sure you have a firm grasp on reality and not a false set of expectations so that we can be clear about what your starting place is for your journey. That starting point might be a scary wild cat, and thus your journey is a daunting one—maybe even unrealistic or impossible—or it might be a sweet, tail-wagging dog, and your journey feels easy. Either way, I'm here to help you access that starting point.

The most obvious example of how this works in reality is the confusion in your twenties caused by too many opportunities, too many options, too many distractions, too many directions. In most first- and second-world countries, we are taught that education is the key to success. We learn as individuals how to be successful inside academic institutions that prepare us to take exams and absorb vast amounts of data. This is not what employers want or what will make you successful in your career, unless you want to be an academic. So, there is built-in dissonance between the expectation that is set versus what is required in reality—in the outside world of commerce. Many people, both talented and less so, are stunned and confused by this but have no way to analyze and describe themselves and to figure out what they want and what journey they should embark on.

Figure 5: Seven Steps to Success Across This Book

*You will tackle one step to success in each chapter of this book, beginning with Step 1, which is addressed in this first chapter. Source: Moo Pie Advisors Inc., 2025.*

As you learned in the introduction, we will follow a simple methodology consisting of a series of seven Steps to Success (see figure 5). This will guide you from an initial broad range of possibilities to a short list of rational, probable opportunities to finally deciding what you really want. Think of this as an inverted pyramid of your choices that works as follows.

Step 1. Initiate: Prepare for your journey. What do you need? In Step 1, we discuss all the things you will need to prepare, including: sharing your journey with friends and family; selecting waypoints or stepping stones for check-ins and celebrations; designing and preparing for a marathon, not a sprint; understanding that the process will be iterative and not linear; and knowing that it is your journey, no one else's, and that you are 100 percent responsible for your own actions and emotions when pursuing your path (a responsible mindset).

Step 2. Insight: Know yourself. Who are you? What is your identity at this time—internally and to the world? How do you think of yourself and your brand? (Remember that your identity is going to change as you go through life changes, partly as a result of things that happen to you and around you, and partly because you consciously shape your identity over time.) In Step 2, you will use my Four Axis Framework (see figure 6) to hold up a mirror of reality to yourself. The framework asks a series of questions that will help you form an accurate picture of who you are as a person and where you are in your career. We will go through the theory and detailed exercises of this in Step 2. For now, I just want to introduce you to the axes as part of your preparation for the journey. They are:

**Competency:** What skills and capabilities do you have? How good are you at them? What do you enjoy? What have other people noticed you are good at?

**Context:** In what context? What organizations, teams, departments, and companies have you worked in? Which environments did you like?

**Culture:** What are your values? What cultures have you worked in? What makes you feel supported?

**Mindset:** What are your motivations? What are your aspirations and goals? What are your limiting beliefs? What is your decision-making process?

Figure 6: The Four Axis Framework

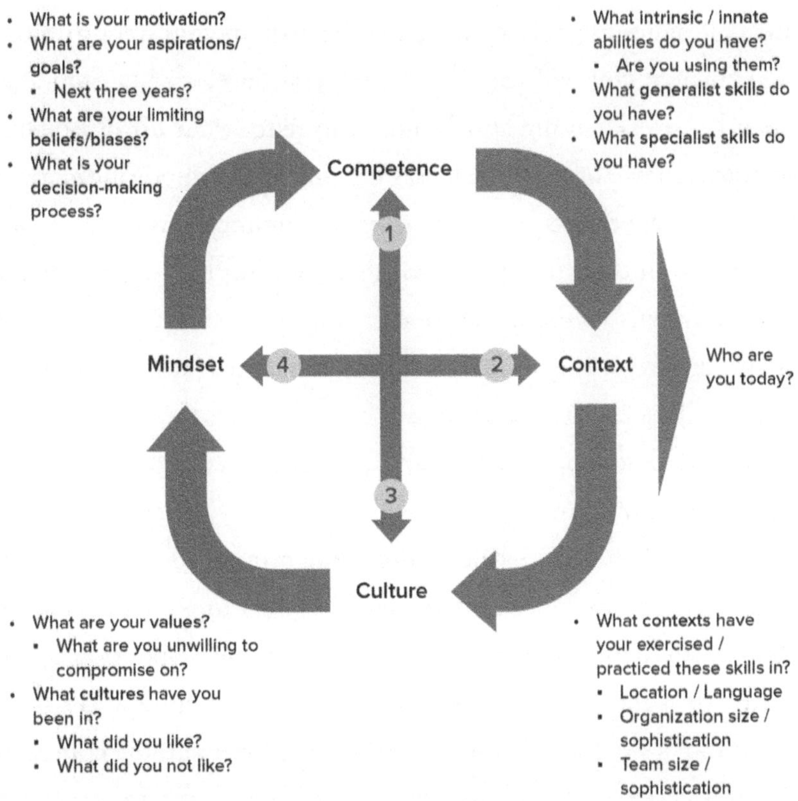


*The Four Axis Framework is your map for taking stock of your current reality, which you will do in the next chapter. And you will go back through it in Step 3, the third chapter, to identify what you want next. Source: Moo Pie Advisors Inc., 2025.*

Step 3. Imagine: Know your options. What do you want to be? In Step 3, we will use the answers you developed in Step 2 for two of the axes, Competency and Context, to help you formulate a list of possible career opportunities. You will then filter them based on probability and pragmatism to get to a shorter list.

For instance, are you really a world-class expert in … ? Do you really have distinctive skills in … ? You'll use honesty and realism to narrow the field of possibility. In terms of the ikigai model, this allows you to think about what you are good at and what you would actually be able to get paid for. You can share this with family, friends, and colleagues to get feedback on the realism of your opportunities.

Further, you will use the answers you developed in Step 2 for the other axes, Culture and Mindset, to refine your list of probable opportunities. Through the lenses of your values, motivation, aspirations, limiting beliefs, and decision-making process, you will be able to think about whether your probable opportunities align with two other elements of the ikigai model: what you want (are passionate about) and what is needed in terms of impact on those you love and care for. This can be turned into a bifocal approach—a set of short-term goals or developmental steps to get you started and a longer-term aspiration or objective.

Step 4. Investigate: Know your value proposition. Why you? In Step 4, you will take your completed answers to the four axes and apply them to form a picture of your current value proposition against what you want. Essentially, this involves examining how close you are to the desired profile for a potential employer and the competencies and keywords, or, if you are an entrepreneur, for an investor or potential clients. My experience, together with polls of headhunters, corporate recruiters, and hiring managers, has revealed that employers are most interested in four factors:

- **Credibility:** Do you have demonstrable competency and mastery (expertise and experience) with examples and references?
- **Relevance:** Beyond credibility, what is your particular angle or specialization that makes you stand out?
- **Fit:** What experiences have you had in environments with teams and organizations, and with cultures/values, to enable you to say that you will be successful?
- **Motivation:** Why would an employer believe you will stay? Why are you motivated to grow, learn, and be successful? Why will you go the extra mile?

This will help you develop a compelling resume, cover letter, and elevator pitch to assist you in asking for what you want. In Step 4 and on my website, you'll find formats for all of these and exercises to help you practice.

Step 5. Implement: Know your plan. What is your focus and action plan? In this step, we will build an action plan that does the following:

- Maps what you want (desired goal) to opportunities (role, industry, function, and location)
- Maps opportunities to channels (e.g., friends and family, headhunters, academics, intermediaries)
- Maps channels to your network and individuals
- Maps individuals to messages (elevator pitch) and desired conversations (what do you want from them?)

We will walk through the principles of responsible mindset, radical focus (to keep you engaged, driving to your goal), and ruthless execution (to work on the granularity of achieving your goals and not mistaking effort for success). Working your plan thoroughly and iteratively will allow you to achieve your goal.

Step 6. Increase: Know your success. How will you celebrate, learn, and reflect? In this chapter, we will ask how you will measure your life. How will you know you have succeeded, and what effect will it have on you? Are you living an identity that you want at this stage of your life? Do others see you for that identity as opposed to being stuck in outdated impressions of who you are and what you do? Many of the entrepreneurs, executives, academics, and politicians I coach have difficulty answering these questions, and so, despite being very successful by almost any measure, they take little joy or satisfaction from their achievements.

Step 7. Inspire: Move From I to We. In Steps 1 through 6, the focus is on clarifying and pursuing what *you* want. But lasting success usually requires working *with and through others.* Whether you're building a business, launching a project, or advancing inside an organization, your progress will hinge on your ability to lead people and teams. So Step 7 introduces the principles of relationship-centered leadership and offers a preview of the team-focused methodologies I'll expand on fully in my next book.

## BEFORE YOU SET OFF ON YOUR JOURNEY

This chapter has focused on preparing for the journey you are about to embark on by giving you a sneak preview of the route. In the chapters that follow, you'll dig into the journey, from figuring out your Next, to making a plan to reach it, to executing that plan, to reflecting once you get to your destination. Before I send you off on that journey—before you zip up the suitcase, so to speak—please consider a few final tips.

## Don't Go It Alone

The journey to determining and reaching your Next is not a solo trip. So, be thinking about friends and family you'll invite to take the trip with you. You will need their support, perspective, and resources. When you get into the chapters that follow, you'll discuss your findings and progress with them. In my twenties, I made the mistake of not talking and sharing with my parents about my career. I also failed to do this with family and friends in my thirties and forties. I could never really explain what I did and so could never get an "attaboy" or congratulations, nor insight and resources that might have been helpful. This might have come from a place of competitiveness, or maybe there was simply no time because of other topics we tended to gravitate toward, but I always felt isolated and did not have support in both the good and bad times. I have now advised hundreds of other people at all stages of their careers, and this is always something I emphasize: Share your journey!

## Watch for Waypoints

You will need some waypoints—stops to break up the journey and help you continue to track yourself on a map. These waypoints will come in the form of a roughed-out personal development road map. How to put this together will be covered in detail in Step 4. Also, key learnings, tips, and milestones will be summarized at each chapter's end.

## Timing Your Journey

Reaching your destination is likely to be a marathon, not a sprint. And the process is iterative. You will not get what you want all in one go. It might take multiple steps and several years. You will almost certainly have to come back to the Four Axis Framework multiple times in your life and go through the exercises again to prepare for and succeed in life's transitions. Individuals who are successful in managing transitions have a set of personal characteristics that they work on, consciously and subconsciously, throughout their journey (we will speak more about these in Step 5).

## Six Superpower Character Traits

Over the last five years, as I have done the field research for this book with hundreds of people from every walk of life, I've observed six common traits among people who have successfully navigated career transitions: positivity, curiosity, adaptability, consistency, persistence, and kindness. These are not necessarily innate personality traits but rather behaviors that can be cultivated and strengthened. Adopting a mindset built around these six behaviors provides you with the inner drive and resilience you'll need to push forward and stay focused even when faced with obstacles or setbacks. Let's look at these in more detail.

### POSITIVITY

Your mindset should be rooted in the fundamental belief that achieving your desired outcome is possible. This belief should underpin your responsible mindset to aid you in achieving your goals and self-actualizing. This mirrors the conviction seen in successful athletes who believe in their ability to win. Positive mental attitude is a well-documented and studied phenomenon among athletes and others. Managers love team members who have it, and team members follow leaders who have it. Be positive; it is a leading characteristic of success.

## CURIOSITY

An active desire to explore, learn, and understand will lead you to uncover new opportunities, gain valuable insights, and adapt your approach effectively.

## ADAPTABILITY

The capacity to adjust your strategies and methods in response to feedback, unexpected challenges, or changing circumstances is critical. Rigid adherence to an initial plan can be a barrier to progress.

## CONSISTENCY

Maintaining steady and regular effort makes a world of difference. Success is often the result of consistent small actions that accumulate over time.

## PERSISTENCE

Persistence is the ability and willingness to continue pursuing your goals despite difficulties, opposition, or those times when reality doesn't immediately conform to your aspirations. This behavior is a vital component of grit.

## KINDNESS

Having a genuine interest in being helpful to others and solving problems for them fosters positive interactions and more authentic relationships. The simple concept of small kindnesses makes people more likely to engage with you and offer assistance. Business culture is always shaped by trends in leadership style, and in recent years, one of those trends—especially in Silicon Valley—has been toward a model of pure self-manifestation: the idea that success comes from relentlessly pursuing a founder's vision, with others working in service to that vision. My experience tells me otherwise. Over three decades, I've seen that the leaders and colleagues who achieve the most meaningful and lasting success are those who care deeply about others and ground their work in kindness. Kindness is not weakness.

Cultivating these six characteristics and behaviors provides the psychological foundation necessary for the demanding task of rigorous implementation. Think of these as muscles to be exercised regularly. What are you doing on a daily or weekly basis to grow these? The more you use them, the higher return you will get, and the more they will stand out to others. As you go on your journey to your Next and become the identity you want, remember to always include these six characteristics.

## You've Got This

Lastly, remember that this process is yours. No one is doing it for you, and no one is giving you a grade. There are no correct answers to the questions posed in this chapter and the rest of the book. You own your answers and your process. You own the actions you take and the thoughts and emotions that those actions produce.

Remember that young accountant who didn't enjoy his work? In his competency analysis, he articulated his innate ability with scent (what a nose!) and his long-standing interest in wine. He started to think about possibilities that would fulfill more of what he wanted and about what was holding him back. He realized that what was keeping him frozen in his current situation was his parents', friends', and colleagues' desires for him. He came to see that he had to focus on his own desires and not theirs. He had to take ownership of his life. He thought about what he really wanted and decided to pivot away from the corporate world and follow his nose—literally. He took an initial wine course, did a huge amount of networking and research, and then, enlisting his network of friends and family, committed himself, sat for his exams, and reached his new goal of working as a sommelier at a famous restaurant in New York. He is over the moon about his career now.

## CHAPTER WAYPOINTS

Clarity is key to success.

Confusion can trigger the brain's fight, flight, or freeze response, hindering rational thought and leading to negative emotions, which makes it harder to get clarity.

The Seven Steps to Success, introduced in this chapter, will guide you from assessing where you are now to determining where you want to be in the future, to understanding your value proposition, to making and implementing an action plan, and, finally, to celebrating and building on your success.

The Four Axis Framework is a tool you will use to reflect on your current reality and envision where you want to go in your professional life. The four axes are Competency, Context, Culture, and Mindset.

Sharing your journey with friends, family, and colleagues is essential for support along the way.

The journey to your next destination is a marathon, not a sprint, and requires an iterative process.

You are entirely responsible for your own choices, actions, and success. This book is your hitchhiker's guide to provide waypoints along your journey.

Celebrate your completion of Step 1! You now have clarity around how you are going to approach the task of finding your Next and making it happen.

# STEP 2

## Insight: Know Yourself

> **"If you don't know what you want, you will probably never get it."**
>
> **—Oliver Wendell Holmes Jr.**

The best way to start figuring out what you want is to take stock of your current reality. Who are you today? What are your strengths? What are your preferred contexts in which to use those strengths? What are your values? What motivates you? In Step 2, you will hold up a mirror to answer those questions based on your current reality.

So, get ready to be active—to do, not just to read. You're going to complete exercises to establish who you are and where you are now.

Figure 7: Focus on Step 2

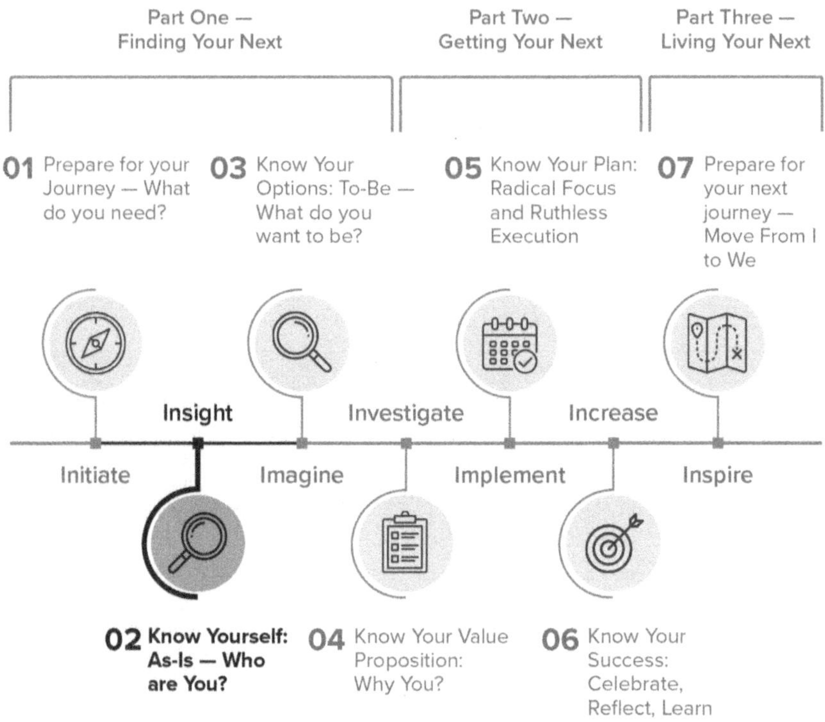


*In this chapter, we are focusing on Step 2—Insight, taking stock of who you are today.*

*Source: Moo Pie Advisors, Inc., 2025.*

## Head North for Insight into Your Competency

The first place your hitchhiker's guide is sending you is to assess your competency. Competency is a measure of how well you do things and is a key part of navigating your Next. Competency describes your ability to get things done, which is made up of your skills, your capabilities, and your experience and expertise with them. It is a measure of your level of mastery of acquired skills and your actualization of innate abilities.

## Figure 8: Finding Your Current Reality in the Four Axis Framework

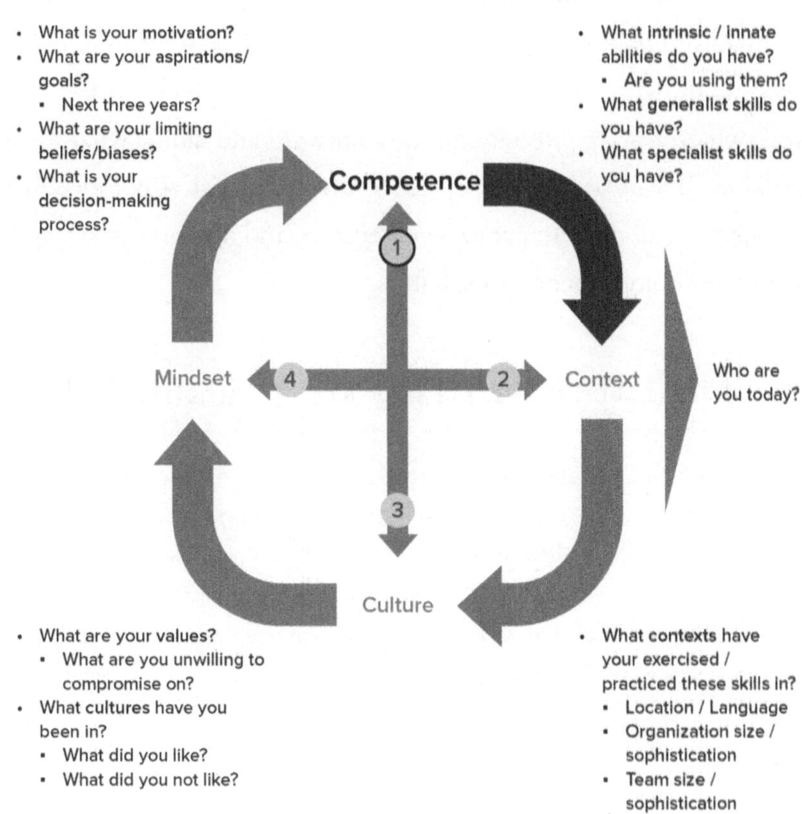


*Step 1 introduced the Four Axis Framework. In Step 2, you'll analyze your current reality through four perspectives: competency, context, culture, and mindset. You'll answer questions in each quadrant based on who you are today. Then, in Step 3, you'll apply the same framework with a future orientation, focusing on how you want to develop and what you aim to achieve. Source: Moo Pie Advisors Inc., 2025.*

We care about competency because employers look for evidence that you've applied your skills and capabilities. Understanding your own competency allows you to see how far up a skill or experience tree you have come and what further development you need to gain mastery of it. Further, competency enables other people to see what makes you distinctive. In terms of ikigai, it is what you are good at and what you can get paid for.

We're biologically wired to ignore the things we're best at because humans are habit-forming creatures. From birth, we mimic people older than we are to learn how to survive. The problem is that when we copy others, we put our attention outward and ignore what we are good at. If you truly want to understand what you're competent at, switch your attention to your own behavior and notice your strengths, weaknesses, and unconscious habits.

### COMPETENCE OR COMPETENCY? WHAT'S THE DIFFERENCE?

These words are often used interchangeably, but there are nuances of difference. Basically, ***competence*** is the general ability to do something, while ***competency*** is a measure of how well you exercise that competence. For our purposes, we are mostly looking at your competencies—those competence areas where you have achieved a high level of skill, knowledge, or even mastery, and those behaviors you've demonstrated that show you can perform a competence well.

## Competency in Three Parts

Competency comes in three types: intrinsic capabilities, generalist skills, and specialist skills.

**Intrinsic competencies** are an essential part of you, often from birth or a very young age. Examples include intelligence; charisma; a heightened sense of smell; perfect pitch; physical skills, such as running or hand-eye coordination; artistic talent; and logical thinking.

## INTRINSIC OR INNATE? WHAT'S THE DIFFERENCE?

*Innate* refers to a capability or talent that is present in you at birth. *Intrinsic* means something that is essential or inseparable from you. Intrinsic is often used in relation to aspects of the universal human condition, such as the intrinsic need for a sense of belonging, or an intrinsic need to feel loved.

As you think about your competencies, some of those might be clearly innate—your father has perfect pitch, and you apparently inherited his genes for that because you never miss a note when singing. But we are also looking at those abilities, capabilities, and talents—or "gifts," you might call them—that are not necessarily genetic, or not entirely, but may have become ingrained in you at a very young age. These are so much a part of you—your acumen for mathematics, your skill at organizing, your talent for persuading anyone to do anything—that they are intrinsic to you.

**Generalist competencies** are versatile skills that can be deployed across multiple functional roles, industries, or work settings. These are sometimes referred to as transferable skills. They are highly correlated to management and leadership activities in successfully forming and guiding teams and organizations. Examples include project management, organization, problem-solving, active listening, persuading or motivating, spoken communications, writing, coordinating, and collaborating.

**Specialist competencies** are skills that are specific to an industry, a functional area, or a technology or process. They are areas in which we have detailed, in-depth knowledge or skill that creates value. You might have specialist competencies related to technology, process, industry, or function. Examples would be expertise in insurance (industry), sales (function), and negotiation and client development (processes).

Much of the language we use now to describe competency comes from guilds that flourished in Europe from the eleventh to sixteenth centuries. Guilds were groups of artisans and tradespeople brought together by the level of competency reached in certain sought-after skills, such as pottery, masonry, carpentry, goldsmithing, and weaving. The guilds policed quality standards, set prices, developed training techniques, and sponsored apprenticeships.

You joined or apprenticed to a guild and were taught relevant skills that enabled you to earn a living, and that gave you a badge or accreditation symbolizing quality and a level of achievement, such as apprentice, journeyman, and master. We do not have guilds anymore, other than loosely through professional associations, but the principles of competency and mastery are built into our language and the way we evaluate each other professionally, whether one is a metalworker, lawyer, engineer, musician, electrician, academician, banker, consultant, writer, or works in any other field with a body of knowledge and required skill set.

Many large organizations build or utilize competency models to describe the skills required to be successful for a role or a job, so it's good to be able to describe yourself accurately using terms you can then use in emails, job applications, and conversations. In becoming a coach and continuing to develop as one, I have had to follow competency models laid out by the International Coaching Federation and the European Mentoring and Coaching Council Global. Those models help me understand which skills I need to learn and to what standard. I can be generally good across competency categories, or I can specialize over time in one or more to make myself distinctive.

As you work through the elements of the Four Axis Framework with exercises that start in the next section of this chapter, you might find it helpful to follow the stories of three people who have walked the same path. Let's call them Pierre, Rachel, and Caroline.

Pierre is thirty-four years old, French, and lives in Montreal, Canada, but would like to move back to Paris to be closer to his extended family. He has a young family, is a manager with a major consultancy, and is facing a turning point in his career. He has worked for large insurance companies in the past and is wondering what he should do. Stay in consulting? Go back to insurance? Try something entrepreneurial?

Rachel is a twenty-nine-year-old woman living in New York. She and her husband are parents to a young child and hope to grow their family. Rachel has a background as a web designer and design team leader. She is torn between her roles as a mother, designer, and career woman. Rachel is leading a significant initiative at her firm but feels stymied and misunderstood in terms of her input and ability to be creative. She has a few months until maternity leave and is wondering if she should return when the leave is over or if she should pursue her dream of becoming an interior designer. She worries about helping to support her family and is considering moving to another city where the costs would be lower.

Caroline, a fifty-year-old American woman, lives in London and has two children in college. She speaks English, French, Polish, and German fluently and is head of the legal department at a Fortune 100 company. She has lived in Paris, Geneva, and Warsaw and has practiced arbitration law for more than twenty years. Caroline is trying to decide if she wants to be a general counsel and a board director, taking all that would entail in terms of career coming first and dealing with interpersonal politics, or if she wants to leave the company or change careers and go have an adventure working in another country.

## Identifying Your Competencies

Our first part of the Four Axis Framework is competency, so it's time for you to take out a pen and paper, or a digital device of your choice, and get ready to complete some exercises around your competencies. These exercises work well set up as electronic documents or as a spreadsheet, but you might find you do your best thinking in a comfortable chair with the tactile sensation of a spiral notebook and a favorite pen—or even standing in front of a whiteboard.

Whichever method you choose, you will complete a written exercise for each of the three types of competencies: intrinsic, generalist, and specialist. And in each of those categories, you'll indicate your level of competence for each and how much you enjoy using each one.

## EXERCISE: MY INTRINSIC COMPETENCIES

Worksheet setup: Set up three columns. Label the left-hand column Intrinsic Competencies, the middle column Strength, and the right-hand column Enjoyment.

1. Competency listing: List your intrinsic competencies on the left. Remember, these are abilities, talents, and strengths that you feel like you were born with or that have been a part of you for as long as you can remember. They are "the essence of you." Don't worry about how often you get to use them currently; just think about how easily they usually come to you and/or how others have rated or given you feedback in these areas.
2. Utilization rating: Moving right to the next column, Strength, indicate how strong you consider your "muscle" for each intrinsic competency by writing (or typing) high, medium, or low. Low indicates the competency is present but not utilized. Medium indicates usage on a regular basis and noted by others as a talent you possess. High can be described as distinctive in some way; you use this on a regular basis and have external validation that this competency is best in class or particularly remarkable.
3. Enjoyment rating: In the right-hand column, indicate how much you enjoy using each intrinsic competency by writing (or typing) high, medium, or low. Again, don't worry about how often or how recently you've used the competency; just imagine how much you enjoy it when you do use it, enjoyed it when you used it in the past, or might enjoy it if you have an opportunity to use it in the future.

Once you've completed the My Intrinsic Competencies worksheet, see if you are satisfied with how you've filled it out. You can share it with people who know you well for ideas of what you might have missed. Past performance reviews from jobs or internships are a helpful source of ideas as well. Keep in mind that other people, or your reviews, might mention generalist and specialist skills, not just intrinsic competencies. If so, save the generalist and specialist ones for the exercises that follow.

Next, let's move on to generalist competencies. Remember, these are versatile, transferable skills that enable you to work with, coordinate, manage, or lead others. They can allow you to be an excellent individual contributor or capable manager or leader. The examples listed in Appendix A: Generalist Competency Examples give ideas for your worksheet. And, once again, talking to others, reading old performance reviews, looking back over descriptions of jobs you've held, or reading your own resume or skills list in your LinkedIn profile can help you with this exercise.

## EXERCISE: MY GENERALIST COMPETENCIES

Worksheet setup: Make yourself three columns. Label the left-hand column Generalist Competencies, the middle column Strength, and the right-hand column Enjoyment.

1. Competency listing: List your generalist competencies down the left-hand column.
2. Utilization rating: Moving right to the next column, Strength, indicate how often you practice each skill by writing (or typing) high, medium, or low. Low means the competency is present but not utilized on a daily or weekly basis. Medium is for use on a daily or weekly basis and noted by others as a talent you possess. High means this competency is distinctive in some way—you use this talent on a daily or weekly basis, and it is likely to be known as something you do heavily and do well.
3. Enjoyment rating: In the right-hand column, indicate how much you enjoy using each generalist competency by writing (or typing) high, medium, or low. Again, don't worry about how often or how recently you've used this skill; just imagine how much you enjoy it or would enjoy it.

Now let's move on to the last competency exercise—specialization, which is structured just like the intrinsic and generalist ones. Keep in mind that specialist competencies are tied to your industry, technical, and functional knowledge (skills you have accumulated through your education or training and jobs you've held). Once again, there is a list at the back of this book to help you out—Appendix B: Specialist Competency Examples.

### EXERCISE: MY SPECIALIST COMPETENCIES

Worksheet setup: Label the left-hand column Specialist Competencies, the middle column Strength, and the right-hand column Enjoyment.

1. Competency listing: List your specialist competencies down the left-hand column.
2. Utilization rating: Moving right to the next column, Strength, indicate how strong each specialist competency is by writing (or typing) high, medium, or low.
3. Enjoyment rating: Now, in the right-hand column, indicate how much you enjoy using each specialist competency by rating it as high, medium, or low. Again, don't worry about how often or how recently you've used this skill; just think about how much you enjoy it or would enjoy it.

## Reflections on Competency

For each of the competency sets you've listed and rated in your three worksheets, you should now have a clearer sense of your current reality regarding what you do well or have the capability to do well. Are you seeing that some competencies stand out as particularly differentiated from the others on your lists, i.e., you are especially well versed in them and very much enjoy employing them? High differentiation represents a competency area in which your level of knowledge or skill is so distinctive that no conversation or decisions on that topic should happen without you being in the room.

### IKIGAI AND COMPETENCY

The concept of ikigai continues to inform your self-assessment process as you identify and reflect on your competencies. Remember that the goal of ikigai is to find the place where what you love to do, what you are good at, and what the world needs and will pay you to do converge. With the exercises around competency completed, you are uncovering what you are good at and which of those skills and abilities you love to use.

## The Curse of Competence

If you're highly competent and have high standards, you might fall into the trap of assuming that you should always do well. In your mind, having high levels of competency is not a cause for celebration; it's only the minimum level of reasonable performance. Anything less than victory would be a failure, and victory itself becomes nothing more than acceptable. Congratulations: You might be very successful! Condolences: You might be very miserable.

To avoid this curse of competence, keep in mind that you are wired this way for a reason. Our earliest ancestors were made up of the most goal-driven, insecure overachievers in history. They had to be that way to meet their most basic needs of food, shelter, and safety. So how could you be any other way? Hundreds of years ago, success meant accumulating food and resources, and now it means accumulating money and accomplishments. And the number of ways your success-seeking system can be hijacked is greater than ever. Extrinsic rewards and temptations are pushed on us everywhere, all the time.

## Examples: Pierre, Rachel, and Caroline

So, how did Pierre, Rachel, and Caroline do with this exercise? (Let's focus on the things they found were medium and high.)

### PIERRE

Intrinsic: intelligence (high: degree from École Normale Supérieure in France, MBA from McGill University in Montreal, Canada); physical (high: long-distance runner)

Generalist: project management, team leadership (high); program management, multiple teams (high); problem-solving (medium); distributed teams/global teams (medium); written communication (high); spoken communication one-to-one (high: French, medium: English)

Pierre observes that he likes working on strategic long-term problem-solving and really enjoys collaborations with distributed, multicultural teams to solve big problems.

Pierre realizes he does not enjoy project-based consulting.

Specialist: life insurance industry (medium); consulting industry (medium); corporate strategy function/process (medium); product strategy function/process (medium); sales function/process (medium)

### RACHEL

Intrinsic: intelligence (high: degree from Rhode Island School of Design); artistic (high: accomplished painter and graphic artist)

Rachel observes that she loves being creative and talking about ideas and design but does not get to exercise this muscle in her daily leadership role.

Generalist: project management, team leadership (medium); problem-solving (medium); distributed teams/global teams (medium); written communication (medium); spoken communication one-to-one (medium)

Rachel observes she is not distinctive at team leadership and does not enjoy it.

Specialist: consulting industry (medium); graphic design (high); design thinking process (high); web design process (high); interior design (medium)

## CAROLINE

Intrinsic: intelligence (high: degree from Georgetown Law, LLM from Sorbonne University in Paris); languages (high: English, French, Polish, and German)

Generalist: team leadership (high); functional leadership, multiple teams (high); problem-solving (high); distributed teams/global teams (medium); written communication (high); spoken communication one-to-one (high: French, English, Polish, and German)

Caroline observes that she does not really enjoy senior leadership responsibility or politics. Caroline loves working with multicultural and multinational teams on complex legal problems.

Specialist: commercial arbitration (high); legal function/process (high); compliance function/process (high); retail industry (medium); contract negotiation (high); European/international contract law (high)

Caroline realizes she would be considered distinctive as an international/European contract lawyer.

Now that you see how the competencies inventory played out for Pierre, Rachel, and Caroline, see if you want to go back to your own results of the competencies exercises to make any changes or additions. Don't forget that, at this stage, you are simply listing all your competencies and rating your level of expertise in them. Later, in Step 3, you will work on which competencies you want to develop and why. But first, let's move to the second quadrant of the Four Axis Framework to continue your assessment of your current reality, now with a focus on contexts you've worked in.

## Head East for Insight into Context

Now we move to the east quadrant of the Four Axis Framework, to context. For our purposes, context refers to the situations and environments in which you have demonstrated and built your competencies. Specifically, we're going to be looking at two aspects of your current and past contexts: teams and organizations.

You'll be thinking about the kinds of teams you've been a part of and the scale and size of those teams. Which types of teams have you been most drawn to and how have you succeeded with them? You'll also be looking at the kinds of organizations you've been drawn to and how you've succeeded in them. We're trying to understand both how you perform in teams and which environments you prefer, based on your experiences in participant and managerial roles across teams and organizations of varying sizes, from very small to large-scale.

If you have been more of an independent worker or individual contributor and don't think of yourself as having a great deal of team experience, that's not a problem. You have still been part of larger group efforts. Even if you've done entirely freelance work or been a solo entrepreneur, you have been part of a "team" of colleagues, suppliers, providers, customers, or clients.

If you are just getting your career off the ground and do not have much work experience in teams or employment in organizations to base your context analysis on, no worries. Think about internships, summer jobs, extracurriculars in high school or college, sports teams, and group class projects where you experienced teamwork at various scales or were part of a larger system or organization.

## Why Employers Care About Context

In my thirty-plus years of experience as a hiring manager and an executive leading teams, I have found that most employers consider three overarching questions when deciding to bring somebody into the organization.

### CAN YOU DO THE JOB?

Do you have the skills and capabilities required to be successful? Your competency lets them know you can handle the basic responsibilities of the role. But are you uniquely qualified for this role? Can you add value in a specific way? By knowing both your competencies and the context in which you've practiced them, employers can determine your credibility and relevance to their needs.

For example, if you are going for a marketing operations job, are you an expert in pricing? Because that's an area of the organization's marketing ops that needs some improvement. If you are going for a territory manager job in healthcare sales, are you deeply knowledgeable of a particular public policy matter that the organization too often bumps up against?

### WILL YOU FIT IN HERE?

Most job interviews beyond the first screening are about assessing fit. Do you share our values? Have you worked in organizations like ours? Research has shown that fit contributes heavily to success over time. Knowing and articulating your context and talking about how experiences were or were not a fit for you can demonstrate fit for the organization in which you want to work.

Does this team need a dreamer or a doer? A number cruncher or a writer? Is this organization filled with people who have exceptionally high standards, all striving for excellence? If you have only ever worked in Fortune 50 companies, will you fit in a startup?

## ARE YOU MOTIVATED TO GROW WITH US?

The best employers don't want you to come and warm a seat, as 50 percent of why they hire you is for what you can do today and 50 percent is for what you will become. They want you to stay and grow, to see your future career development with them. By knowing and talking about the competencies you enjoy applying and the context in which you thrive, you can show employers you would not be there just for a paycheck but to help create a great product, serve clients, and so forth.

## Figure 9: Focus on Context

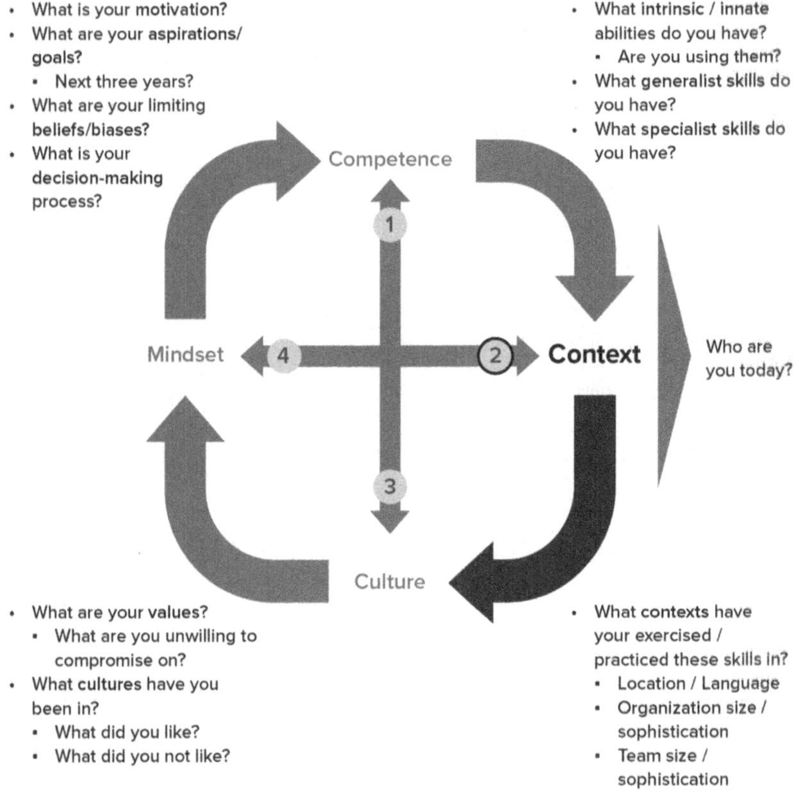


*We are now focused on the Context quadrant of the Four Axis Framework. Source: Moo Pie Advisors Inc., 2025.*

# EXERCISE: MY CONTEXT—TEAMS

Worksheet setup: Whether by hand on paper or in a document or spreadsheet on your computer or tablet, make five columns. Label the left-hand column Team, then, moving to the right, label the next column Type, the next one Size, next one Role, and the final column Enjoyment.

1. Teams list: Under the Teams heading, list all the teams you can think of that you've been a part of. Don't worry about the order, though you might start with your current or most recent work experiences and work backward. Your teams might have had an official name. If not, don't worry about what to call each team. Just jot down something that helps you remember which one you are talking about.
2. Type of team: Under Type, make note of the nature of each team. What was the scope of each team that you were on or led? Department? Division? A functional area? Project team? Client-focused team? Product team? A whole company? A portfolio of teams across multiple companies?
3. Team size: Moving right to the next column, indicate the size of each team. Since this exercise is just for you and there are no hard-and-fast rules about how to do this, use a size categorization system that works for you. You might say small, medium, large, or very large. You might give a range representing the number of people on the team, such as 2–5, 6–10, 11–30, 31–50, and so forth. Or you may choose to list an exact or approximate number of team members.
4. Team role: What was your role on each team? Leader? Manager? Participant? A particular functional role you fulfilled? Other?
5. Enjoyment rating: Now, in the far-right column, indicate how much you enjoyed each team experience by writing (or typing) high, medium, or low.

## Reflections on Team Scale and Scope

Look over your team exercise results and see what patterns emerge. Which scale of team environment are you most drawn to and likely to succeed in? In what sorts of team roles do you thrive most? We're going to move on here to a similar context exercise but focus on the organizations in which you've worked. Then, you'll reflect on context overall.

### EXERCISE: MY CONTEXT—ORGANIZATIONS

Worksheet setup: Make four columns. Label the first left-hand column Organization, the next one Type, the next one Size, and the right-hand column Enjoyment.

1. Organizations list: Under Organization, list the names of all organizations you've worked for (companies, nonprofits, governmental organizations, academic institutions, and so on). If you have extensive paid employment experience, you may want to list only that, but feel free to list organizations you've been significantly involved with in other capacities, such as board roles or volunteer work. Don't worry about the order you list them in, though you might start with your current or most recent experiences and work backward.
2. Type of organization: Indicate the type of organization each name on your list represents. This is where you specify public, private, nonprofit, NGO, governmental, academia, and so forth. You might also add to any of those: startup, early stage, or even self-employment (entrepreneurship, freelance, private practice, gig economy).
3. Organization size: Moving right, indicate the size of each organization. As with teams, you may be specific or give a range (e.g., 0 to 200 employees, 201 to 1,000, and so forth), or you might say small, medium, large, or very large.
4. Enjoyment rating: Now, in the final column, indicate (with high, medium, or low) how much you enjoyed (or currently enjoy) working in each organization.

## Reflections on Organizational Scale and Scope

As you look over this worksheet, what are your reactions? Which experiences did you enjoy or feel most comfortable in, and which did you not? Which sorts of environments are you drawn to? Be curious about why. Write down your reasons and insights.

### SMALLER OR LARGER TEAMS AND ORGANIZATIONS—WHICH IS YOUR PREFERENCE?

An affinity for smaller environments, whether a team or an overall organization, is generally predicated on a focus on relationships (lots of high-touch iterations with people to build engagement and trust), while an affinity for larger environments is generally predicated on a focus on tasks (emphasizing outcomes based on shared process and content).

Social anthropologists have found that if you grow up in a small family unit, say, with parents, a couple of kids, and minimal extended family, your predilection is toward getting things done via relationships. Why is this? Well, it turns out that tens of thousands of years ago, when we were wandering around, the world was a very dangerous place for children and adolescents. And so you could not afford to lose a family member; you had a high degree of dependence on the small number of people around you. You developed a reliance on getting things done through affinity, trust, and engagement with your small world. If you grew up in a very large family unit, perhaps with cousins, uncles, aunts, and so forth around you, you may have often found yourself in a role of coordinating among all the various entities. So now, if you come from a large family, your predisposition is likely to be toward task orientation, coordinating among lots of people to get things done.[2]

## EXPLORING IDEAL TEAM SIZES—THE WORK OF ROBIN DUNBAR

If you're curious about the science behind ideal team sizes, a key figure to explore is Robin Dunbar, a British anthropologist and evolutionary psychologist on the faculty of the University of Oxford (www.psy.ox.ac.uk/people/robin-dunbar). Dunbar's research focuses on human social behavior, particularly how our brains manage relationships. His work led to the development of Dunbar's Number, a theory that suggests there are cognitive limits to the number of people with whom we can maintain stable social relationships.

Our brains are designed to handle social connections in layers, with our innermost circle consisting of our closest five people—typically our loved ones. Beyond that, we have good friends (15 people), then friends (50 people), and expanding further, we have meaningful contacts (150 people). As the number of people grows, the strength of the relationships generally weakens. Beyond the 150 mark, we move into the realm of acquaintances (500 people), and at the outermost layer, we have about 1,500 people we can recognize.

So, what does this mean in terms of teams and organizations for you? Do you prefer small teams and organizations in which things get done because groups are close-knit, highly engaged, and communicating from a place of mutual trust and inter-reliance? Or do you prefer larger contexts, in which you have lots of people around you, lots of energy you can harness and coordinate to work in systems and processes, all focused on tasks?

---

2 Robin I. M. Dunbar, "The Social Brain Hypothesis," *Evolutionary Anthropology* 6, no. 5 (1998): 178–190.

You can now view your credibility relative to your competencies because you have a complete view of the contexts in which you've exercised those competencies. You can also now start thinking about how you are drawn to particular types of contexts in which to use your competencies.

So, how did our three friends Pierre, Rachel, and Caroline do with this exercise?

## PIERRE

Context—Teams: Pierre has worked in mostly small expert teams, both in consulting firms and in industry (insurance), and feels comfortable in them. One of the things he observes is that he does not enjoy constantly having to build new relationships as teams break up and reform in consulting work. He is happiest when he has more permanent and deeper relationships. He likes having direct access to decision-makers and so wants a senior executive boss. He also has experience in sports (small long-distance running teams in college) and in academics working on projects. He does not really know large team environments.

Context—Organization: He has worked in very large, complex organizations (Fortune 1000 insurance companies) and in some scale-up organizations in Paris, New York, and Montreal. He likes large company environments that have lots of problems to solve and lots of opportunity and that have distributed, multicultural teams.

## RACHEL

Context—Teams: Rachel has worked as an individual contributor (designer or design partner) and as a leader and manager of small expert teams. Her one experience working in a large cross-functional, international team was unpleasant, ridden with politics and conflict.

She is nervous about changing context, as she knows the people she currently works with well.

Context—Organization: She currently works in a large, complex organization driving a complicated project across many business units and functions and is not enjoying it all. She has also worked in a design partnership and liked the simplicity and directness of getting things done but disliked the personal influence the two owners' personalities had on the team's work and culture. She is curious about what it would be like to work for herself.

## CAROLINE

Context—Teams: Caroline has worked in small team environments (as a general counsel to a Polish private equity firm) and in large team environments (many years of work in top UK law firms in London, Warsaw, and elsewhere in Europe). She does not have a preference either way. She does want to be the leader in a team context and wants a seat at the table in decision-making.

Context—Organization: She currently works in a Fortune 50 company and runs a large and complicated department. She has lots of experience and competency doing this across multiple organizations. She is more of a corporate, practical, process-oriented lawyer than a partner in a legal firm. She hates the politics of her current organization and thinks she would like to work in a smaller, less complicated environment.

Do you see anything in the findings of Pierre, Rachel, and Caroline that jogs your memory of your own context analysis? Anything additional or different you want to say about your context preferences?

Having completed your competency and context exercises, you should be starting to see what is possible (what you could do, maybe) and what is probable (those things that you are most likely qualified for and a fit for). We'll take a deeper dive into your possibles and probables in Step 3, but for now, there is no harm in giving thought to your possible or probable options.

## Head South for Insight into Your Culture

We experience each other during those interactions as a series of values. We observe and build pictures of each other both consciously and unconsciously. Are we kind? Are we curious? Are we persistent? Are we thorough? Are we positive or negative?

So, what we want to understand is who you are from a values standpoint. How do you show up? And what is important to you in how others show up? What does that mean for your teamwork and leadership style and your fit for various contexts?

## Figure 10: Focus on Culture

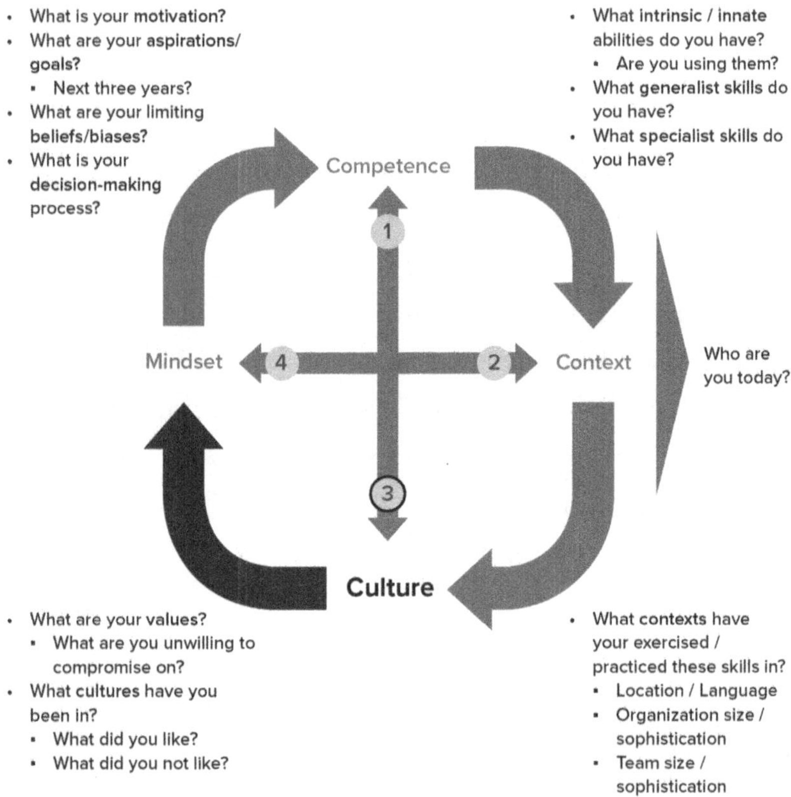


*We are now focused on the culture quadrant of the Four Axis Framework. Source: Moo Pie Advisors Inc., 2025.*

## EXERCISE: VALUES AND CULTURE

Worksheet setup: Make two columns. Label the left column My Values and the right column Culture.

1. Values list: Under the My Values heading, list all your personal values. See the list in appendix C for ideas of values. These are things that you stand for, things you consider important.
2. Top values: Which of the values you listed are most important to you? Which ones would you stand up for and not compromise on? Pick your top five and mark those in green.
3. Organizational cultures: Now skim through the list of organizations in the My Context—Organizations exercise and the list of teams in the My Context—Teams exercise. For each of those experiences, think about the culture you experienced in the organization or with the team. You can think of an organization's or team's culture as its collective values. Now, in the Culture column of the current worksheet, make a list of cultures you have worked in. Has the culture been very competitive? Collaborative? Has it been customer focused? Sales intensive? Product or engineering focused? Has it had high or low integrity? Has it been very time focused?

## Reflections on Values and Culture

Look back over your own list of values. Have some of these been important to you all your life? Have some changed over time? Are the ones you've marked as your top five truly the ones you are willing to take a stand on, while the others you'd be more willing to compromise on? Make any adjustments to your list that might be needed now that you're reviewing your values list in its entirety.

Now look at the cultures list and consider these questions:

Do you see an overlap with your own values or hardly any? Did you feel comfortable in the contexts where the culture fit your values? How did you feel in the context that had values not on your own list?

Which of the cultures in which you've worked have felt most positive and comfortable for you? How did they fit with your values?

Which of your cultures/contexts have you felt negative about or least comfortable in? Why did they not fit your values?

Write down as many details as you can when reflecting on the issue of culture because this area is likely to be the canary in the coal mine as you determine which types of cultures you want to—or do not want to—work in. Culture is critical for describing what you may be most interested in regarding future options.

Here's what Pierre, Rachel, and Caroline found out about their values and cultures.

### PIERRE

Values: Pierre's values are family harmony, financial security, learning, collaboration, kindness, control, organization, and integrity. Pierre is happiest when surrounded by people who are family and children focused, and who are organized, collaborative, and kind. He thinks about these in relation to his opportunities.

Organizational culture: He has worked in several culture types: highly competitive, highly collaborative, and both highly centralized and highly distributed decision-making. His strong preference is for organized, collaborative, and diverse organizations with clear and reliable decision-making.

### RACHEL

Values: Rachel's values are financial security, creativity, independence, freedom, family harmony, and respect. She is very focused on taking care of her growing family and being financially secure. She wants to have a creative career with independence to make decisions and work on projects with clients she cares about.

Organizational culture: She has worked in several culture types: a highly centralized, hierarchical, competitive design partnership and a highly collaborative, collegial, and distributed global management consultancy. She does not really enjoy either and thinks she would prefer to work on her own or with one or two other people.

## CAROLINE

Values: Caroline's values are respect, integrity, kindness, accomplishment, control, and social impact. She cares about her status and brand and wants to break the glass ceiling with the career achievement of being a major company's general counsel. She also wants to ensure her children are taken care of and successfully transition from college. She is interested in having more social impact once this is achieved.

Organizational culture: Caroline has always worked in large organizations with competing functions, geographies, and business units. She enjoys complexity and having control over her organization but dislikes the politics. She likes leadership and managing large teams. She worries that if she cannot break the ceiling, she will be limited to smaller companies in order to get her spot in the C-suite. She would like to prepare for a future when she can give back and use her competencies to serve others.

Having completed and reflected on the two exercises, you should be able to describe what your most important values are and which types of cultures you are most drawn to, a strong potential fit for, and likely to be successful in. This will come in handy for Step 3, when you close in on what you want your Next to be.

## Head West for Insight into Your Mindset

The final element of our Four Axis Framework is mindset. Mindset refers to your established set of attitudes concerning motivation, goals, beliefs or biases, and decision-making. Your mindset is essentially how you play both the inner and outer game of life; your inner attitudes drive your outwardly visible and measurable behaviors. In the exercises that follow, you'll gain a clearer understanding of your current mindset. We'll begin with motivation and then move through goals, beliefs, and decision-making.

## Figure 11: Focus on Mindset

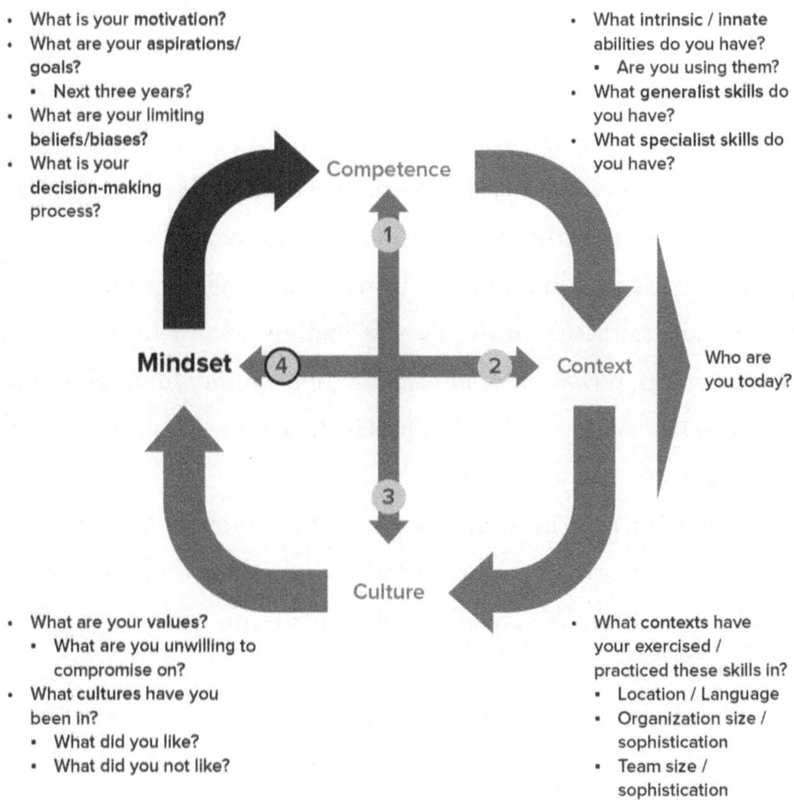


*We are now focused on the final quadrant of the Four Axis Framework: Mindset, which includes motivation, goals, beliefs, and decision-making. Source: Moo Pie Advisors Inc., 2025.*

## Motivation: Intrinsic and Extrinsic

What motivates you currently? Think of motivation as a large circle, a set of all sets of motivation, in which there are two mutually opposed subsets of motivations. This is depicted in figure 12.

Your first subset of opposing motivations can be described as intrinsic and extrinsic. This is your way of thinking about your reward mechanism—what motivates you to get things done. Both intrinsic and extrinsic motivations are about the wealth you seek, but not just financial wealth. Intrinsic motivations are you-focused wealth, such as personal mastery, achievement, curiosity, learning, creating, freedom, and good health. Extrinsic rewards include wealth in the form of money, status, power, title, admiration, opportunity to travel—things that are external to you. More complete lists are available in Appendix D: Examples of Motivations.

While intrinsic motivations may sound more noble, they are not inherently better than extrinsic motivations. There is no judgment of good or bad here. We are all wired and conditioned to seek certain rewards. What matters is what motivates you.

The second opposing subset of motivations is the creative or reactive subset. This subset involves how you create impact in your ecosystem and how your ecosystem in turn influences your motivations. Creative motivations reflect your desire to have an outward impact on your ecosystem (your family, friends, colleagues, and so on). These include being of service, having social impact, contributing to sustainability, protecting your family, and creating wealth for your family.

Reactive motivators are things that your ecosystem (other people, such as your family, friends, or colleagues) wants to have and that act as an influence for you. Your friends or colleagues may want you to compete more. Your family may want you to do only a certain type of job or to stay in a particular kind of location or make lots of money. Reactive motivations include drivers such as fear, shame, guilt, compliance, peer pressure, and recognition. More examples of creative and reactive motivations are in appendix D.

Figure 12: The Set of All Sets of Motivations

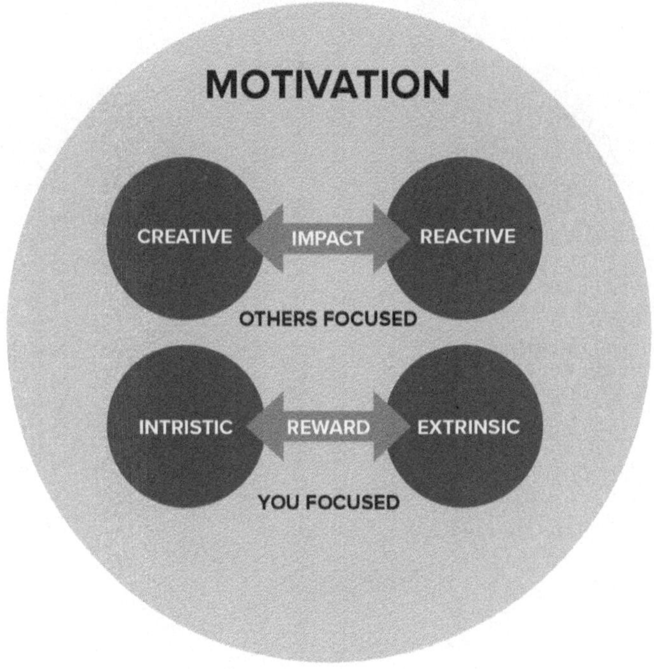


*This set of all sets of motivation relates to your reward mechanism—what motivates you to get things done. Source: Moo Pie Advisors Inc., 2025.*

As you think about what motivates you, it can also be helpful to think in terms of the primary "pillars" of your life, as you see in figure 13, and what is important to you across those life areas, as you can see in figure 14.

Figure 13: Life Pillars

**'Life Pillars' - Identifying dependencies and balance in how you measure success**

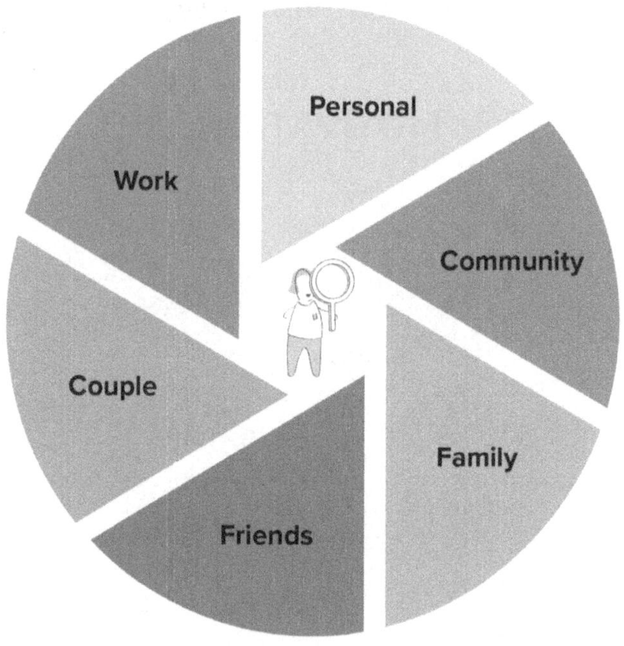


*Consider these primary areas of your life as sources of your motivations. Source: Moo Pie Advisors Inc. and Hudson Institute, 2025.*

## Figure 14: What Do You Want: Identifying and Understanding Intrinsic Motivation

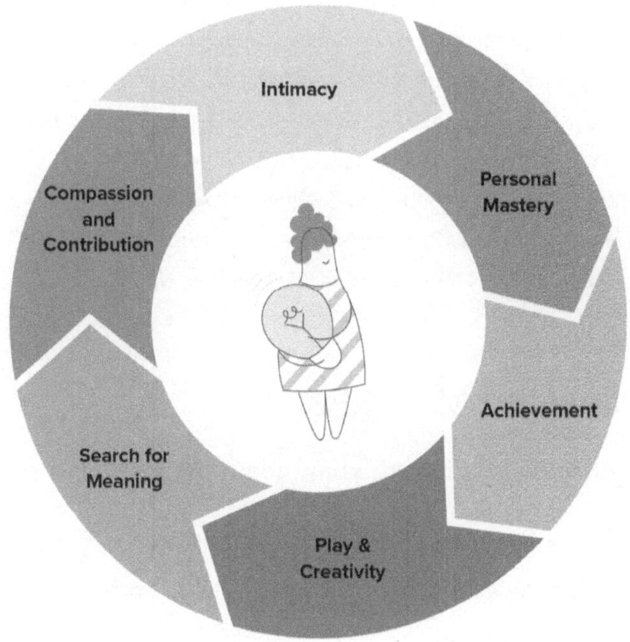


*What is important to you in life? Source: Moo Pie Advisors Inc. and Hudson Institute, 2025.*

## EXERCISE: MY MOTIVATIONS

Worksheet setup: Get a piece of paper or set up a digital document and orient it to portrait. Divide the page into four quadrants. Label the left-hand top box Intrinsic and the right-hand top box Extrinsic. Label the left-hand bottom box Creative and the right-hand bottom box Reactive.

1. Intrinsic/extrinsic motivations list: Write down all the intrinsic and extrinsic motivations you can think of. Don't worry about the order, the ranking of importance, or whether they are intrinsic or extrinsic, creative or reactive. Just get them all down in the top two boxes.
2. Creative/reactive motivations list: Now, write down all the creative and reactive motivations you can think of. Again, don't worry about the order, the ranking of importance, or whether they are creative or reactive. Just get them all down in the bottom two boxes.

## Reflections on Motivations

There are three main things to know about motivation as you reflect on yours:

- Tension between what you want and what other people expect of you is normal.
- Motivations change over time; they are not static.
- Understanding the connection between motivation and what you want is key to achieving goals.

Let's first look at that tension. You are a part of several systems—family, friends, work colleagues, your professional field or industry, society at large, and so forth. What is the tension between what you want for yourself and what members of these systems want for you? How has this driven decisions you've made in your life and career?

The second factor to keep in mind as you reflect on your motivations is that they are mutable. In this process, we are taking your motivations from being subconscious to being something you are aware of. This lets you examine and change them if you want to. For example, you can decide whether your parents' need for you to be financially secure is still a relevant need for you, or if you have different priorities. Your motivations will alter with your changes in context and life stages. What you care about and the ways you think about spending your time both change.

The third thing to understand is that motivations connect to what you want. You've done your competency analysis, contextual analysis, and cultural analysis. Now, where does motivation come in for you? What drives you forward?

Consider the example of Novak Djokovic, one of the world's greatest tennis players. Before he ranked number one in the world, he was getting trampled by the big three leaders of that sport (Roger Federer, Rafael Nadal, and Andy Murray). He didn't have a big serve, or a big forehand or backhand. Murray had the better backhand. Nadal and Federer had better forehands, and Federer had a better serve, so Djokovic couldn't win. He was very ambitious and really wanted to win but couldn't manage to make it work. Eventually, he sat down with a coach who noted that his distinct advantage was his motivation, his will to win, and that he could beat those guys by being willing to work harder and be fitter and never get off the court, never let a point get past him, and never give up. He would outlast them. He has now won more majors than all of them.

Thinking of Djokovic's example, is there something you are motivated to get better at? What might be your distinctive advantage that can help you achieve great levels of mastery?

## Aspirations and Goals

If you go to the CEO or president of a business and ask them what their goals are for the next year or two, and they can't articulate them, you will think that it is a poorly run business. How would you handle the question regarding your own goals and aspirations? Too often, we don't know our goals, or we have too many. What you want to do here is look at your current trajectory—your goals and aspirations as you can currently think of and articulate them. (In Step 3, you'll be guided to develop much more specific goals—your most probable career or life options.)

### EXERCISE: MY CURRENT GOALS

Worksheet setup: Make four columns. Label the left-hand column Goal, the next column Priority, the next column Possible/Probable, and the final column Horizon.

1. Current goals list: In the first column, list all your current goals, both personal and work related.
2. Priority: Consider which goals on your list are the highest priority. Mark those with a 1 in the Priority column. Then, assign 2 or 3 to reflect the middle priority goals and the lowest priorities.
3. Realism: How likely is it that you can achieve each goal? Is it only possible but not probable, meaning you might not have the competencies needed or prior experience in relevant contexts? Is it probable, meaning you can do it and you'll be a good fit? In the Possible/Probable column, mark each goal as possible or probable.
4. Goal timing: Think of three horizons stretching out from now. Horizon 1 means you could likely achieve this goal in a year's time. Horizon 2 goals might take two years, and Horizon 3 goals, three years. For each goal, assign a 1, 2, or 3 in the Horizon column.

## Reflections on Current Goals

Was it difficult to prioritize your current goals? Difficult to sequence them with a horizon designation? Whether you've got too few goals or too many, you are going to need to lay them out over time. No one can achieve everything at once. Think about your capacity to get things done—ability, time, and resources. What will you work on first? In Step 5, you'll learn about and implement the critical keys to success in activating a plan. For now, just start reflecting on how your current goals might need to spread out over time and how you might need to make some tough decisions around priorities, which you'll get help with in Step 3.

You might also ask the following additional reflection questions:

- How many of your goals are only possible, and how many are probable?
- How do they relate to your motivation?
- Do you see any of the four types of motivations reflected in the goals?
- Are there some goals stemming from reactive motivations? What do you want to do about those?

## Beliefs or Biases

Our third element of mindset is the beliefs and biases you hold. These two concepts are related, but beliefs are more personal and narrative based. They are the stories you tell yourself, often shaped early in life, that define what you think is possible, acceptable, or meaningful. These may include ideas such as "I'm not a creative person" or

"Success means working for a big-name company." Some beliefs serve you; others can constrain you.

Biases, on the other hand, are cognitive shortcuts. They are automatic, pattern-driven ways of interpreting the world. Biases help us make fast decisions, but they also distort our thinking. These include things such as negativity bias (focusing on what could go wrong), sunk cost fallacy (sticking with something because you've invested in it), or confirmation bias (favoring information that supports what you already believe).

So, while beliefs are deeply held and often identity shaping, biases are mental tendencies that affect how you process information and make decisions. The goal here is to make both conscious so you can question, reframe, and take more purposeful action.

## COMMON COGNITIVE BIASES EXPLAINED

**Anchoring Bias:** Relying too heavily on the first piece of information encountered (the "anchor") when making decisions.

**Availability Bias:** Estimating the likelihood of events based on how easily examples come to mind.

**Confirmation Bias:** Favoring information that confirms your existing beliefs while ignoring contradictory evidence.

**Hindsight Bias:** Believing, after an event has occurred, that the outcome was predictable, even if it wasn't.

**Self-Serving Bias:** Attributing successes to internal factors (such as skill) and failures to external factors (such as luck).

**Overconfidence Bias:** Having more confidence in your abilities, knowledge, or judgment than is objectively warranted.

**Status Quo Bias:** Preferring things to stay the same rather than making changes.

**Loss Aversion:** Preferring to avoid losses more strongly than acquiring equivalent gains.

**Framing Effect:** Making different decisions based on how information is presented, rather than on the facts themselves.

**Bandwagon Effect:** Adopting beliefs or behaviors because many others do.

**Dunning–Kruger Effect:** Tending to overestimate confidence despite low ability in a domain.

**Negativity Bias:** Giving more weight to negative experiences or information than positive ones.

**Sunk Cost Fallacy:** Continuing a course of action because of previously invested resources (time, money, effort), even when it's no longer the best option.

**Recency Bias:** Giving undue importance to recent events over historic ones.

**Affinity Bias:** Favoring people who share similar interests, backgrounds, or experiences.

**Optimism Bias:** Believing that you are less likely to experience negative outcomes compared to others.

To identify your biases, consider these questions:

- Do you believe that the world is full more of opportunity or danger? (negativity bias)
- Do you believe that there are only certain locations that are good or acceptable for you to live? (location bias)

- Do you view the world as a glass half full or half empty? (opportunity bias)
- Do you believe that people are fundamentally honest or dishonest? (availability heuristic, bandwagon effect, or halo effect)
- Do you believe that you have access to all the resources you need or that resources are scarce and unavailable? (scarcity bias)
- Do you believe it's more important to win at all costs or to play the game? (outcome bias)
- Do you believe you have free will agency in the world or that your fate or actions are predestined? (agency bias, victim/responsibility belief)
- If income were not a concern, do you believe you can take time off or that you must always have a job? (urgency fallacy belief)
- Do you believe the only good jobs are of a certain type? Are the only worthy jobs in engineering or being a lawyer, banker, doctor, social worker, or teacher?

These are examples of beliefs that keep you in place and prevent you from changing your trajectory or career. They are neither good nor bad, but they either serve you or they don't. They can be self-limiting or opportunity expanding. What we are interested in understanding is what kind of beliefs you have, how they are serving you in your life, and which of them you want to change. Beliefs that limit you are constrained beliefs, while those that give you freedom to grow, achieve, and take calculated risks are unconstrained beliefs.

## EXERCISE: MY BELIEFS/BIASES

Worksheet setup: Make two columns. Label the left-hand column Belief and the right column Constrained/Unconstrained.

1. Beliefs/biases list: In the first column, list all your current beliefs, both personal and work related. Use the sample questions above as prompts, but feel free to add other beliefs.
2. Constraint: Consider if each belief is constrained or unconstrained and label it accordingly in the other column. You might know the classification immediately because you are aware that a particular belief has held you back in the past or could hold you back. Others might not be so obvious and will require some thought.

## Reflections on Current Beliefs, from Perception to Perspective

A key shift in mindset is to move from a focus on perception, which is our own interpretation of the world, to perspective, viewing the world from a certain angle, including others' viewpoints. This approach gives you an informational advantage, as most people remain trapped in their own perceptions and beliefs. By understanding others' perspectives, biases, and beliefs, you can win arguments, advance your career, and improve relationships. Perspective is an edge available to us all but that few people utilize.

## Decision-Making

The final element of mindset is decision-making. Are decisions easy for you or difficult? What is your approach, typically? This is an important reflection because you want the process you use for decision-making to correlate to the role you end up pursuing.

To explain the role of decision-making in navigating your Next, let me tell you about my own entry into decision-making and my observations. I was running strategy processes, corporate development processes, and board processes. What I found was that teams are mostly ineffective. First, they have a bunch of biases they don't recognize, and so they have blind sides. Second, they tend not to be explicit about what process they're using to make decisions, so they get confused because they have different mental models they're trying to utilize—inductive versus deductive, for instance. Third, their members don't look at information the same way. Some people, for example, regard opinion as fact. A classic example is the clash between salespeople and product people. The product people want facts. The salespeople want client anecdotes and regard those as facts, and therefore, the two sides are not on the same page.

I started to do up-front work with my teams to set the conditions for successful decision-making. We would agree to have a single source of truth around facts we could all rely on. We could have differences of opinion but not of fact. We would agree to a common, collaborative process for the way we were going to make decisions together. And we had to recognize and be explicit about our biases. We got those things out on the table because the kind of decisions we were involved with were not tactical day-to-day ones. They were "bet the firm" decisions we had to get right. We were going to be held accountable by shareholders and employees.

Throughout all this experience, I became more aware of my own decision-making style. I like to have a lot of information. I like to take my time and not be rushed. I talk to other people to get their input, but I don't involve them in my final decision. I like to see my decisions as patterns over time. I look at all the risks versus rewards. That approach has served me tremendously well as a strategist but would serve me poorly if I were a day trader, factory manager, or field commander. Much of my success as a strategist has resulted from the high degree of correlation between my decision-making style and my chosen career. I was able to be right about decisions and to align the way I made them more than 50 percent of the time.

So, how do you make decisions? Under what conditions or with what process are you most successful? Does this match what you are currently doing in your role or have done in your recent roles?

**If you want to take a deeper dive into some of the innovative thinking around decision-making, The Chicago School's work in behavioral economics is a great place to start. Check out its articles in its online *INSIGHT* Magazine at www.thechicagoschool.edu/insight.**

## EXERCISE: MY DECISION-MAKING PROCESS

Freeform writing about my decision-making: Whether by hand on paper or in a digital document or spreadsheet, write down everything you can think of about your decision-making style or approach. There are no columns in this journaling style of exercise!

## Reflections on Current Decision-Making Approach

After completing the exercise, read what you wrote. As you do that, consider these questions and jot down your thoughts.

- Do you need more or less information?
- Do you make decisions quickly or need time?
- Are you an intuitive decision-maker or focused on data?
- Do you rely on emotions or logic to make decisions?
- Do you make decisions on your own or refer to others' opinions?

Consider any additional patterns and tendencies you can spot in your decision-making process and add those to your document.

What does all this tell you about what you're really suited to do and what you are doing now? If, for example, you're a highly intuitive decision-maker who likes small amounts of information and a fast pace and who wants to focus on action, then a research or development job is going to be a bad fit. Are you making decisions in a way that aligns with your competencies? Is your decision-making approach valued and in alignment with the contexts and cultures in which you've been working? Do you need to make some adjustments?

So, how did our three friends Pierre, Rachel, and Caroline do with these exercises concerning mindset?

### PIERRE

**Motivation:**

Intrinsic/extrinsic: Pierre is motivated by financial wealth creation, status, and control (all extrinsic).

Creative/reactive: He wants financial security for his family (creative) and is aware his family wants him to return to Paris to be near them (reactive). He is competitive with his friends and colleagues and wants to have the status of working for a famous brand company.

**Aspirations/goals:** He has an existing plan of (1) leaving his consulting company, (2) moving from Montreal back to Paris, and (3) working for a large financial services firm there. He wants to focus on developing his strategy and business unit planning competencies while working in insurance and with a global organization. He is unsure what he wants to do longer term.

**Beliefs/biases:** Pierre has a strong location bias (his own and his family's), a strong urgency fallacy bias, and a strong opportunity bias.

**Decision-making process:** His decision-making process is well aligned with being a corporate strategist (lots of information, collaborative, risk-focused, takes his time, consultative, long-term focused, balanced, etc.).

## RACHEL

**Motivation:**

Intrinsic/extrinsic: Rachel is motivated by her need to provide financially for her family (extrinsic) and by her interest in becoming an entrepreneur and having freedom over her career (extrinsic).

Creative/reactive: She wants financial security and work-life balance for her family (creative). Her family wants her to stay in New York City and work for a prestigious company. Her husband wants her not to work as hard and for them to have access to excellent healthcare and benefits for their expanding family.

**Aspirations/goals:** Rachel has no clear current goals and is confused about how to go about getting what she wants.

**Beliefs/biases:** Rachel has several biases, including urgency fallacy bias, location bias, negativity bias, and sunk cost fallacy (her current position).

**Decision-making process:** She is an emotional decision-maker with a highly intuitive and creative process for decision-making. She likes to talk with her friends and family and is swayed by others' opinions. She finds it hard to stick to unpopular or difficult decisions, revisiting them multiple times.

## CAROLINE

**Motivation:**

Intrinsic/extrinsic: Caroline is driven by a love of learning and being of service (intrinsic) and by a need for personal recognition and status and being associated with or employed by well-known brands (extrinsic).

Creative/reactive: She is influenced by her affinity for and need to support her children as they launch into adulthood (creative) and by her desire to give back and be of service to her community/ecosystem (creative).

**Aspirations/goals:** She has an existing plan of (1) being appointed general counsel at her Fortune 100 company and being appointed to the board, (2) looking for a more satisfying role with another more internationally focused player as a general counsel, and (3) getting appointed to other board roles. She wants to focus on developing deeper recognition for her international business law competency and to spend more time building her reputation. She has a vague plan about quitting and doing NGO work if she cannot get what she wants.

**Beliefs/biases:** She has a strong negativity bias against her current work environment, a strong location bias against being in London, and a strong spotlight effect bias about her current role and its drag on her perception of advancement.

**Decision-making process:** Caroline is a considered, careful, cautious, logical decision-maker. She takes her time, gathers facts and opinions, compares options, and uses both risk and reward to come to conclusions. She has more difficulty doing this with her own situation than professionally.

## TESTING, TESTING

You've done a lot of reflecting on who you are in Step 2, including your competencies, motivations, and values. But you may find that you'd benefit from some formal assessments to gain a more complete picture of who you are. Appendix E: Assessments lists recommended tests and tools and how to access them.

## Ready for Step 3

You have done some hard work in this chapter! Taking stock of your current reality by working through the Four Axis Framework is a key foundation for deciding on—and moving toward—your desired future reality, your Next.

Before moving on to Step 3 in the next chapter, look back through all of your exercises from each of the four quadrants. Reflect on what you've written. Does it all make sense? Does it capture who you are? Anything you want to add? What are you curious about?

Discuss the output with family, friends, and colleagues who have known you for a long time and have had exposure to you in different situations. They can help you go from self-assessment to a sort of 360-degree analysis, ensuring your results represent you and your reality.

In the Culture quadrant, you identified your core values and assessed your comfort levels and fit with past work cultures.

In the Mindset quadrant, you explored your attitudes, including motivations, goals, beliefs, and decision-making.

You have reflected on your output and shared your findings with trusted family, friends, and colleagues for their input on your current reality.

Celebrate your completion of Step 2! You now have clarity around your current reality, which is a critical first stepping stone toward determining what you want to be different in your career.

## CHAPTER WAYPOINTS

Step 2 of the Seven Steps to Success is about taking stock of your current reality by understanding who you are today to determine where you want to go next.

You have worked through the Four Axis Framework to examine your current reality from four perspectives: competency, context, culture, and mindset.

Competency was assessed by exploring your intrinsic capabilities, generalist skills, and specialist skills, and rating your strength and enjoyment in each area.

You examined your Context—teams and organizations in which you've built or utilized your competencies. You should now have a clearer sense of contexts that fit you well and a foundation for articulating your credibility and relevance to employers.

# STEP 3

## Imagine: Know Your Options

> **"The first principle of success is desire—knowing what you want. Desire is the planting of your seed."**
>
> **—Robert Collier**

Now that you've taken a close look at your current reality in Step 2, we can move on to Step 3, in which you'll imagine what you want your new reality—your Next—to be. If you're worried about how you're going to figure this out, you're in good company. In my experience, most people struggle with deciding what they want. They struggle in one of two ways. They get stuck with confusion caused by too many possibilities, wondering how to tell what they really want. They also get stuck by being overwhelmed by the gap between their desired future and current reality. "It's too far. I cannot do that." This sense of being overwhelmed usually stems from not knowing what is probable and how to take small, purposeful actions that build confidence and lead to longer-term achievement.

Experience, personal insight, many conversations with recruiters and human development specialists, and pattern analysis of the five hundred or so clients I have worked with over the last five years have led me to two conclusions about overcoming these struggles.

First, even if you don't know your purpose, you almost certainly know your desires. You can articulate and list all the things you want for yourself, for the person you would like to be. Your desires are the seeds of discovering purpose. Whether ten years, five days, or three minutes from now, think about a future that inspires you to action. In career terms, breaking this down into stepping stones—what you want to learn and experiences you want to have, in what context, and with whom—is the path to clarity.

For example, in my early thirties, as I was leaving McKinsey & Company, I was dazzled by the number of possibilities open to me. Should I focus on go-to-market strategy, on corporate development, or on services and support? I had spent years coming up with plans for clients, half of which were ignored or never implemented properly. I knew that I wanted more control (responsibility and accountability) over outcomes and that I desired to prove my own ideas in a big business. I wanted to demonstrate that my recommendations were right. Through conversations—interviewing the role—I realized that I needed to develop myself further in strategic and planning roles before taking on general manager roles. I wanted a seat at the table "in the room where it happens." I ended up going to Hitachi Ltd (a three-hundred-thousand-employee company) to run strategy and corporate development. My possibilities were filtered and made a practical reality.

Second, gaps are overcome by taking purposeful actions. To understand this, consider the goals you identified as your current aspirations in Step 2. You might find yourself daunted by the gap between your current level of competence and your aspirational level. As an example, imagine you're a very talented tennis player who consistently wins at a junior club tournament level and aspires to go to the Olympics in four years. But you need a much bigger and better serve to stand a chance. Your starting point is not trying to serve the ball 140 miles an hour today; that's the goal, not the first step. Instead, a purposeful action you might take is practicing tossing the ball a little higher and seeing how that improves your impact, or bending your legs more and jumping into the ball, or using more angle on your racket as you hit. All these actions may improve results, and testing them will tell you what works for you and how well. You will make progress toward your goal and build confidence, giving you better options as you move forward.

Actions that are attached to your motivation and aligned with developing competency are purposeful. Fill your life with purposeful actions and grow real competencies, and at the end of your life, whether you found your purpose or not, you will feel that you have lived a purposeful life, a life worth living. If you want different results, you must do different things.

Taking purposeful action is a skill you can learn. Deliberate and sustained practice of an action that leads to your goal is purposeful and helps you transform yourself through changing habits and behaviors for the better. Doing something for three days is an idea. Doing something for three weeks is an attempt. Doing something for three months is a habit. Doing something for three years develops a core competency, mastery. The actions you take today will help you do better work tomorrow.

In addition to action, mindset is key. Feeling sad or overwhelmed when you compare the life you have today with what you desire is normal but not useful. This is not manifestation or motivation. It's destructive. Get excited about how you could become better today and succeed tomorrow. Live a life of desire backed by competence, and you will become an indomitable force of nature!

## The Essence of Step 3

In this chapter, you will:

Review the work you did following the Four Axis Framework in Step 2.

Use the Four Axis Framework a second time to articulate your desires regarding competency, context, and culture and turn them into a list of possibilities. What do you want to be different, better, or more meaningful?

- What do you want to spend your time doing (competency and experience)?
- Where do you want to do this (location, company, size of team)?
- With whom do you want to do it (people with what sorts of values and cultures)?

Where does this lead you in terms of desired and potential possibilities?

- There are several potential versions of you. For example, I have been a management consultant, a general manager of software and services businesses, a functional leader, a territory sales leader, and a leadership coach.

Filter your possibilities to get to probable options.

- Look at your level of aspiration or ambition. Does a tennis player want to stay at a club level? Play at a city level? Or try for the Olympics?
- Look at your credibility, relevance, and fit. Does that tennis player have the serve required to succeed? Or the backhand? The motivation to practice and compete?

Break down the gap between your current reality and desired state by understanding the actions you need to take to improve to the mastery level you want over time.

Prioritize the actions that feel worth taking and that connect to your motivation, and sequence them by relevant factors (difficulty, availability, cost, etc.).

A physician I coached is a good example of moving from assessing one's current reality to understanding desires, generating possibilities, filtering those to the probable, and taking purposeful action. This doctor was well respected, wealthy, the recipient of many accolades, and happily married but wholly unsatisfied in his career. He had been a GP, had run hospital departments, and for the last fifteen years, had run an integrative medicine practice supporting a Native American tribe. He was sixty-five years old, and he could not envision how he could make a change at his stage of life, being so entrenched professionally, but he had come to loathe his day-to-day life.

I worked with him through the Four Axis Framework, and he began to see which aspects of his current reality were not what he wanted or needed. He realized that his overdeveloped sense of responsibility (reactive motivation) was keeping him frozen, but he could not see how to let go of his ties to the tribe and the people he served. He knew he was not ready to retire, but he could not imagine making a career change. It seemed overwhelming.

He took leave from work and went on vacation with his wife to visit their adult children and to spend some time thinking about what he really wanted and the options that might fit those wants. He came to some conclusions, the first of which was that his current reality was not sustainable and he had to make substantial changes. He had to stop feeling responsible for all the health issues of the tribe (reactive drivers of his motivation) and some of their leadership decisions that he considered dysfunctional (misalignment of culture and values). He had to disentangle himself from his patients' lives and live his own. He realized he had to quit his position and spend more time with his family and on his health—he had had a mild heart attack (intrinsic and creative motivations).

He was thorough and exacting in listing his future possibilities: clinical consultant, hospital operations expert, medical ethics teacher, coach for early career doctors, health podcaster, or entrepreneur. He decided to utilize his deep competencies as both a medic and a deer and game hunter (he owned a large amount of land and enjoyed deer hunting) to focus on building a business, as this was most likely to achieve his desires and was the most probable option.

His desired context was to be an entrepreneur leading a small team in a small organization with no boss and a more balanced lifestyle. His desired work values and culture were to work in an environment that had integrity and freedom and was supportive. He aligned his mindset, being motivated by being of service to others, caring about animals, and being deeply curious about the issues that affected them. With a goal of owning his own business, he overcame limiting beliefs about his ability to change and do new things. He took purposeful, actionable steps.

Pragmatically, he knew he needed help, support, and greater expertise than he had on his own. He needed a team. He joined up with two genetic research scientists he had known for many years and began systematically asking groups of hunters and animal farmers about the problems with keeping livestock. By doing research, they quickly came up with a short list of issues, at the top of which was disease diagnosis in wild herds. They checked to see if the animal farmers would pay for testing and if the state and federal authorities thought this was a big need. He founded a genomics research group focused on disease diagnosis in herds of wild animals.

Today, he is a successful CEO and happy individual with terrific family relationships and a compelling way of learning and giving back. He got what he wanted by examining his desires, understanding his possibilities, filtering them to the most probable, and taking pragmatic, actionable steps.

Figure 15: Focus on Step 3

*In this chapter, we focus on Step 3—Imagine: Know Your Options. Source: Moo Pie Advisors, Inc., 2025.*

## Articulate Your Desires

Imagine you are holding a funnel through which you are going to pass your possible opportunities. First, you will use your findings from the competency, context, and culture axes in Step 2 to formulate a list of desired possible career opportunities (different versions of you) that you will pour into the funnel. You will then filter those down to a shorter list of probable opportunities and, eventually, to your next pursuit. You'll use probability and pragmatism (related to competency, context, and culture) for that funneling process, together with real-life constraints such as location and family commitments, moving from options that are only possible desires to those that are probable. You'll also be mindful of your mindset, watching out for how your motivations, goals, beliefs, and decision-making style uncover your real desired pursuit and how they may help or hinder you in the process.

Figure 16: Funnel of Options from Possible to Probable

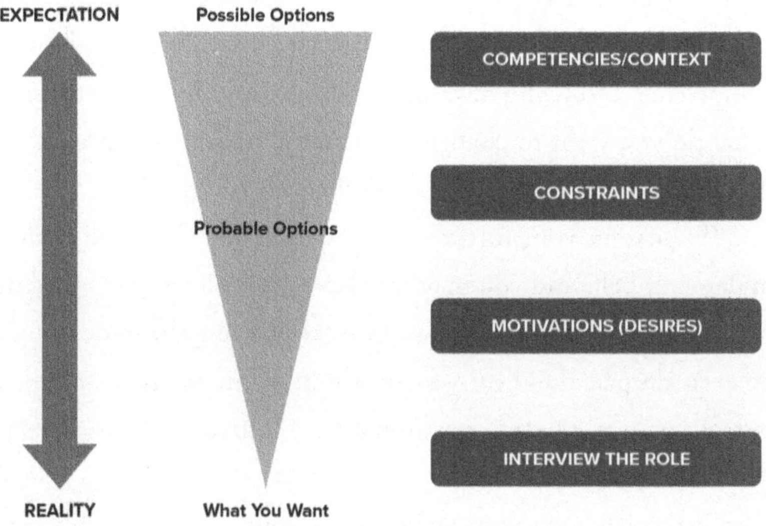


*Moving from possible to probable options. Source: Moo Pie Advisors, Inc., 2025.*

What you want is going to vary by your age group. If you're doing this in your twenties, you want to focus on your desired competence. What are you going to be good at? What do you want to be known for? Getting good at anything typically requires a time commitment to achieve mastery. Many believe it takes approximately ten thousand hours to reach a level of mastery.

The ten thousand hours concept is based on research by Anders Ericsson, a psychologist who studied expert performers in various fields (sports, music, etc.), finding a strong pattern of consistent, persistent, focused practice among high achievers. In his book *Outliers*, Malcolm Gladwell popularized this concept, which makes the important distinction between simply spending time doing something and engaging in "deliberate practice," which involves focused effort, feedback, and continuous improvement.[3]

If you're doing this in your thirties, you likely already have your ten thousand hours or are getting close. How is this working for you? Are you on the right trajectory? Are you enjoying your deepening competence and being rewarded both intrinsically and extrinsically? What do you want to change, stop doing, or add? What would you do differently? Where does your desire lead you next?

If you're in your forties or fifties, your ten thousand hours are under your belt, and you may well have multiple deep competencies. Now you're wondering if you want to keep doing the same thing and go even deeper, build on your learning or move on to an adjacent pursuit, or even pivot to start something different. Where does your desire lead you?

By the way, ten thousand hours is a handy round number, backed up by research, but I caution you against getting too caught up in that figure. Your own talents, innate aptitude, and access to resources play a role in how long it will take you to achieve mastery. The key idea here is that you not only have to put in however many hours you need to reach a certain level, but you have to spend those hours deliberately. You have to practice and build your skills and knowledge in a way that promotes learning and growth rather than simply going through the motions. So, the quality of your practice, access to resources such as good coaching or mentors, and your own individual capabilities might mean that you achieve mastery in far fewer than ten thousand hours, or it might take you a bit longer.

---

3 Malcolm Gladwell, *Outliers: The Story of Success* (New York: Little, Brown and Company, 2008).

## Don't Aim for Mediocre

There is someone out there with half your talent but ten times your self-belief making five times the money. Ninety-nine percent of people in the world are convinced that they're incapable of achieving great things, so they aim for mediocrity. So you're insecure? Guess what: The rest of the world is too! Do not overestimate the competition and underestimate yourself. You are better than you think.

## Finding Your Desired Competencies

This involves factoring in your competency and context to come up with your big list of possible options. Then, you bring in your level of aspiration, credibility, relevance, and fit to start funneling down to probable options. So, let's get into the action of Step 3, starting with the information you already have on hand.

### EXERCISE: MY DESIRED COMPETENCIES—WHAT I WANT TO DO

Worksheet setup: As with prior exercises in Step 2, you may choose to set up a worksheet on paper or in a document or spreadsheet on your computer or tablet. Either way, make three columns. Label the left-hand column Desired Competencies, the middle column Strength/Enjoyment, and the right column Wants.

1. Competency listing: Review your lists of competencies from the three exercises in Step 2 in which you identified intrinsic, specialist, and generalist competencies. In the left column of this worksheet, list all the competencies you want to bring to your next career move and life situation from across all three of the competency categories.

You will most likely automatically want to include competencies that you rated high for both Utilization and Enjoyment. And you might want to include those you were low or moderate in for Utilization but high in Enjoyment, as these are ones where you may wish to develop and grow (do more of or do differently). And you might consider listing some competencies where your enjoyment was only moderate but Utilization was high, as these could come in handy in your job search or entrepreneurial development as highly marketable skills you possess that you don't love but don't mind using.

You will most likely not bring over to the current worksheet those competencies you want to stop using or use much less because your enjoyment of them is low or you consider them no longer very marketable or relevant.

2. Desires/wants: In the right column, make notes about what you want to do with each competency. Examples may include the following:
    - Do it differently: Become better at this skill area through practice, training, formal education, mentoring, or other means because I enjoy it and it is likely to get me where I want to go.
    - Do it more: Become better by using this competency more. It's a real strength of mine, and I want to use it more often.
    - Start doing it: I have not had a chance to use this competency at all, so I would like to start doing so.
3. Progress versus progression: Which are you looking for? Which do you desire? Progress or progression? Progress involves bringing about meaningful change in yourself—growing, learning, getting better at the things you want to do more of. Progression can be important to you, but it is more the window dressing—promotions, advancement, more prestige.
    - What would this look like for you? Can you picture what your lived experience doing that would be? Is that what you desire?
    - As an example, in my career, I wanted progression when I was in my twenties and thirties: more responsibility and authority, and more focus on practicing leadership and decision-making. In

my forties and fifties, I wanted progress, to be as good a strategist and advisor as I could possibly be. I shifted away from my ability to solve, direct, and control to a more collective and collaborative approach requiring different skills and modalities, more facilitation and coaching of a team in articulating its vision.

- Do you want to move up in the organization or go deeper into your competency/functional area?
    - Progression: What would you need to be promoted? Can you do that in your current organization, or would you need to move?
    - Progress: What would you need to learn or experience? Current organization/team or a new one?

Once you've completed the My Desired Competencies exercise, set it aside for the moment and complete the next exercise: My Desired Contexts.

## EXERCISE: MY DESIRED CONTEXT—WHERE I WANT TO DO IT

Worksheet setup: Make three columns, labeling them left to right: Desired Contexts, Enjoyment, and Wants.

1. **Context listing:** Review your lists of team and organizational contexts from the two Step 2 exercises in which you identified your current, recent, and/or past contexts. In the left column of the current worksheet, list all the types, sizes, and scopes of teams and organizations you might want to consider for your next career move.

   You will most likely automatically want to include team and organizational contexts that you rated high for Enjoyment. You might want to include some contexts in which your enjoyment was moderate but you sense it could be high if you were better equipped to work within them (e.g., with more experience, training, knowledge, or leadership support).

2. **Desires/wants:** In the right column, make notes about what you want to do in context.
    - Figure out the types of work environments—types of employers, industries, etc.—in which you could work on this type of team more often or as your primary focus.

    Consider industries, niches within industries or sectors, types of products, and types of services that would put you in these organizational contexts.

    List locations: Where do you want to live and work? Countries, cities, towns; town versus countryside? Remote or in-office?

    - Figure out the type/size/scope of teams you really want to be on.
    - Small, medium, or large?
    - Project-based versus ongoing operational?
    - In the office, remote, or hybrid?
    - Hierarchical or flat and democratic?
    - External (customer, partner, or supplier) or internal?
    - Very accountable (sales, marketing, or product) versus administrative (HR, finance, operations, etc.)?
    - Figure out the types of roles you could seek that would put you on this type/size/scope of team more often:

    Do you want to be a subject matter expert or advisor?

    Do you want to be an individual contributor?

    Do you want to manage people (drive others in ensuring an outcome)?

    Do you want to lead people (drive others in defining and achieving outcomes)?

    - Identify what you need to bridge the gap between where you are now and where you want to be.
    - What would you desire/want to do next (a stepping stone or next step)?

## Filling the Funnel of Options

In Step 2, you explored your goals—aspirations you have that might involve competencies you want to develop, contexts you envision yourself being in, and so forth. Remember that Step 2 was about your current reality. All you had to do was daydream or brainstorm about your goals. You didn't have to determine how attainable they are or figure out how you would get to them. You didn't even have to narrow them down.

Now, in Step 3, we are being both more pragmatic and more aspirational, considering specific options—career pivots, types of jobs to go for, lifestyle changes—through the lenses of feasibility, desirability, and priority. We are funneling from the possible to the probable.

But first, you need a solid list of options to consider, a funnel of possible Nexts. As you evaluated your current reality in Step 2, some clear options might have emerged as you thought about your broad goals—too many, perhaps. No worries: We'll sort through those. Or maybe not enough options, or even no options, came to mind. No worries about that either. There are ways to generate options that fit with what you desire using a variety of sources, from pure brainstorming (alone and with trusted people) to more detailed data analysis, with the data being both your insights from Step 2 and information available out in the world.

Look at what you've entered in both your desired competency and context worksheets. Is anything missing because you might not have thought of it at Step 2? Add it now! While each step in our seven-step process builds on the prior one, you do not have to limit yourself to what you thought of in a prior step. One way to expand beyond your initial lists of competencies and contexts is to reflect on activities, tasks, or goals that you have engaged in either personally or in professional or educational settings and that give clues to what you really want to do and in which contexts.

Whatever you have written down, whatever your point of view, consider these questions and see what they bring up for you:

- What competency or activity have you done, or currently do, that causes you to lose track of time when you are in the thick of it (in "flow")?
- What activity or competency causes you to look forward to starting your day as you wake up each morning? Which days do you dread, and why?
- What do you daydream about doing while you are doing the things you have to do? If you could drop your responsibilities, how would you spend your time?
- What would you spend your time doing if you could not fail at it, if there were no trade-offs of cost or responsibility?
- In what sorts of environments or settings do you lose yourself?
    - Outdoors?
    - Alone with your thoughts at a desk or in a creative studio?
    - With people? Making things in a hands-on way or simply being around others who are making things?
    - In a formal corporate environment or a laid-back setting?
- If you didn't have to make money, what would you really want to do?
- What kinds of people really give you energy, and where do you find those people?

- In five years, what do you want to learn? How do you want to grow? What do you want to know how to do? What are you excited about?
- Who are five people you admire, and what do they do?
- What do you really want to do but you're just too embarrassed to tell anyone?
- If you knew you wouldn't fail, what would you dare to do?

Some of your answers might sound impractical. If you need or want to keep doing paid work, you can't necessarily drop everything to pursue hobbies. But you don't have to worry about that yet in our process of exploration. Those ideas might not make it through the funnel when you filter from possible to probable. But for now, they provide valuable clues to what you might want. That physician who found a way to combine his professional background and knowledge in medicine, healthcare, and science with his hobby related to hunting and being outdoors is a great example.

The bottom line here is that you took stock of your current reality before, and now you are asking what you want to be different and why. This is your road to clarity about your future, to the turns you might want to take to move away from your current reality. Or, in the words of Bugs Bunny, "I knew I shoulda taken that left turn at Albuquerque."

You probably already have ideas of what you might want to do next in your career and life. Perhaps you came into this process with some options that you just need to narrow down. Or maybe, while working through the Four Axis Framework, specific ideas have come to mind. Now is the time to write those down, if you haven't already.

To spark your thinking, let's revisit Pierre, Rachel, and Caroline.

## PIERRE

**Possibilities—What Pierre Wants**

Competency: He has competencies for four possibilities: business strategy, business unit planning, operations, or insurance product development. He wants to develop deeper expertise in strategy and business unit planning but needs more information to make a final decision. He is concerned he could be pigeonholed and will not have other options if he does this.

Context: Where does he want to do this? His desired location is Paris, near his family and in the thick of the French-speaking financial world. He wants to work for a large, complex multi-line corporation and to lead a small team. He would prefer a multi-line insurer or a financial services group with global reach.

Values and culture: With whom does he want to do this? He wants to work with intelligent, hardworking, logical, and ambitious colleagues. He wants to feel part of an elite group working on issues that will create impact in the company with people who care deeply about outcomes.

Desires and motivations: What is driving him? What does he desire? Pierre wants financial security for his family (creative) and is aware that his family wants him to return to Paris to be near them (reactive). He desires the status of working for a famous brand company (extrinsic).

## RACHEL

**Possibilities—What Rachel Wants**

Competency: Rachel has several possibilities based on her competencies: become a more senior design team leader, focus on being a subject matter expert, be an individual contributor web designer, or become an entrepreneur in interior design.

Context: Her family wants to stay in New York City and have her continue working for a prestigious company, but she wants to move to Austin and have a larger home in a more relaxed community. She desires to work for herself or at least in a small creative team but is stuck in the gilded cage of her existing global team leadership role.

Values and culture: She wants to work in a diverse team culture in which design thinking and creativity are respected. She would like to be in an environment that values integrity, meritocracy, and entrepreneurialism.

Desires and motivations: Her real desire is to be an interior designer; however, her primary motivations are financial security and work-life balance for her family (creative), and she is concerned that leaving the security of her corporate job will endanger this.

## CAROLINE

**Possibilities—What Caroline Wants**

Competency: Caroline could stay the course and become general counsel at her Fortune 100 company (generalist leadership competency); look for a general counsel role with a more internationally focused player, leveraging her European business law experience; or leave the safety of large corporate life and join an NGO in Eastern Europe, leveraging her contract and employment law experience.

Context: Her family wants to stay in London, but Caroline would like to move back to Paris or Geneva or even to Eastern Europe. She wants a small team. She likes large corporate environments and questions whether she can be successful in smaller environments with fewer resources.

Values and culture: She likes people who have high integrity, are committed, have an aspiration to be the best, and are kind, fair, and patient. She likes diverse, multinational environments with highly educated people. She dislikes political, nondiverse, homogeneous, hierarchical cultures.

Desires and motivations: Caroline is torn by two competing desires: a need for personal recognition and status and being associated or employed with well-known brands (extrinsic), which drives her to stay at her company and become general counsel, and a love of learning and being of service (intrinsic), which drives her to change her life and work for an NGO.

If you are still at a loss for options for yourself, don't worry. This can be a good time to involve trusted friends, family, or colleagues again. You won't be coming to those conversations empty-handed; you're bringing clear insights into what you want and have to offer. Your broad-brush picture of what you are going for can help them provide specific suggestions.

You could host an "idea party" by having friends and family join you in a room with sticky notes and pens to explore your opportunities and desires. This is a strategy developed by the late Barbara Sher, considered by many to be the "godmother of life coaching." You can find more on this strategy and her work at barbarasclub.com. Similarly, browse job postings (just for ideas, not to apply), read LinkedIn profiles, and follow industry news to get ideas.

## Finding Your Probables

If I had answered the question "What do I really want?" when I was in my thirties, the answer would have been to be a gentleman sheep farmer. I've always liked spending time alone outside in beautiful surroundings. I like peace and quiet. I like taking care of animals and being with dogs. I like reading books on the side of a mountain.

My specific dream was to own many acres of beautiful hill or mountain land where I would herd the dark-colored Merino sheep that produce the wool called Pecora Nera (literally "black sheep"). They are Italian, as the name would suggest, and very rare. Only two pure flocks exist, both in New Zealand, and the woman who owns them is now in her eighties. The wool is very valuable and is acquired exclusively by Loro Piana, a famous Italian garment company.

My dream made some degree of sense: I'd have a company that wants to buy all my wool at a high price, and sheep don't take a lot of maintenance. You get some Great Pyrenees dogs, drive the sheep up to the top of the mountain in summer, drive them to the bottom of the mountain in winter, and otherwise, just leave them alone. So, this dream was "possible."

There is just one hitch: I'm completely unsuited for this line of work. I have no credibility as a shepherd or livestock farmer of any kind. I didn't grow up on a farm, so I have no context for the work. I don't know how to handle livestock. I have no relevant training or competency. And even if I could learn those things, I do not like getting covered in mud and would not want to climb a mountain every day. I do like reading books and hanging out with dogs, but I can do that by my fireplace in California. Also, I cannot move to New Zealand. My wife's company is here in California, my daughter is in college in the US, and my friends are all in Northern California and Europe. Could I buy the flocks and move them to California? Not feasible. And so, being a Pecora Nera shepherd remains only a dream. It was possible, but not probable.

## From Possible to Probable

As you look at all the options you've poured into your funnel, are some comparable to my shepherd dream? Are they technically possible but very unlikely? Do you have some options on your list that are not so far-fetched, but you have an inkling they might not make practical sense because you don't possess the competencies needed for that option or the innate ability to gain them? Do you have any relevant experience or education? If not, that might not be a problem, but it does make the road to getting to that option much longer and more circuitous. The point here is to use honesty and realism to narrow the field of possibility. In terms of the ikigai model, this allows you to think about what you are good at and what you would be able to get paid for. Once again, share your options with others to get feedback on the realism of your opportunities. (In Step 5, you will learn more about the best ways to do this.)

## Finding Your Next

To take some pressure off this part of the process, know that you are still not narrowing to one thing, to that one next move. You just want to whittle your options to a manageable number, such as three to five. Many people get stuck at this point. This is usually because the options are often very different things. You could be a strategist, you could be in operations, you could be in business development, you could be in customer service, or you could open a dance studio (those twinkle toes!).

Here's a secret: You are not going to figure this out just sitting there wrestling with choices on your own. You have to talk to people who are doing the things you're considering. Identify people who are at least a few years ahead of you. Ask them what their life is like. What do they do on a daily or weekly basis? What do they enjoy? Not enjoy? You are basically interviewing your future self, which allows you to narrow down from the probable to what you want to go for. Go interview the job first, before you get interviewed.

A big part of the decision to go in a certain direction is considering what that would take. What would be your next steps? Can you go straight into conducting a job search? Would you first have to get better qualifications? Would you look for a mentor? Would you stay where you are but go for a promotion or a reassignment? In Steps 4 and 5, you'll get into these and related questions more purposefully as you devise and implement a plan. For now, gather this information as part of your due diligence on how the various options would play out for you, and use the information to inform your decisions around which options to begin ruling out and which make the even shorter list.

At this point, you want to bring in the other axes, Culture and Mindset, to refine your list of probable opportunities. Through these lenses, consider how your probable opportunities align with what you want (are passionate about) and what is needed in terms of impact on those you love and care for. This can be turned into a set of short-term goals or developmental steps to get you started and longer-term objectives.

Pull out your worksheet from Step 2 regarding values. Which of these are nearest and dearest to you? Those should help in the apples-to-oranges quandary of your diverse choices. Which options are most likely to put you in roles and work settings in which you can live and work in alignment with those most treasured values?

Next, go back to your mindset exercises around beliefs, motivations, and goals. Remember the consulting associate partner who left to start a charter boat company? She had a constraining belief that almost held her back from making a change. She worried she couldn't be successful doing something on her own. Her father was a longtime IBM employee, an old-style devoted "company man." He ingrained in her a belief that one must be employed in a large, stable company to have career security. And so, she had to have the courage to step back and imagine how life could be different if she moved past this constraining belief.

Which career options would be open to you if you decided to challenge the mindset issues that might be holding you back? Which of your motivations are truly yours versus simply reactive ones? How could you let those drive your choices? Which of your goals could be realized if you let yourself go in a direction where those could be achieved?

## But Honestly, How Do I Really Decide?

Finding your Next will require managing real trade-offs. Caroline wanted to give back and join an NGO, but she also wanted what comes with being a board director or general counsel in a Fortune 50 company. She was torn between doing good in the world and achieving her personal career ambitions. Rachel wanted to have the money, security, and control that come with being at a bigger company, but she also wanted to see if she could be an entrepreneur. What are your conflicting desires like those Caroline and Rachel experienced? What will your tiebreakers be?

Often, the decision is made for you because the answer lies in what you are best at. Sometimes, the power of location, where you want to be, drives the choice. Sometimes, the power of relationships, with whom you want to be, determines it. Sometimes, there's just a pragmatic consideration about whether you can actually make something happen. In Rachel's case, she ended up not believing she could be successful as an entrepreneur, so she stayed where she was in a great role, being highly paid and taking care of her family. Caroline got promoted to general counsel but hated it so much that she quit and went to work for an NGO. Pierre was not bedeviled by these issues. He knew he wanted to move to Paris. He knew he wanted to take care of his family. So he got a job with a former boss who was the head of strategy at a large French multi-line insurer.

### TESTS WON'T TELL YOU WHAT TO DO (BUT THEY CAN HELP)

In Step 2, you might have used one or more of the assessments listed in appendix E to help clarify your current reality. As you now move into exploring your future options, it's a good time to revisit those results or to consider taking additional assessments.

While no single assessment can tell you what to do (only you can decide that), the career matches they generate, along with insights into your personality, strengths, values, motivations, and decision-making style, can help you get closer to defining what you want next.

## The Power of Regret: Future-Proofing Your Decisions

You don't want to build your life only to look back and wish you had made different decisions. That's the power of regret—it helps you clarify what matters most before it's too late, and you have an opportunity to harness that power here. There are four major types of regret as identified by Daniel Pink:[4]

- **Foundational regrets:** "If only I had done the work." These tend to be small decisions that compound over time and have a significant impact on achieving your goals and creating your identity. As we will discuss in Step 5—Implement: Activate the Plan, discipline is the antidote. Just do it. Doing is being.
- **Boldness regrets:** "If only I had taken the chance." These decisions are about not making decisions. Today's procrastination and prevarication, fear and doubt, breed regrets

4 Daniel H. Pink, *The Power of Regret: How Looking Backward Moves Us Forward* (Riverhead Books, 2022).

tomorrow. This category is the most prevalent and powerful among all respondents in the study.

- **Moral regrets:** "If only I had done the right thing." These decisions are about being out of alignment or integrity with yourself, such as by lying, cheating, or hurting someone. The more you align and live with your values and other people who share your internal compass, the more you avoid these regrets.
- **Connection regrets:** "If only I had spent time with so and so . . ." Not allocating time to those who matter most in your life—parents, siblings, friends—hurts us over time. People give us meaning and context.

In a survey of more than twenty-three thousand people about their biggest regrets in life, Pink found that regret is age related. People in their twenties and thirties tend to regret both action and inaction. In other words, wishing they had done something different or in a different way (action) or wishing they had done something at all rather than not taking action (inaction) contribute about equally to the regrets they hold at that point in life. But as we age, the balance tips sharply toward regretting what we didn't do—the chances we didn't take, conversations we didn't have, time we didn't spend in certain ways or with certain people.

As you make decisions about your Next, use these regret categories as lenses to future-proof your decision. If you're not sure what you want, ask, "Which choice will I regret not taking?" Then imagine that regret—"How would I feel if I didn't do this?" Not "What would I get?" but "What would I feel?" That emotion brings the decision into the present, making it no longer abstract but real and personal. Use this approach to stem the tide of regret before it shapes your future.

## BEFORE YOU MISS WHAT MATTERS

The wisdom of Clayton Christensen, renowned Harvard Business School (HBS) professor and bestselling author of *How Will You Measure Your Life?*, is a powerful compass to keep in mind early in your journey to help you avoid regret later.

Christensen's book grew out of a now famous 2010 talk he gave to graduating HBS students, a lecture inspired by his own confrontation with mortality after a cancer diagnosis. Health challenges prompted him to reflect more personally and philosophically on success, not just in terms of career, but in life: What gives it meaning? How do we prioritize our relationships? How do we live with integrity? In his talk, he posed three deceptively simple questions:

1. **How can I be sure I'll be happy in my career?**

   Christensen encouraged students to look beyond money or status and define what truly brings satisfaction and meaning to their work.

2. **How can I be sure my relationships with my spouse and family become an enduring source of happiness?**

   He emphasized that love and connection are not things we "find" once but must be continually invested in through consistent choices.

3. **How can I be sure I'll stay out of jail?**[5]

   Though this sounds tongue in cheek, Christensen meant it seriously: Many well-intentioned people make small ethical compromises that compound over time. His

---

5 Clayton M. Christensen, James Allworth, and Karen Dillon, *How Will You Measure Your Life?* (New York: Harper Business, 2012).

point was to stay aligned with your values in all circumstances, even under pressure.

Answering these questions for myself had a profound impact on me and on my journey to writing this book. Christensen's work reminds us that regret often comes not from failure but from losing sight of what really matters. His insights will come up again in Step 6, when we explore how to measure and celebrate success once you've reached your Next.

## Happiness Is a Choice

Yuval Noah Harari makes the point that much of what we pursue as happiness is built on "imagined realities."[6] These are the stories and beliefs we choose to live by. In other words, happiness isn't something handed to us; it's something we decide to step into. One way we make that choice tangible is through celebration.

Marking small victories by treating yourself—or better yet, celebrating with others—turns happiness from an abstract idea into something lived. Yet most of us don't do it. We reach a goal and immediately move on to the next one, never pausing to acknowledge where we are.

Celebration is a practice that reinforces happiness, builds energy, and strengthens connection, but it has become surprisingly rare. I'd like to see us normalizing celebration.

If you accept those two points—that happiness is a choice and that we don't celebrate enough—then a simple formula follows. Ray

---

6 Yuval Noah Harari, *Sapiens: A Brief History of Humankind* (Harper, 2015).

Dalio reduces it all down to three essentials: meaningful relationships, meaningful work, and something to look forward to.[7]

Put all this together and the through line is clear: Choosing happiness, practicing celebration, and then grounding yourself in relationships, work, and the future are elements that sustain progress and will give your Next both meaning and momentum.

## Deciding from the Outside In

Another way you might find your Next is to reverse the process. Instead of being driven inductively by your desires and aspirations, instead of designing your Next as a hypothesis, consider letting availability make the decision for you. Be deductive. Put the decision in the hands of the market.

Let's say you have three options and can't bear to bump any of them off your list. Deeper analysis of your motivations, competencies, and so forth doesn't help you shorten the list. Maybe some options are more probable than others, but the differential is not enough. What do you do? Put yourself on the market! Apply for and do your best to secure interviews for jobs in each of the areas of your options. You are letting the market decide whether you are credible or relevant and whether you are a fit.

Many variables affect whether someone is invited to interview, advances in the process, and ultimately gets an offer. Relevance, credibility, and fit are going to be on the line and will play a huge role in determining which opportunities come along. You can take the decision out of your hands in a proactive way. You're making it an externalized, pragmatic, market-based decision, which is a form of purposeful action.

---

7 Ray Dalio, *Principles: Life and Work* (Simon & Schuster, 2017).

## What Are You Not Going to Be Anymore?

> **"Tranquility comes when you stop caring what they say, or think, or do, only what you do."**
>
> **—Marcus Aurelius**

A final way you might find your Next is to be reductive. Instead of being driven by your desires and aspirations, you can decide by elimination what you are no longer prepared to do or who you are no longer prepared to be. What repels you or angers you about your current life? What are you no longer prepared to tolerate about yourself or others? Think about that.

Here is a good checklist of questions to ask yourself and reflect on:

- Is your biggest fear not fulfilling your potential?
- If the next ten days end up looking exactly like yesterday, would you be closer to or further away from your dreams?
- If aliens came down to earth and studied your routine, what would they assume your priorities are?
- What's the biggest lie you tell yourself about why you aren't where you want to be?
- If twelve-year-old you met you today, would they be in awe of and inspired by where you are and who you are?
- If ninety-year-old you met you today, would they be proud or disappointed?
- What's the first thing you're procrastinating on that you know would change your life?

- Have you been consistent enough to deserve the results you want?
- If you knew you couldn't fail, what dream would you go all-in on?
- Are the people around you pushing you forward or holding you back?

Sometimes, it is easier to see in the negative. Remove things from the table. What do you reject? What do you resist? Many people I have advised have used this method to eliminate actions, habits, current competencies, people, and influences from their lives, and by doing so, have freed themselves up to be what they really want.

## Interview the Role

Applying and interviewing for jobs as one way to let the market determine which path you should take is not as passive an approach as it might sound. In their book *Job Moves*, Bernstein, Horn, and Moesta advocate looking beyond titles and companies for a broader view of what a potential job can do for you.[8] Rather than simply being interviewed so that the employer can determine what you can do for them, think of yourself as interviewing the role so you can determine where it could take you. How does it align with your aspirations, goals, and desires? Learn more about this approach at www.jobmoves.com.

---

8 Ethan Bernstein et al., *Job Moves: 9 Steps for Making Progress in Your Career* (Harper Business, 2024).

## From Step 3 to 4

You should now have a clearer view of your Next, but if not, reread this chapter, review or even repeat the exercises, talk to more people, have that idea party. Keep working at it until you have made a decision about your longer-term goals or have narrowed them down to one or two options to actively explore. You will get to a point where your Next is defined! You will have clarity around what you want and the purposeful actions you're going to take to get there. Remember that this journey takes a bifocal approach—focusing on the goals that might be a few years out while just as importantly focusing on a short-term set of purposeful actions, the stepping stones, that will add up to your longer-term goal. This is the tennis player breaking down the components of a serve to become a better player competing at higher levels.

You'll never find clarity if you keep telling yourself, "I don't know what I want." Because the moment you say that, you give yourself permission to not find the answer. But here's the real reason you're stuck: If you do know what you want, you'll have to act on it, and your brain doesn't like that because familiar equals safe. So, instead of saying, "I don't know," ask yourself, "What scares me about knowing?" Because once you remove that block, you clear space for answers to land and clarity to come through.

If you were the main character in the movie of your life, and you have an audience watching the movie, what would the audience be screaming at you to do? What is it, and what needs to change?

With that clarity and sense of purpose, you will get out and test your decision to make sure it's truly the right direction and to know how you are going to get there. This leads us to the next chapter, Step 4, where you will define your value proposition. You will articulate "This is what I am, this is what I want, this is why I am suited to do this, and this is why I'm interested in this particular opportunity." Being able to articulate your value proposition is critical for enlisting the help of others along your journey. Remember that employers and investors are interested in your credibility, your relevance, your fit, and your motivation, all of which should be articulated in your value proposition as you take purposeful action toward your Next.

Before moving on to Step 4, I want to leave you with two final observations.

First, in my experience, when trying to find their Next, people spend a lot of time stressing and being anxious about outcomes. They focus on the result, not the journey, often frozen by a fear of failure, and do not achieve their goal. Looking for stepping stones to your goal, actions you can take that you desire and will enjoy, can unfreeze you.

Second, people focus on things outside themselves instead of working on what they can control—things inside themselves. I hear things like, "I can't move forward in my life until the economy is better." Focusing on the exogenous is natural, but you can't control those things. Increased success comes when you focus on the things you can affect and not the ones you can't.

## CHAPTER WAYPOINTS

In Step 3, you moved from the current reality assessment of Step 2 to a forward-looking approach to generating options for your Next.

You utilized the Four Axis Framework again, this time to envision your desires across competency (what you want to do), context (where and with whom you want to do it), and culture (the values you seek in your work environment).

Filtering an initial list of possibilities to more probable options involves considering aspiration, credibility, relevance, and fit while being honest and realistic about current capabilities and the feasibility of options.

Taking purposeful actions bridges the gap between your current reality and a desired state.

You were encouraged to brainstorm broadly, alone and with others, about what you desire.

Celebrate your completion of Step 3! Crack open a bottle! Hug the cat! Call your friends! You now have clarity around what you want and some stepping-stone strategies—purposeful actions—for getting there.

# PART 2

# Getting Your Next

# STEP 4

## Investigate: Why You?

> **"Identity is cause; brand is effect, and the strength of the former influences the strength of the latter."**
>
> **—Larry Ackerman**

Meg was puzzled by the fact that she kept getting interviews but no job offers. She was smart, credible, and relevant to her chosen field. But as she told her story to me, her coach, I saw the problem: Her story was flat. Nothing about it engaged me, and that's because she was not engaged in it herself. She was highly motivated to land the types of jobs she was going for and was confident that she could do them well, but her ability to convey why she was *the one* for the job was sorely lacking.

Good stories don't just have beginnings, middles, and ends. They are connected by a why. They have an arc that brings the listener along, riding the ups and downs of the message. They show a transformation in the protagonist—the why. Meg was on her best behavior in interviews, answering all the questions and not fumbling her words, but she had not adequately conceptualized why the things she had done in her career, or how she had done them, should be of interest to anyone.

Her problem was one of not understanding that hiring managers wanted to hear her *story*, not just a set of unconnected answers to questions that gave no clue as to who she really was and what her value proposition was. She had not connected and crafted the story of her value proposition and learned to deliver it with heart and enthusiasm. She lacked confidence in herself because she had not internalized the reality that others would want to hear her story. When she did those things, connected her value proposition to her why, her confidence grew, her story became compelling, and job offers resulted.

Figure 17: Focus on Step 4

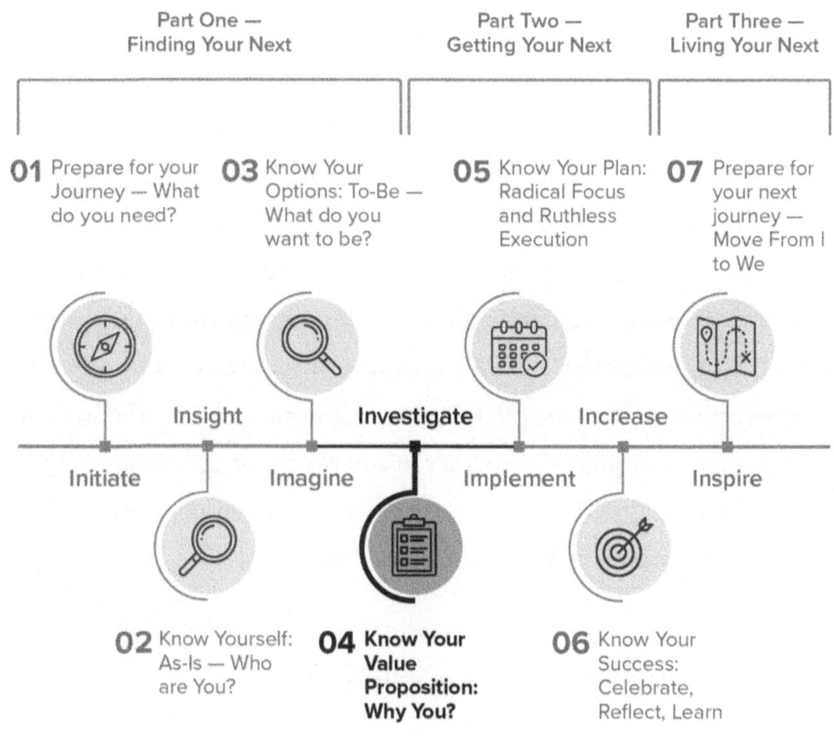


*In this chapter, we focus on Step 4—Investigate: Why You?*

*Source: Moo Pie Advisors, Inc., 2025.*

## Your Story Is Your Ticket to Your Next

So, you know what you want next, at least directionally—where you want to go, what you want to do, who you want to be. Now you have to get there. How to do that?

Well, your story is your ticket. Construct your story. Learn to tell your story well. Figure out whom to tell it to so that people know you and can help. Focus and build a plan of purposeful actions to execute and make progress. Live your story every day.

In this chapter, Step 4, you're going to take all the hard work you did in Steps 2 and 3 around preferred competencies, contexts, mindset, and more, and use that knowledge to articulate why you are the one for the job, the promotion, the successful business investment, admittance into a new career field, or whatever your Next entails. Remember that employers and investors are interested in your credibility, your relevance, your fit, and your motivation, all of which make up your value proposition. Being able to articulate your value proposition is not only for job interviews or investor pitches; it is critical for enlisting the help of others along your journey, whether in a networking, advisory, or other supportive capacity. Telling the story of your value proposition is a way of taking purposeful action toward your Next.

## Story Development Simplified

Both Steps 4 and 5 on the way to achieving your Next involve lots of drafting, testing, refining, telling, and retelling of your story. To ensure you don't get lost along the way, here's the story development process in a nutshell:

**Clarify your value proposition—the "bones" of your story:** The foundation of your story is a concise narrative that covers three questions: *Who am I?* Your background and identity. *What do I want?* Your goal or next career move. *Why me?* The unique value you bring.

**Frame your story:** Think in terms of a beginning (your current situation), a middle (the complication you're solving), and an end (the resolution or impact you intend to achieve).

**Practice and refine it:** Tell your story to yourself, hearing yourself say it out loud, maybe recording it and playing back the audio or audio/video. Tweak and revise as needed. Also test it out by telling your inner circle—close friends, family, very close colleagues—and further revise it. Ask for feedback on your story.

**Expand your channels:** Once your basic story is in pretty good shape, translate it to the various media in draft form—elevator pitch, resume, cover letter, social media profiles. Remember, the elevator pitch, resume, and cover letter are all custom depending on the opportunity—the stepping stone you want; the social media profiles are all static, focused on representing the identity/brand that you are becoming.

**Seek next-level feedback and conduct A/B testing:** Present your story and digital documents to a small group of mentors or former managers who understand you and your work but can be candid. Ask specifically, "Does this resonate?" and "What feels unclear?" Their insights will help you tighten your narrative and enhance your delivery. Try out variations of your story (known as A/B testing in the marketing world and described in an upcoming section of this chapter).

Next, map people you don't know so well against the opportunity you are pursuing (same industry, same company, competitors, etc.), such as fellow alumni of your alma maters, members of professional associations you belong to, or senior leaders at your company or in your industry. Call, email, or InMail them and arrange virtual or in-person coffee meetings. Go see them, tell your story, and ask for their help and feedback. Refine. Listen for deeper nuances—perhaps they'll clarify industry jargon, point out skills you need to highlight, or suggest resources for upskilling. Use this input to refine both your language and your proof points. Always ask what you can do to be helpful and if they have any suggestions as to other people to talk to.

**Field-test your story:** Expand your audience to increasingly important people who are closer to the Next you're aiming for. Schedule informational chats with a few recruiters or headhunters who specialize in your field. Present the now much more polished version of your story and ask, "How does this fit what companies are currently seeking?" Their perspective might reveal any gaps between your narrative and actual job openings. They may highlight emerging trends, such as a rising emphasis on data analytics for product roles, or advise you on which keywords or metrics resonate best. You will be getting incrementally smarter and more comfortable with each meeting.

**Iterate until polished:** Consolidate feedback and revise your story—tighten phrasing, swap out vague claims for concrete examples, and fine-tune the "Why me?" section based on what resonated. Keep practicing for a smoother, more compelling delivery.

**Maintain a closed-loop mindset:** As you iterate through these steps, track which audiences raised similar questions or objections. If a theme recurs (e.g., "How did you measure impact?"), add a concise example to your narrative up front. In other words, close the loop on all that has come up through the process. Track everything (who introduced you, when you first contacted them, what their notes were, etc.)—use a spreadsheet.

In Step 5, you will take your story on the road, identifying the people you're going to tell your story to, those who can really get you where you want to go. You'll learn how to approach the conversations you'll have (and that includes job interviews, since a job interview is really a conversation between two or more people). And you'll learn how to persist, telling your story over and over, always refining and customizing it, until you get to your Next (and even thereafter).

But for now, let's focus on Step 4 and the initial development of your story.

## The Value Proposition–Story–Brand Connection

Your value proposition is the bones of your story, why you are distinctive in some way. As you tell your story, the story expresses your brand. Personal brand is talked about a great deal, and I believe that we have lost sight of what a personal brand means, especially as social media has muddled the notion of brand. A brand is not a few viral pieces of content. It is not a slogan, a logo, or a color. A personal brand is built on trust. You build that trust with consistent messaging, presentation, and execution. Inconsistency in how you tell your story—and how you live it—is death by a thousand cuts when it comes to brand.

Your personal value proposition is a brand promise—a promise of trustworthiness made up of your credibility (competency, quality, consistency, and persistence), relevance, values, and motivation.

**Your personal value proposition is a brand promise—a promise of trustworthiness made up of your credibility (competency, quality, consistency, and persistence), relevance, values, and motivation.**

Your brand expresses your value proposition and tells others:

- **This is what I am:** This is my competence and credibility. I am a good "product" that is useful, functional, and well designed.
- **This is what I want:** This is my desired clear outcome, role, or personal goal. These are the problems I want to solve and the opportunities I want to have.

- **This is why I am uniquely suited to do this:** This is my relevance and fit. This is what the experience of working with me is like. This is the user experience (UX) and user interface (UI) when working with me. This is how I am like strong customer service, a great purchase delivery, and an ideal unboxing experience.
- **This is why I'm interested in this particular opportunity:** This is how it connects to my story. (This is the hook of your story.)

You will tell these things in a way that people actually want to hear. You will tell a story they connect with; they want to find out what happens next. They want to be involved in getting you to *your* Next! And that's where the magic happens—getting people to help and support you, to open doors for you. In Step 4, you're going to construct your value proposition, defining and preparing to express your brand using elements you already have from the exercises in Steps 2 and 3.

Then, you'll learn how to talk about it, which means articulating your value proposition using tried-and-true storytelling tactics in a multichannel way (elevator pitches, resumes, cover letters, and social media presence).

And finally, you are going to refine your story by telling it over and over to get feedback and feel more confident with it.

Then, in Step 5, you'll figure out whom you are going to tell your story to, continue to refine how you tell your story, map out action steps to get to your Next, and execute a plan to make things happen.

## The Why of Your Value Proposition

After reaching the point of knowing what they want, many people struggle with taking action. They might settle into the doldrums of not believing in themselves, experiencing imposter syndrome, overwhelm, or other roadblocks. So even if they've put a great deal of effort into figuring out what sort of career transition they want to make, they never get there. In Step 5, we'll talk about your mindset and how you're going to have absolute focus on ruthless execution to get to your Next. But, here in Step 4, you can lay the groundwork for that focus by remembering your motivation. What is motivating you to keep moving forward toward your Next? What is your *why*? Your why keeps you focused and able to execute.

Examining what makes you distinctive can be highly motivating. Crafting your value proposition and telling the story of it will remind you how important this transition is to you and why you deserve to get where you want to go. When you step onto an unconventional path, your mind will always try to convince you not to do it. It will bring up all the fears you've been conditioned to believe. And the only way to move past those is to challenge your assumptions. *I'm too old. It's too late. I need to get a new degree to do this. It's too risky.* Is this true? The truth is, most people don't get stuck because they're incapable. They stay stuck because they never question the old stories that keep them paralyzed. They need to build a new story with themselves as the main character. Start questioning the old story about yourself because, the moment you do, you realize that most of it is no longer true or was never true to begin with. Create a new story with your value proposition for what you want, and tell it and live it every day.

Let's say your Next involves landing a new job. You apply, go through initial interview rounds, and make the short list that might consist of you and one or two candidates, or the short-ish list that has several candidates. You've all reached the later interview round because you all have roughly the same competencies and relevance for the role. You're all roughly going to be at the right calibration in terms of culture and fit.

Those qualifications and qualities got you to this point, but they don't win you the job. What wins is the *why* of *you*. Your unique relevance and your motivation to tell the story convincingly get you the job. Job seekers are so often puzzled as to why they didn't land a particular role. "But I was perfect for it," they say. But they weren't; they didn't tell an engaging and memorable story that made it clear why they were *the one* for the position.

Once you have a job, according to Harvey Coleman's PIE (performance, image, exposure) Model, your performance at work only accounts for 10 percent of your career advancement. The other 90 percent is driven by your image or how people perceive your professional competence (credibility, relevance, and fit) and your exposure (who knows you).[9] The key to exposure is learning how to tell your story so that the right people are aware of what you can do, what you want, and the value that you can create (value proposition).

## Crafting Your Value Proposition Story

The qualities you share with candidates who are going after the same next move as you would be called brand attributes in the language of product marketing. To identify your value proposition, you have to go beyond those to figure out what makes you—your brand—distinctive.

---

9 Harvey J. Coleman, *Empowering Yourself: The Organizational Game Revealed* (AuthorHouse, 2010).

I had dinner with a client of mine who is a very senior executive at Universal Music Group. After developing brand strategies for more than a hundred different artists, he told me that these are the exact questions he asks to unlock a musician's authentic brand:

1. **What is your *why*?** Don't tell me what you do. Tell me why you do it.
2. **What emotion do you want fans to feel when they discover you?** Don't say "inspired" or "happy." Be specific with a moment. For example, "I want to be the artist they play at two o'clock in the morning on the way back from the club after they finally got out of a toxic relationship."
3. **What do you want to be known for?** Not your sound, not your aesthetic, but your impact. Most artists build their brand around what they create, but the best artists build their brands around why people need them. Think about it: Taylor Swift isn't just a songwriter and artist. She's the friend who helps you process heartbreak. And your brand isn't just the aesthetic that you show them. It's the role you play in their life story.

Why do you want to spend so much time on your story, making it authentic and interesting? Dopamine is the chemical of motivation. It's the chemical of pleasure and excitement, and when you're asked about things that make you feel excited (not just what you're doing but why), you actually produce dopamine, and you create what are called mental markers.

Dr. John Medina calls these markers mental Post-it Notes that you make when you're with someone and they ask you a dopamine-sparking question. Research has found that when we produce dopamine in conversation, it actually makes us more memorable to the other person.[10] Your brain goes, *Oh, this person makes me feel good. I'm going to remember them.* Think about the brands of Coca-Cola and Pepsi. Both are carbonated drinks—brown colas, sugary, give a caffeine jolt. But what is different about them? Some might say it's the recipe. Sure, there are differences in taste, but what really distinguishes them from each other is the brand. Coca-Cola is typically positioned as classic and timeless, with an emphasis on nostalgia, togetherness, and tradition. Pepsi's marketing conveys younger, trendier energy, often aligning with pop culture, music, and innovation. The stories the two products tell evoke very different feelings in us. What story do you want to tell, and what feelings do you want to evoke?

## THE EMOTIONS OF VALUE PROPOSITIONS

Consider some famous brand examples that illustrate what value proposition can mean on an emotional level:

- Disney sells *memories*, not roller coaster rides.
- Amazon sells *convenience*, not products.
- Richard Mille sells *status*, not watches.
- Hermès sells *exclusivity*, not handbags.

People buy emotions!

So, how do we produce dopamine? You literally use dopamine-triggering words. An example: Do not ask people what they do. Replace that with asking them about what they are working on that gets them excited. That's a very, very simple swap, but it allows someone to be drawn out of themselves. You want to do the same

10 John Medina, *Brain Rules: 12 Principles for Surviving and Thriving at Work, Home, and School* (Pear Press, 2008).

in framing your story. You want to substitute autopilot answers for dopamine-producing ones. Charisma is not about being extroverted; charisma is about being interesting and interested.

**Charisma is not about being extroverted; charisma is about being interesting and interested.**

Crafting a story that conveys your value proposition in an interesting way starts with completing three basic prompts, which you'll do in the following exercise.

## EXERCISE: MY VALUE PROPOSITION STORY WORKSHEET

Take out a pen and paper or open up a digital document and write out your thoughts on these three prompts, referring to what you already know about yourself from prior exercises.

1. *I am ...*

   My *core* competency—what people come to me for

   My *complimentary* competency—the relevant skill from my background that creates this rare and complementary combination with my core competence

   My *compassion* competence—my human relationship skills

   My *context* competence—the context in which I do my best work

2. *I want to ...*

   Here, jot down wording that will describe the Next you identified in Step 3. Be descriptive and avoid speaking only in labels. "I want to be a product manager in AI" is not unique or interesting. "I want to be a curious, data-driven manager who guides product teams through insight into action and who helps them be more creative and productive utilizing AI tools" is a bit more interesting, wouldn't you say?

If you need some inspiration, go back to the Filling the Funnel of Options section of Step 3 and reflect again on those questions that might have gotten your juices flowing.

As you craft this part of your story, consider having a short-term "I want to ..." (this year) and a longer-term "I want to ..." (next three years).

## Refining Your Value Proposition Story

Look at what you wrote on your worksheet and see if anything is missing. Where could you provide more detail? Where did you say more than is needed? Beware of being redundant or including irrelevant or unflattering information. Edit as necessary.

Get clear on your whys. How do they relate to what you want? What is the relationship between the you that you are depicting in answering these questions and what you want? How would you explain that to another person? Now you are storytelling.

Also, is your story true? Is it an old story, or does it authentically tell the tale of who you are now and what you want?

You should now have the makings of an actual story. Think about the classic hero's journey that is the basis of so many tales from the beginning of time. Our hero accepts a challenge, goes into the desert, overcomes the challenge, comes back, and gets the thing they want. In this case, you are the hero. What is the hero's challenge in your story? What are you striving for? Why do you want it? What is the background you bring? (People love an origin story.) What will success look like?

## Solving for the Right Problem

In Step 3, you did a great deal of work around figuring out what you want to do next. To get to that point, you had to identify the problem you are solving for. By that, I mean you had to determine the competencies you want to use or develop, the context and culture you want to be a part of, the motivations driving your desire for a change, and the goals you are aiming for. At the heart of this was figuring out what you want to change about the current reality you identified in Step 2. That is the problem you are solving for. This needs to come through loud and clear as you tell your story.

## Tailoring to the Audience

You will likely be telling your value proposition story in a wide range of situations. You want to get your story out there. If you are not known or discoverable, how can people find you or help you? (This will be mapped out in Step 5.) You might tell your story in networking settings and job interviews, tell it to friends and family who can help, and tell it to professional colleagues.

You will make adjustments along the way to tell your story in a particular way that resonates with each audience. Some people will want to hear more about the specifics of your unique skill set, while others won't have the technical or functional expertise to make sense of that but will want to hear more about the industry shift you want to make so they can think of people to introduce you to. For some people, it will be the deeply personal motivation that will strike a chord. The point is to be flexible with your story and emphasize aspects—competency, relevance, fit, and so forth—that will resonate with and engage the audience at hand.

### TAILORING YOUR STORY TO YOUR AUDIENCE

These are my three favorite ways to customize a story:

1. Share achievements in building competency—credibility, relevance, etc. (personal and professional)—as context to keep people informed.
2. Make all achievements "others-oriented." How have you helped other people succeed, or what are you doing to help them?
3. Numbers don't lie. Using metrics to quantify achievements takes the emotion out of it and makes achievement more objective. I used to record all of my projects and achievements in an interview-ready format. This provides the evidence needed to advocate for yourself, to bring up in performance reviews, and to serve as conversation springboards. And doing so will make it even easier to create all sorts of compelling personal brand content.

## Hearing Your Own Story

Take the words you've jotted down on your worksheet and start speaking them. Say them to others, record them for yourself—just vocalize them in some way. This will help you see where you may have gaps to fill in or areas where you could cut it down. Does the story have an arc? Will it bring listeners along, making them want to know more, or will it strike them as generic and uninteresting?

The story must explain *"Why you?"* at a fundamental level. You can have a great value proposition, but a compelling story puts you into motion. If you don't have a great story, it's hard to get people motivated to help you, to work on you, and to invest in you.

## A Multichannel Approach to Telling Your Story

The "who I am," "what I want," and "why me" elements of your story can be plugged and played in various formats for various purposes. These include

- spoken elevator pitches, shorter and longer versions;
- cover letters and emails;
- resumes or CVs; and
- social media profiles.

You do not have to start from scratch with each of these channels. Think of this as a scaffolding process. You have crafted your basic value proposition story, and now you will build out or "remodel" that basic foundational story for the various channels of communication and various audiences. The shortest versions of your story are likely to be your LinkedIn profile headline and your short elevator pitch. Those versions might be retooled and expanded somewhat to create an executive profile or opening summary section of your resume. You can expand that to write your About section in your LinkedIn profile bio or a cover letter.

Throughout it all, you are keeping in mind that the core of your story is "This is who I am, this is what I want, and this is why me."

Detailed guidance on these topics is outside the scope and purpose of this book, but here I want to offer you some strategic tips for each channel, an example of each, and suggested resources for more specifics.

## Elevator Pitch

Your elevator pitch, or elevator speech, is used when speaking directly to someone in person, by phone, or in a video meeting. It can also be useful for leaving a voicemail or sending a LinkedIn InMail (direct message).

It is much like the story you've already crafted in this chapter, but now you want to consider the context. Is this a networking appointment? A brief chance encounter with someone? A social occasion where you don't want to go too far with mixing business and pleasure? A speed dating–style networking gathering?

The short version usually takes about thirty to sixty seconds to say, or even briefer if it's being left as a voicemail message. This version is best for those situations in which it's not appropriate to tell the full story, such as at a party, or when you don't have scheduled time to sit down with the other person and just want to whet their appetite for knowing more about you and how they can help.

The longer version, which is often about one to two minutes but could go to about three minutes if it is engaging and moves at a brisk clip, is for those times when you have a more captive audience. This might be a scheduled conversation, the "tell me about yourself" prompt in an interview, or a networking event with structured mingling.

### ANATOMY OF AN ELEVATOR PITCH

You might find it easy to turn your story into an elevator pitch by using the "Name, Same, Fame, Aim, and Game" framework:[11]

**Name:** What is your name?

11 Daniel Priestley, *Key Person of Influence: The Five-Step Method to Become One of the Most Highly Valued and Highly Paid People in Your Industry* (Capstone, 2010).

**Same:** State what you do in terms that make it easy for the other person to understand. For example, someone in an uncommon marketing role or with an unusual job title might say, "I'm in the same space as social media strategists, designing campaigns that boost engagement and drive clicks."

**Fame:** Fame is what makes you interesting—what makes you fascinating. Which big brands have you worked with? What interesting projects have you landed? Relate anything that would make you stand out—big numbers, awards, names to drop.

**Aim:** Aim is what you want right now, in the next 90 to 120 days. These might be stepping-stone roles or other requests.

**Game:** This is your bigger, longer-term vision. What do you want to achieve in the next three to six years?

I suggest adding to this paradigm consideration of the other person. How can you be helpful to them?

## AN ELEVATOR PITCH EXAMPLE

Here is a sample of an elevator pitch that a fictitious job seeker, Taylor, might use when meeting someone at a university alumni networking event. Taylor works in healthcare product management, and the other person has a background in retail and e-commerce.

**Name:** Hi, I'm Taylor Morgan. Thanks for asking what brings me here today.

**Same:** I'm currently an associate product manager at CareConnect Inc., where I support our flagship product—a secure messaging platform for hospitals. I translate clinical workflows into actionable user stories, work closely with engineering and UX teams to deliver new features, and help optimize client retention through data-driven insights.

You can think of this as being like working at a retail company to launch a new loyalty rewards program, in which you might gather feedback from store managers, define how the rewards system should function, coordinate with developers to build it, and then analyze purchase data to see customer engagement.

**Fame:** I built a tool that lets our clients easily see how their users interact with our platform, which boosted sales by about 15 percent and kept nearly 20 percent more customers on board. I also led the effort to connect our product to the two big hospital record systems, which made our partnerships about 20 percent more valuable.

**Aim:** I want a holistic, end-to-end life cycle product manager role where I can own strategy and road map for an entire digital health product. My goal is to work on initiatives that meaningfully improve patient outcomes and streamline clinical workflows at scale.

**Game:** Ultimately, I want to direct multiple product teams in developing end-to-end cardiovascular healthcare solutions—tools that clinicians and patients actually love to use—and help shape the future of how cardiovascular care is delivered. My father died of heart disease, and I want to spare other families the sadness that mine went through.

**Help:** I'd love to hear any ideas you have about how I might make this move or to be connected to anyone you think I ought to get to know. I also want to hear more about ways I could support you.

## RECOMMENDED RESOURCES FOR CRAFTING YOUR ELEVATOR PITCH, RESUMES, COVER LETTERS, AND SOCIAL MEDIA PROFILES

Free and low-cost advice, templates, and samples are available through these sources:

Greg Langstaff's website

https://greglangstaff.com/

LinkedIn Learning, Coursera, and Udemy offer short courses in their career categories.

## Cover Letters

Cover letters are often the most dreaded aspect of a job application. Getting to your next move is invariably going to involve writing your story in the form of cover letters for jobs and emails for networking requests. The resources cited earlier provide more detailed guidance and samples, but here, I'll share some key ways to frame your thinking and strategy for these communications.

Think of your cover letter as a strategic narrative that bridges your track record with a prospective employer's most pressing challenges:

- Open with a concise statement that puts you on the map and conveys the specific impact you've made, ideally quantifiably.
- Rather than recapping your resume, choose one to three signature accomplishments that illustrate how you've navigated complexity, led change, or unlocked new opportunities—whatever is relevant for the goal at hand—and then

make a clear connection between each story and the outcomes this organization needs to bring about.

- Weave in evidence of your industry savvy by mentioning a trend or obstacle you know the organization is facing and articulating how your expertise (and your personal brand's *why*) positions you to address it.
- Keep each paragraph lean and purposeful: Frame the challenge, name your approach, and highlight the result you've achieved in the past or could bring about for them.
- Conclude with a forward-looking proposition—an invitation to discuss how you might replicate that success in their context—so your closing serves not just as a courtesy but as a clear next step in a conversation you're already framing.

Above all, avoid extraneous verbiage, filler and fluff, overly flowery language, and clichés.

You can see how this plays out for Taylor in figure 18.

## Figure 18: Tailoring Your Cover Letter

# TAYLOR MORGAN

Product Management | Product Operations

(xxx) xxx-xxxx | Charlotte, NC | emailaddress@email.com | linkedin.com/in/your-linkedin-URL

March 12, 2026

Sarah Nguyen
Hiring Manager
MedFlow Innovations

Dear Ms. Nguyen,

As a healthcare-focused product leader who consistently excels at boosting engagement and revenue through clinical solutions, I am excited to apply for the Product Manager, Population Health Solutions, position at MedFlow Innovations.

Over the past year at CareConnect Inc., I launched a real-time analytics dashboard that drove a 15% upsell increase and improved client retention by nearly 20%. In parallel, I led our Epic and Cerner integration effort, raising partner lifetime value by 20%. These outcomes demonstrate my ability to deliver data-driven features that align directly with MedFlow's goal of expanding user engagement and maximizing revenue for your population health platform.

I understand that one of the primary challenges MedFlow faces is turning disparate clinical data into actionable insights while ensuring seamless interoperability. At CareConnect, our HIPAA-compliant messaging platform required not only secure communication but also deep EHR connectivity. When hospital clients struggled to monitor platform adoption, I championed the development of a usage-metrics module by collaborating with engineering, UX, and clinical stakeholders. We gathered requirements through clinician shadowing sessions, designed intuitive dashboards in Figma, and conducted iterative UAT cycles, ultimately reducing implementation feedback loops by 30%.

I am especially impressed by MedFlow's recent expansion into risk stratification analytics for ACOs, as the industry works to identify high-risk patients without overburdening care teams. My personal commitment is to build technology that clinicians trust and patients value, and I believe my track record of translating complex clinical workflows into revenue-driving features positions me to help MedFlow accelerate product adoption and drive measurable improvements in population health outcomes.

I would welcome the opportunity to discuss how my experience scaling interoperability and analytics solutions can support MedFlow's roadmap. Thank you for your time and consideration. I look forward to speaking with you.

Sincerely,

Taylor Morgan

*This sample cover letter demonstrates how to tailor a value proposition to the recipient's needs and goals. Source: Moo Pie Advisors, Inc., 2025.*

## Resumes

If your Next is a new job, a career field change, a promotion, or other employment shift, you will need to update and perhaps substantially revise your resume or CV. Even if going into entrepreneurship, a resume may be needed for investors or marketing.

Out of all the ways in which you'll tell your story, a resume is arguably the most complex and hotly debated one. This book is not a resume guide, and so I refer you to the guidance and examples of the Greg Langstaff website cited earlier for more detail. Here, I will share some high-level tips on resumes.

I have spent more than thirty years writing, reviewing, presenting, and discussing resumes with hiring managers, recruiters, and headhunters. I have been part of many hiring processes and hired well over five hundred people at various levels. Here are my best practices:

- Think of your resume as a strategic marketing document that tells your story and presents your value proposition as tailored to a specific role, not as a laundry list of jobs.
- Lead with a short professional summary, a very brief paragraph of two to five sentences that crystallizes your unique impact. Example: *Senior product leader, specialist in new product introduction. Ten years as a manager of global software teams, delivering 30 percent revenue growth through AI-powered features.* You'll see an example resume in figure 19.
- List areas of expertise. These are competencies/skills that you are differentiated in and have credibility in. Be specific and highlight competencies/skills that are relevant to the role you want or are applying to.

- Be tactical with your professional experience section:
    - If making a significant career change, organize your roles thematically around core strengths (e.g., "growth leadership," "cross-functional collaboration," "innovation and scale") rather than listing jobs strictly chronologically, so that a hiring manager immediately sees your pattern of success.
    - Or, if your search is more straightforward and you are not departing significantly from your past experience, stick with the chronological listing.
    - List the company first with length of tenure and location. Then provide a brief snapshot of the role to convey scope, level, and areas of responsibility. This can include team size, to whom you reported, budget, technologies, and more. Follow that with a few bullet points that spotlight key achievements using the STAR framework: Name the strategic challenge, outline your approach or action you took, and quantify the result in clear business terms.
    - Skip day-to-day tasks unless you feel they are needed to match the keywords of the job posting; weave those into your STAR points or into the role snapshot.

You can see this in action in the example provided below for Taylor.

## Figure 19: Tailoring Your Resume

# TAYLOR MORGAN

Product Management | Product Operations

(xxx) xxx-xxxx | Charlotte, NC | emailaddress@email.com | linkedin.com/in/your-linkedin-URL

### PROFESSIONAL SUMMARY

Results-driven product management professional with five years of progressive experience in healthcare technology and digital health solutions. Coordinates cross-functional teams to deliver user-centric, revenue-generating products. Adept at translating business requirements into actionable roadmaps, optimizing workflows, and improving patient outcomes.

### AREAS OF EXPERTISE

- Product Road Mapping and Prioritization
- Use-Case Development
- User Research & Usability Testing
- Project Planning & Time Management
- HIPAA, GDPR, and CCPA compliance
- Clinical Workflow Optimization
- Telehealth Systems
- Agile and Scrum Certified
- SQL, Excel, Power BI, Tableau
- HL7/FHIR standards and EHR integrations (Epic, Cerner)
- Figma, Balsamiq

### PROFESSIONAL EXPERIENCE

**Associate Product Manager** | July 2024 – Present
**CareConnect Inc.**, Charlotte, NC
Reporting to the Product Manager of this mid-sized health IT vendor specializing in interoperability solutions, provide support for the flagship secure messaging platform. Role scope encompasses requirements gathering, backlog management, and coordination of design and engineering teams to optimize clinician-to-clinician communication.

- Serve as the primary liaison between hospital clients and the internal dev team, translating complex clinical workflows into user stories and acceptance criteria. Delivered two major feature releases to-date with zero high-severity bugs.
- Launched an in-app analytics dashboard that provided usage insights to hospital admins, which drove a 15% subscription upsell and improved client retention by 18%.
- Conducted competitive analysis and market research that informed the roadmap for integration with major EHR systems (Epic, Cerner), contributing to a 20% increase in partner CLTV (Customer Lifetime Value).
- Organize and facilitate weekly Agile sprint ceremonies (planning, stand-ups, retrospectives) and manage the Jira backlog for a team of six engineers and two UX designers.

**Business Analyst** | September 2021 – June 2024
**MediSystems**, Charlotte, NC
Gathered and documented requirements from clinics and hospitals, supported implementation projects, and performed gap analyses for EHR system upgrades for this healthcare software consultancy.

- Conducted process-mapping workshops with clinical staff to identify inefficiencies, resulting in recommendations that improved inpatient discharge times by an average of 12%.
- Developed functional specifications and use-case documentation for a custom lab-ordering module, which was rolled out to three regional medical centers within timeline and budget constraints.
- Created Excel-based dashboards and Power BI reports to track project KPIs, such as deadlines met, budget variance, and client satisfaction, allowing leadership to proactively address issues and maintain a 95% on-time delivery rate.

### EDUCATION

**Bachelor of Science Degree, Information Science,** University of North Carolina at Chapel Hill | 2021

- GPA: 3.5/4.0; Dean's List four semesters

*This sample resume tells the story of a rising leader who is ready to move to a position of increased responsibility. Source: Moo Pie Advisors, Inc., 2025.*

## Social Media

Social media platforms are one of the most important places to tell your story. Pick the platforms most aligned with your brand and your goals. LinkedIn works for just about everyone as a platform in North America and Europe but does not cover some professions well, such as law or medicine. You might also use Instagram or Facebook if those fit the culture of your Next.

### ONLINE PLATFORMS TO SHOWCASE YOURSELF AS AN ENTREPRENEUR

AngelList (https://angel.com)

Crunchbase (https://crunchbase.com)

Gust (https://gust.com)

XING (https://xing.com)

Opportunity Network (https://www.opportunitynetwork.com/)

Alignable (https://alignable.com)

Chief (https://chief.com)

ExecuNet (https://execunet.com)

Startup Grind (https://startupgrind.com)

## ONLINE PLATFORMS TO SHOWCASE YOURSELF AS A FREELANCER

Upwork (www.upwork.com)

Fiverr (www.fiverr.com)

Freelancer (www.freelancer.com)

Guru (www.guru.com)

PeoplePerHour (www.peopleperhour.com)

Toptal (www.toptal.com)

99designs (www.99designs.com)

Dribbble (www.dribbble.com)

Behance (www.behance.net)

Contently (www.contently.com)

## LINKEDIN PROFILE TIPS

Treat your LinkedIn profile as a static showcase of your unique value or brand (because you won't be tweaking and tailoring your LinkedIn profile as often as you do your elevator pitch, cover letters, and resumes). Be careful to tell one story, not several—trying to be a consultant, an executive, and a writer will just leave everyone confused as to who you are and make you look less than competent.

Craft a headline that does more than state your title and place of employment (which is the default headline LinkedIn will give you based on the current or most recent entry in your Experience section). Distill your core promise into a bold, benefit-driven phrase.

In your About section, weave a concise narrative arc—what you do, why it matters, and how you deliver results—backed by one or two high-impact metrics or signature achievements.

Elevate the entries in your LinkedIn profile's Experience section by spotlighting outcomes over tasks. Frame each role around a strategic challenge you solved, the behaviors you modeled, and the tangible gains you drove.

Select and add to your profile three to five multimedia highlights—case studies, published articles, or speaking reels—that reinforce your brand story and ensure every recommendation you request speaks to a distinct dimension of your expertise.

Finally, curate your own posted or shared content with intention: Follow and engage thought leaders in your target domain, share or comment on their insights sparingly but meaningfully, and position yourself not just as a connector but as a go-to resource in your field.

## A LINKEDIN HEADLINE AND ABOUT SECTION EXAMPLE

Taylor's headline, for example, could be:

*Data-Driven Healthcare Product Manager | Lifecycle Product Management | Revenue Growth and Patient Engagement Driven by Analytics Insights*

Taylor's About section could tell this story:

*My passion is to work on healthcare solutions, combining clinical needs and technical execution for cardiovascular complaints.*

*I'm a healthcare solution product manager with several years of experience creating clinical software solutions that improve patient care and operational efficiency. I enjoy collaborating with physicians, nurses, engineers, and designers to turn complex requirements into user-friendly features.*

*At CareConnect Inc., I'm involved with efforts to enhance interoperability and build data-driven tools that boost client engagement and retention. Earlier, as a business analyst at MediSys Systems, I streamlined clinical workflows to reduce discharge times. My approach is rooted in listening to end users, validating assumptions with data, and iterating quickly.*

*I'm now aiming to step into a full product manager role where I can own strategy and road maps for impactful digital health products. Let's connect if you're looking for someone who balances compliance, usability, and business impact.*

## The Importance of Feedback

Earlier, you told your story to yourself to hear how it sounded so that you could tweak it for greater impact. You might also have shared it with close family or friends to get early feedback. The thing about telling your story to people close to you is that they are usually great about giving pats on the back, as they want to be supportive, but you don't always get the level of feedback that's needed for refining your story for your ultimate audiences. They might not have the industry or technical expertise to be able to give precise feedback about your story's content and delivery. Your inner circle is helpful, but you'll need to listen carefully for moments when they hesitate or ask clarifying questions.

Now that you have progressed with shaping your story for the various channels in which you'll share it, it's time to get out there and tell it again to get to a deeper level of refinement. You might call upon some of the same people who helped you brainstorm options for your Next, but you should also think of some new folks who haven't been part of your journey thus far and maybe those who are more likely to give candid, constructive criticism and not just offer "attaboys" or "attagirls." Having fresh eyes and ears as you tell your story or share your LinkedIn profile or resume can be beneficial, since they will receive your story as the same open vessel that they are when reading a novel for the first time.

You want to learn what resonates with them. Do they find it believable? Succinct enough? Interesting? You will take their feedback and keep practicing your spoken story and revising your digital versions. Remember that a dream unvoiced is just a dream, but a dream shared is a new reality.

## A/B Test Your Story

Think of the refining of your value proposition story like a marketing department determining which email subject line or layout is going to get the most recipients opening it or get the most click-throughs to a website. Craft two distinct versions of your story—version A might include more about your origin story, your relevant career history, and the *why* behind what you want to do, while version B might highlight your competencies and the cultures in which you've worked. Share each variant with different audiences (a former colleague, a mentor, or a friend in another industry) and note which version sparks curiosity, prompts questions, or earns you invitations to connect further.

By collecting this feedback—just as that marketing department would track open rates and click-throughs—you'll learn which framing resonates most. Then iterate accordingly. Refine the stronger version, test again with new listeners, and continue sharpening your pitch until you have a compelling story that consistently opens doors.

## Taking Your Story on the Road in Step 5

Now that you've imagined, crafted, refined, and rehearsed your story—knowing your what, your why, and the how that gives your story an engaging arc—you're ready to move on to Step 5—Implement: Activate the Plan. In that chapter, you'll build and implement an action plan that gets you closer to your Next. You'll learn to say no to distractions and say yes to radical focus and ruthless execution, testing new approaches as you go. You'll also expand your network, cultivating relationships and mentors who can serve as gateways to your next opportunity. And you'll learn about the six success behaviors for making things happen.

All throughout that step, you'll be taking your story on the road, connecting with decision-makers, interviewing for jobs, building key relationships. *New York Times* bestselling author Daniel Pink, drawing on the work of many scholars, including anthropologist Polly Wiessner,[12] says we are natural storytellers, with that talent handed down from our ancestors millennia ago when they sat around campfires weaving narratives that forged social bonds.[13] So, storytelling is baked into you as well. Take your story on the road and tell it! I know you can do it!

---

12 Polly W. Wiessner, "Embers of Society: Firelight Talk among the Ju/'hoansi Bushmen," *Proceedings of the National Academy of Sciences* 111, no. 39 (2014): 14027–35, https://doi.org/10.1073/pnas.1404212111.

13 Daniel H. Pink, *To Sell Is Human: The Surprising Truth About Moving Others* (Riverhead Books, 2012).

# CHAPTER WAYPOINTS

In Step 4, you used information gathered in Steps 2 and 3 to articulate why you are the right person for your desired Next.

You identified your value proposition, encompassing credibility, relevance, fit, and motivation.

You learned that your value proposition is the foundation of your story, highlighting what makes you distinctive, while your story conveys your personal brand, which is built on trust through consistency in your messaging, presentation, and actions.

You will tell your story—your why, what, and how—in an engaging way that makes people want to hear it and encourages them to help and support you.

It's important to edit your story for clarity, removing unnecessary details, and ensuring it is true to your current self and aspirations, goals, background, and vision of success.

Ways to customize your story include highlighting achievements (credibility), focusing on how you help others (others oriented), and using metrics (numbers).

The core elements of your story (who you are, what you want, why you) can be adapted for different formats, including elevator pitches, cover letters, resumes, and social media profiles. This process is like scaffolding, where you build upon your basic story for various communication channels and audiences.

A/B test different versions of your story to discover which framing is most effective at generating interest and opening doors.

Whether you realize it or not, you are a natural storyteller, ready to share your story!

# STEP 5

## Implement: Activate the Plan

> **"You have to assemble your life yourself, action by action."**
> **—Marcus Aurelius**

In the summer of 1994, I was on holiday from my consulting job in London, visiting my cousin in the San Francisco Bay Area. In the late afternoon, on a warm September day, I walked the sands of Muir Beach and gazed across the Marin Headlands toward the skyline of San Francisco. Back in London, I'd been grinding away at Andersen Consulting, feeling stagnant and uninspired with both my role and the grim environment of the early 1990s recession. As the Pacific waves rolled in, something clicked. I realized that this was where I wanted to be. I looked at the Golden Gate Bridge glowing in the sunshine and realized it was metaphorically, if not literally, the gate to technology gold, and I wanted some.

I flew back to London with a single focus: land a job in San Francisco and move to the US. This was pre-internet, so I got hold of the *San Francisco Chronicle*'s list of top companies, called the front desks of each and every one, acquired the names and addresses of heads of recruiting, and began my campaign. For each firm, I wrote a personalized cover letter and enclosed a customized resume, mailing those to 250 companies.

I let them know I would be back in San Francisco for two weeks in the near future and would be available for interviews. From that outreach, twenty-five responded, and five asked me for interviews after a screening call. I ultimately accepted an offer from Cambridge Technology Partners, the first publicly quoted management consultancy. Six weeks later, at age twenty-eight, I was unpacking boxes in my new apartment in the city by the Bay.

My tactics look quaint today, no Zoom interviews nor job portal postings, but the fundamentals of what worked remain unchanged: I had clarity of vision about where I wanted to go (just saying "San Francisco" wasn't enough). I conducted systematic outreach; I demonstrated my value, pitching my four years of large-scale enterprise technology strategy experience—skills that were rare in the Silicon Valley of 1994—plus my European industry expertise across both financial services and product companies; and I followed up relentlessly.

With the additional years under my belt since then, I know that networking should have been in the mix, but the key point here is that this story isn't about luck or just being in the right place at the right time (though those help). It's about creating your own opportunity with a strategically crafted plan and focused, persistent execution of that plan.

Figure 20: Focus on Step 5

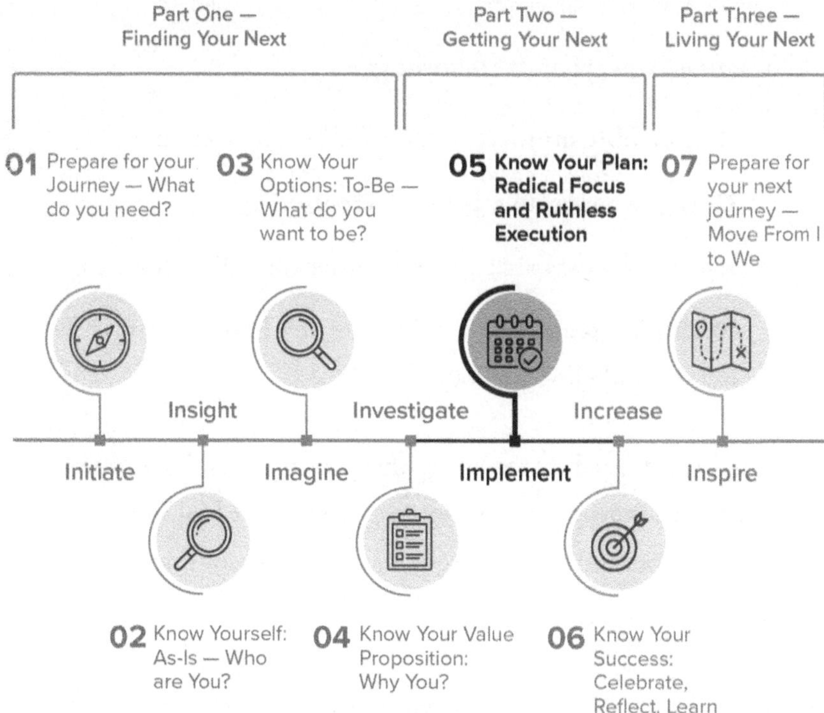


*In this chapter, we are focusing on Step 5, where you will learn how to activate your plan. Source: Moo Pie Advisors, Inc., 2025.*

## Step 5: An Overview

This chapter covers Step 5 of your success journey, focusing on your plan. Think of Step 5 as consisting of two big buckets of things to know and do.

The first is the how—the guiding "meta" core principles that will set you up for success and help you sustain momentum as you develop and activate your plan. These are mindsets and approaches that you must internalize and commit to from the start and must recommit to as you go along in your plan implementation. The second bucket is the what—actions to take to devise and implement your plan in a logical and manageable order.

The ***how*** consists of the following:

- **Responsible mindset**: responsibility and accountability
- **Doing is becoming**: issues of identity
- **Radical focus**: concentrating rather than diffusing effort
- **Ruthless execution**: a deliberate methodology to activate, iterate, and close the loop

You'll learn much more about these four principles and how to apply them to your own journey in the How to Do Step 5: Meta Principles for Successful Plan Activation section coming up next in this chapter.

## Figure 21: Lighton's Four Core Principles for Getting Your Next

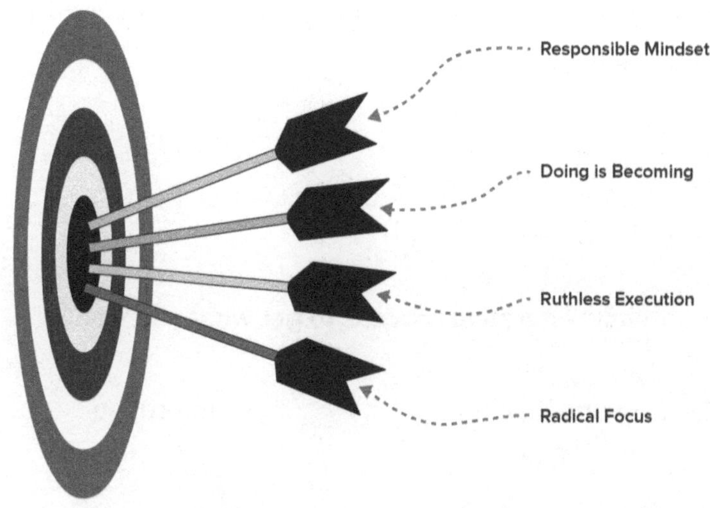


*Key principles that form the how of successful plan implementation. Source: Moo Pie Advisors, Inc., 2025.*

But first, here's a quick overview of the what—the actions to activate your plan. These are all about mapping:

- Map your *destination* (what you want, both short- and long-term goals/objectives).
- Map your destination to *channels*—ways to reach them (types of people, groups, forums, companies, etc.).
- Map those channels to *specific individuals* (specific individuals and the "doors" they are behind).

- Map those people and places to *messaging* that will have you building the right relationships (your story and why that will resonate with them).

Overarching all of this are those core principles that must be followed for all this to work effectively. These are described in the section that follows.

## Figure 22: The Iterative Process from Planning to Execution

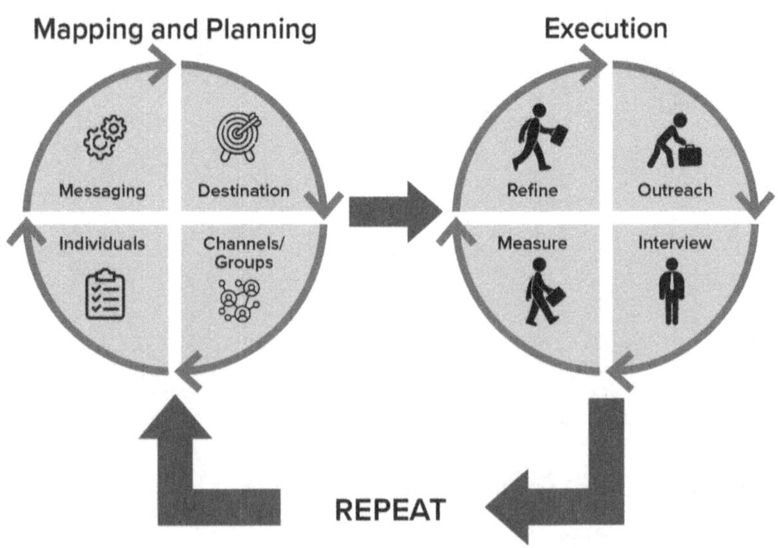


*Reaching your destination is not a one-step leap but an iterative process with multiple steps. Source: Moo Pie Advisors, Inc., 2025.*

## How to Do Step 5: Four Core Principles for Career Success

Let's take a deeper dive into the four key guiding principles that are vital for successfully activating a plan.

### Responsible Mindset

The first of our four meta principles is a responsible mindset. Everything starts with this. You are entirely responsible and accountable for your success and your own actions. You have agency in the world and complete responsibility for getting yourself to take action. Blaming your family, or other people, or your circumstances is not helpful. It disempowers you. You are not a victim. Bad things and bad people happen to all of us. It is what we do about them that matters and determines the course of our lives. Let that sink in and sit with it. Embracing this mindset unlocks the forward momentum to do what needs to be done. You cannot change the past, but you can make different decisions in the present and take different actions that lead to a better future.

#### JUST DO IT

Responsibility and accountability to yourself start by building a non-negotiable standard for yourself, a commitment. I've come to realize this is the only way we can ever grow and improve. When people say that no one's coming to save you, they're not talking about how no one's coming to help you reach your goals. They're talking about how no one's coming to save you from yourself. Without commitment, without standards, we always lose direction, and we always fall back to our lowest automatic systems—self-soothing, procrastination and prevarication, clinging to comfort, and the worst one of all, lacking a desire to change because it's just too difficult.

## PROCRASTINATION

Psychologists describe procrastination as an emotional coping strategy rather than simply a time-management problem. When a task triggers anxiety—whether fear of failure, fear of judgment, or uncertainty—our brains look for quick relief. Avoiding the task temporarily reduces stress, rewarding us with a short-lived sense of comfort. Over time, this habit is reinforced, so the next time we feel the same anxiety, we delay again, even when we consciously know the delay may hurt us later.

Lack of structure intensifies the cycle because clear plans and deadlines give the brain a road map that reduces uncertainty. Without that framework, tasks feel vague and overwhelming, heightening anxiety and making avoidance more appealing. Effective antidotes therefore focus on both emotions and organization: breaking work into smaller, well-defined steps, setting external deadlines, and practicing techniques such as mindfulness or self-compassion that reduce fear of failure. By addressing the underlying anxiety and installing structure, people can gradually replace procrastination with productive momentum. Here are five hacks everyone should know for overcoming procrastination:

1. **Use the two-minute rule**: If a task can be done in less than two minutes, do it immediately. This helps to eliminate small tasks that can build up and make you feel overwhelmed.
2. **Use the one-and-three rule**: At the start of each day, identify one big thing to accomplish and the three actions you need to take to complete the big thing. This was made famous by Steve Jobs at Apple, who used it as a management technique with his team to drive radical focus and action.
3. **Break tasks into smaller pieces**: One reason we procrastinate is that a task seems too big and overwhelming. Make it more achievable by breaking it into bite-size chunks. As an example, Michel Lotito, the French entertainer and stuntman who became famous

as Monsieur Mangetout for his consumption of indigestible objects once ate a Cessna 150 plane by breaking it down into bite-size pieces and washing it down with mineral oil.

4. **Identify your prime time**: We all have individual biorhythms. Notice when you tend to be most focused and energetic, and then dedicate that prime time to your highest priorities. Save mindless processing tasks for your mental lulls.
5. **Use to-do lists**: It sounds obvious, but creating to-do lists focuses and prepares the mind for accomplishing tasks as we imagine doing them. Crossing off tasks as we complete them gives us a sense of accomplishment and progress.

Discomfort has become so distasteful these days, precisely because of the availability of comfort. What separates the good from the great? The most underrated superpower of any athlete is their ability to do "it" no matter what. You're tired. You want to skip the last few reps. You don't want to put up the extra shots. You don't want to meal prep or eat the food that fuels your body. You don't want to stretch.

That's fine. You don't have to want to do it. The superpower comes from doing it anyway. For example, no one likes getting out of a warm bed at five in the morning to go running when it's raining and cold, but someone with a goal of training for a marathon or winning a race and who wants to be successful just does it.

So, create a standard of action and behavior for yourself. Be responsible and accountable to yourself for that standard. Nike's brand and deep significance for athletes are built on this. Just do it. Good old Nike!

## USE THAT POWER OF REGRET AGAIN

Regret was introduced in Step 3 as a powerful way to future-proof your decisions. It's important to understand what leads most people to have regrets at various stages of life—the things they did or didn't do, the chances they didn't take, the times they didn't do the right thing morally, or the connections they didn't forge or maintain. Staving off future regret helps not only with decision-making but also with taking action. As you adopt a responsible mindset to move forward, keep in mind that what you do now, the chances you take, the way you do it, and whom you involve along the way can prevent regrets down the road.

### THE ZEN MASTER'S STICK

Let's use a famous parable to illustrate this. What do you do when you believe there's no play to be made and there is no way out, so you are trapped no matter what you choose? A classic double bind. There's a Zen illustration in which the teacher holds a stick. He says to his student, "If you tell me this stick is real, I'll beat you with it. If you tell me it is not real, I will beat you with it. If you say nothing, I will beat you with it." The student ponders for a second and then reaches out, grabs the stick, and breaks it. The student was completely responsible in the face of an untenable situation and took purposeful action. If a situation is untenable, you break the stick.

Let me give you an example. How did I get to be sitting on Muir Beach looking at San Francisco and the Golden Gate Bridge? I felt trapped. I felt I had nowhere to go and was being beaten by the stick. I had reached the end of my tether. In my job, I was deeply unhappy and not succeeding at Andersen Consulting, was traveling all the time, and was being harangued by unhappy partners. London was in an economic recession, and so there were no new, exciting job opportunities. I was burned out socially. I was not going anywhere and was being beaten down by my context and my ambitions. But as I sat on that beach, I figured out I could break the stick. And so, on Muir Beach that day, I did. I hit the reset button by putting myself in a different environment: new job, new city, new country. And that was the single best thing I've ever done.

## NO ONE CARES. DO YOU?

Let's use a stark accountability and commitment example relevant to all of us: fitness. Fitness is a mathematical equation. Calories in, calories out; muscles worked, strength gained. The problem is, we live in an entitlement epidemic. We think we can cheat and still pass the class—the class being our fitness journey. We think it won't matter if we cut corners. But fitness doesn't lie, and it does matter. The only person you are cheating is yourself.

You're not owed progress because you kind of showed up. You are not owed progress because you said no to one alcoholic drink or one dessert one time. Fitness doesn't care that you hate tracking macros or don't have time. It doesn't care that someone else's genetics are better than yours or other people have it easier than you. Fitness rewards effort, not excuses.

How can people who are always very hard on themselves learn to build up their self-esteem a little bit more? I would argue it's not bad to be hard on yourself as long as you also celebrate when the victories happen. But so many people will tell you, "I have poor self-esteem because when I was a kid, people said this and that to me." They remember the negative messages and conveniently forget any positive ones. To be clear, if you've experienced actual trauma, those negative messages are likely to feel painfully real to you, and your journey to build self-esteem may take longer and require more complex healing.

(In the US, the Substance Abuse and Mental Health Services Administration offers phone and text helplines and directories of mental health treatment providers and resources at samhsa.gov.)

It's more important to realize that self-esteem is earned—by you, with yourself. You're not going to get self-esteem because everybody praises you, and you're not going to lack self-esteem because no one praised you. Self-esteem comes from doing incredibly difficult things in which you push yourself. It's not virtue signaling; it's not telling people about it; it's just doing it. And the more you do things that are incredibly difficult, especially things that are meaningful, the higher that esteem will be. Find something you care about more than yourself, and the self-esteem will follow.

Entitlement is wanting the result without changing the behavior. You want to keep all of your old easy, comfortable behaviors, but you want the new body, or you want the new career. Do you care enough and are you willing to be accountable for achieving your goal or for failing?

## Doing Is Becoming

The second of our principles is "doing is becoming," which is all about identity. Much of your identity is based on what you do for work. In turn, that is based on what you do at work and whom you spend time with—your tribe. Neuroscience shows that your identity is a self-fulfilling prophecy. The first thing you need to know is that your brain will work 100 percent of the time to keep you in alignment with your identity. So, if you're trying to build new habits and achieve new goals but you keep falling off, this is why. You haven't shifted your identity. You will achieve your goals when your identity matches the outcome.

There is a part of your brain called the default mode network, and it's responsible for your default way of thinking, feeling, behaving, and sense of identity. It's also involved in the predictive processing of your reality.[14] So, your mindset, behavior, and reality depend on who you think you are. I say this to my clients all the time: The only reason it takes a long time to achieve your goals is because it takes you a long time to become the version of you that achieves them.

So, if it feels like it's taking forever to reach your goal, ask yourself if you have fully stepped into the identity of the version of you who is already doing the thing. Am I walking, talking, thinking, and feeling like the version of me I want to be? An astronaut might not land on the moon or go for a spacewalk for many years, but they are an astronaut the day they start at NASA in Cape Canaveral. That person's identity is "astronaut" today and every day, even if they have not left Earth yet.

**An astronaut might not land on the moon or go for a spacewalk for many years, but they are an astronaut the day they start at NASA in Cape Canaveral. That person's identity is "astronaut" today and every day, even if they have not left Earth yet.**

## BE, DO, HAVE

So, 99 percent of people live in this order: have, do, be. They think, *When I have more time, more money, more clarity, then I'll do the thing and finally become the person I want to be.* But here's the truth: That's backward. The model that works is actually "be, do, have." You start by choosing who you want to be—your identity. A disciplined person and athlete? A writer? Cool. Now decide you are that person. Then

14 Marcus E. Raichle, "The Brain's Default Mode Network," *Annual Review of Neuroscience* 38 (2015): 433–47, https://doi.org/10.1146/annurev-neuro-071013-014030.

start doing the things that version of you would do. You train, you create, you show up. And over time, you stack results, the habits, the confidence, the life. Not because you waited for permission, but because you started taking purposeful action like the person who already had that identity. Be the person first and let the rest fall into place.

I am the classic example of being talented but inconsistent as an academic or executive or sportsman. My career has been full of examples of winging it and getting things done at the last moment by the skin of my teeth, by luck and by ability, not consistency. For example, I used to hate getting up at five o'clock in the morning in my twenties or thirties. There's no way you would've seen me with my running shoes on in the rain and wind. Now, I am different; I get up at five in the morning most days and am in my office working by half past five or so. I am much more successful at what I care about now, have much less trouble with imposter syndrome, and get more satisfaction from doing things. I learned we have a choice: hard now or hard later. Doing the hard things later inevitably leads to feelings of shame and poor outcomes. Tackling the hard stuff later is very stressful.

On reflection, if I had put in the hours of really doing things properly, I would not only have been successful a lot sooner in my career, but I would've been a lot more confident and not had so much imposter syndrome. I would have reached a much deeper level of mastery much faster.

If you are in your twenties and getting out of college, don't do what I did. You have a chance now to start earlier, doing the hard things sooner. And for those of you in your forties or fifties, it's not too late to change your habits. I've ended up very happy and self-actualized but not where I imagined I would be or on the timetable I would have predicted.

## DON'T EXPECT THE DOING TO BE A STRAIGHT PATH

When I left university, I had a law degree and was supposed to become a barrister. I abandoned doing that, much to my parents' chagrin. I had no idea what I really wanted to be, and I'd missed the boat on all of the graduate recruiting, so I ended up working in a ski shop for the summer. Then, my first foray into a professional career path was working for an advertising firm. I thought this was a fit because I was interested in ads; my sister and brother-in-law both worked in advertising; I was relatively eloquent, presentable, and could problem-solve, and I had basic collaboration and management skills.

I discovered that I was very good at advertising's problem-solving and client relations (generalist competencies), but I didn't like the type of problems I was working on (specialist competency) or the culture and values of the organization (context) I was working in. I had not really learned consistency yet and was looking for where I would fit. By chance, through an ex-girlfriend, I was introduced to a technology startup in London (at a time when there were no startups) at the beginning of the computer revolution. The company's largest client was Apple, and the company I joined focused on solving go-to-market problems using research and information modeling. I really liked what I did and the problems we worked on (specialist competency), but I wanted to affect a greater piece of the solution, not just distribution, marketing, and sales, so I shifted again and went to work at Andersen Consulting, where I could look at whole enterprise strategy problems and how technology could solve them. So, you can see the experimentation and stepping stones I took in my early career. It's not just linear success.

## DOING AND IDENTITY

It's the journey, not the destination. Doing and becoming are what make you what you are. Comedian Jimmy Carr puts this powerfully by defining success in his world not as fame or the standing ovation but the showing up night after night, honing your craft in front of anyone who will listen.[15] It's the work that makes him a comedian. He doesn't perform for applause; he performs because the journey itself defines him. Every set, punchline, or joke that falls flat shapes the comedian he aspires to be. His definition translates well to success in any endeavor. Actions accumulate into not just momentum but also the very essence of who you are becoming. In the doing, you truly become.

### IS IT TRUE?

As we've noted, when you step onto a new career path, your mind will always try to convince you not to do it. It will bring up all the fears you've been conditioned to believe by your ecosystem of family, friends, colleagues, and so forth about yourself. The only way to move past those is to challenge your assumptions. Is it true? Am I too old? Is it too late? Do I really need to get a new degree to do this? Is it too risky? Is any of that actually true?

Remember what we've said about how most people don't get stuck because they're incapable. They stay stuck because they never question the stories about their identity that keep them in that stuck place. Be curious and start questioning because the moment you do, you will realize that most of the stories others tell you about yourself and your identity were never true to begin with.

15 Jimmy Carr, *Before & Laughter: A Life-Changing Book* (Quercus, 2021).

## THE GAP

You're frustrated by how your life and career currently feel versus how you want them to feel: expectation versus reality. That gap closes when you start acting differently. You're frustrated because you haven't grown. Nothing's changed, but nothing's changed because your behavior hasn't changed. To build confidence, you have to take action in the face of doubt. To find peace, you have to learn to tolerate discomfort to create the life that you want. You have to stop waiting for everything to feel easy before you make the move.

The simple fact is that real change and progress come from stepping into the unknown and trusting that what you want is on the other side of the action that you're afraid to take. There's a gap between who you are and who you want to be, how your life currently feels and how you want it to feel.

That gap closes when you start acting differently. You will remain the same until the pain of remaining the same is greater than the pain of changing. You don't have to sit at home and hate yourself, because you can choose whether you want the pain of growth or the pain of staying the same, and the pain of staying the same is when days, months, years have gone by and you realize that you are in the exact same place.

## SELF-RESPECT AND DISCIPLINE

Discipline is remembering, not restricting. Every time you choose discipline, you're not depriving yourself. You're reminding yourself who you said you wanted to become. And it's not about being perfect. It's about showing up for the future. Yes, even when today's version feels tired, distracted, or triggered. Discipline is also another way in which you stop abandoning yourself. You break your own trust every time you say you're going to do something and you don't follow through. You are out of integrity with yourself. That's not a time-management issue. That's a self-worth issue. Real confidence doesn't come from hype, from affirmations and manifestation. It comes from keeping promises to yourself when no one's watching.

Discipline is a love language for your future. You don't need more motivation. You need a higher standard because when you really respect yourself, laziness stops being alright. When you love who you're becoming, your new identity, discipline becomes obvious. You're not forcing it anymore. You're just done betraying yourself. Discipline is nothing but self-respect at the highest level. It's the strongest form of self-love. It's ignoring something you want right now for something better later on. Discipline reveals the commitment you have to your dreams, especially on the days when you don't want to put the work in. The future depends on the current "you" keeping the promises you have made to yourself.

Discipline is boring. Hard work is boring. Studying is boring. Doing the same thing every day is boring. If you want to go far in life, learn how to be bored. Ask yourself, *Who am I when no one is watching?* The basics done daily beat brilliance done rarely, every time. Persistence and consistency. It's not hacks or hustle; it's consistency over intensity, progress over perfection, fundamentals over flash, over and over again. One of my first mentors and clients in the US told me, "Greatness is built in empty rooms." He could not have been more correct.

**If you want to go far in life, learn how to be bored. Ask yourself, *Who am I when no one is watching?* The basics done daily beat brilliance done rarely, every time.**

It may have taken me a while to get traction in my career in my twenties and to figure out what I wanted to do, but when I started giving myself credit for being a great problem solver, for having great pattern recognition allowing me to rapidly figure out business strategies, and for having chutzpah that deserved to be utilized, I started making real progress. When I moved to San Francisco, I got to the point where, at each fork in the road, I said, "OK, I'm going to commit. I'm going to say yes." And I committed (applied discipline) to figuring out a way to do the thing.

## Radical Focus

The third of our principles is radical focus. You can't do multiple things with excellence. You will get confused, and you will fail. Radical focus on one goal concentrates your efforts rather than dissipating them and moves you deliberately toward your Next. Having radical focus means deliberately choosing to concentrate your energy and resources on the purposeful actions that will most directly move you toward your Next and actively saying no to distractions.

Strategy is as much about saying no to things as it is about making the right decisions.

In a world filled with competing demands and shiny objects, staying focused on your plan requires discipline. To do this, take a lesson from Jony Ive, Apple's chief design officer for nearly three decades. Ive built his career, in partnership with Steve Jobs, on a simple premise: Excellence comes not from doing more, but from doing less, and doing it better than anyone else. At the heart of Jobs and Ive's approach was what he calls "radical focus."[16] In practice, this means staying focused on doing the one thing that matters until

---

16 Leander Kahney, *Jony Ive: The Genius Behind Apple's Greatest Products* (Portfolio, 2013).

it is complete and saying no to ideas that tug at your ambition, no matter how exciting and tempting, so you can channel every ounce of creativity and dedication into the project that matters most. Having radical focus means deliberately choosing to concentrate your energy and resources on the actions that will most directly move you toward your Next and then actively saying no to any and all distractions.

You are probably already aware that saying no would free up your time to focus on what matters, but have you thought of saying no as a strategic act of self-care? By saying no, you communicate a clear statement, not just to others but to yourself about your priorities, and you protect your energy and focus. Saying no is hard, but it's a skill you can cultivate.

Build the skill of saying no with these tactics:

- **Make it short and sweet:** A brief, direct refusal, such as "Thanks for thinking of me, but I can't commit to anything else right now," enforces your boundaries without drama.[17]
- **State your values:** Use polite framing, such as, "I appreciate the opportunity, but that doesn't align with my current priorities."
- **Know that assertiveness can coexist with respectfulness:** Understand that saying no doesn't have to be harsh. You can advocate for yourself—holding your boundaries, stating your values—while being polite and respectful.

17 Vanessa Bohns, "Yes, You Can Get Better at Saying No," interview by Angela Haupt, *Time*, November 16, 2023, https://time.com/6332017/how-to-say-no-better/.

## RULE OF THREE

Consider the frenetic pace of a check-the-box tourist as described in Jamaica Kincaid's classic essay "The Ugly Tourist."[18] Kincaid skewers the type of traveler who flits from city to city or site to site without ever truly seeing or understanding a place. These sorts of travelers usually learn nothing and rarely remember much of what they saw. They could benefit from the Rule of Three.

Jobs and Ive often insisted that their team at Apple limited itself to focusing on only one objective at any given time. Ive has described the conversations he had with Jobs, who remonstrated with him because he wanted to look at multiple problems: "If this is the most important priority for us, why would we work on anything else until it is done?" Because of this focus, they designed some of the world's most iconic products: iMac, iPod, iPhone, and iPad.

When I matriculated at Oxford for my undergraduate degree, my admissions tutor was Professor Oliver Taplin, head of the classics department. Speaking to our matriculating class in 1985, he said, "Ladies and gentlemen, my only real piece of advice is this: In the time you will spend here, you are faced with a fundamental choice—how you spend your time and focus. They are finite resources: You can be truly excellent at one thing, you can be good at two things, or you can be average at three things. You have to decide how to spend your time and what your level of aspiration is. The more things you try to do, the less chance of success you're going to have. Choose wisely." It has stayed with me ever since and has remained a fundamental principle in my life.

---

18 Jamaica Kincaid, "The Ugly Tourist," *Harper's Magazine* 277, no. 1650 (October 1988): 41–48; Reprinted as chap. 1 in *A Small Place* (Farrar, Straus and Giroux, 1988).

## DEDICATION

Dedication to something is to consistently and persistently maintain a set of actions in pursuit of a goal to the exclusion of other activities. You should be dedicated to a radically focused set of commitments. Commitments to your goals. Try dedicating the next six months of your life exclusively to your goals and your goals only. Do nothing else. Don't announce it to anyone. Don't tell people on Instagram about it. Don't tell anybody. Just disappear. Do the work and reemerge in six months as a different person. Connections, money, looks, intelligence—those are all great, but you can beat other people who have all of those things if you just have one thing, which is dedication to improve, no matter where you start. It's hard to beat someone who improves every second of every day without giving up. You don't need to be smart. You need to be dedicated.

What does dedication look like in practice?

- A new mindset takes 1 day.
- A new habit takes 21 days.
- A new skill takes 100 days.
- A new body takes 180 days.
- A new life takes 360 days.
- A new you takes 1,095 days.

The thing they don't tell you is that the long way *is* the shortcut, because what looks like the shortcut never gets you there. People quit when things get hard because the thought of things being hard forever feels unbearable. However, that's a lie because nothing's hard forever. You either quit, it gets easier, or *you* get harder. No matter what, the hard always ends, and the only way you lose is if you quit before seeing it through. What I try to tell myself when I'm going through hard times is that this is for now, not forever. It's not permanent; it will pass.

### CHOOSE YOUR HARD

The popular saying "choose your hard" comes from a poem of the same name by Devon Brough.[19] The phrase resonates because it names a truth: Life inevitably presents difficulty, but in many cases, we can choose which difficulty we take on. It's important to acknowledge that not every hardship is a choice: Living with a disability, coping with chronic illness, or enduring systemic injustice, for example, are not "hards" one elects. But when you do face a crossroads where you have agency, remember that the hard path is often the one that leads to growth.

## NOT DOING

Whatever you're not willing to give up is going to be the thing that slows you down from achieving your dreams. If that list is really long, it's improbable that you'll ever achieve anything important. If you are reading this in your twenties, what are you willing to give up to get what you want? Not going out with friends? Not going on that trip? Not buying that car, suit, or handbag? If you are in your thirties, are you willing to give up time with your children to spend time practicing to gain mastery in your chosen pursuit? Or vice versa, if you are a dedicated executive, are you willing to walk away to get to your child's or spouse's event? Will you carve out time for your hobby?

What did I do to become successful? It's not what I did. It's what I didn't do. I took time away from my relationships. I missed a lot

19 Devon Brough, "Choose Your Hard," *Prayables*, December 12, 2024, https://prayables.com/poetry-choose-your-hard-121224/.

of family events. I didn't go to a lot of concerts and shows. I did not sleep in. So, it turns out that if you just get rid of all of those things that hold you back, that's what creates the space for you to become what you want. To be successful.

## Ruthless Execution

Our fourth and final principal for the how is ruthless execution. This is a concept and methodology built at and made famous by Cisco. It is focused on rapid, iterative, collaborative and closed-loop planning and execution. Cisco has been one of the world's most successful companies over the last thirty years, formerly the world's fastest growing and most valuable, and is famous for its operational prowess and ability to get things done very quickly, exactly, and to a standard, predictable outcome. Cisco's culture is based on commitment, accountability, and discipline. As a methodology, ruthless execution has four phases:

- commitment
- planning
- delivery
- measurement

In practicing this vital competency, you will break your objective into incremental steps and persist through uncertainty, discomfort, learning curves, boredom, and anything thrown your way. You might need an accountability partner or coach, and that's fine, but you'll keep at it. Like an athlete honing a tennis serve day after day, you will steadily transform.

Let's look at the four phases of the ruthless execution methodology.

## 1. COMMITMENT

Commit to a goal. Do you really want it? Do you have enough clarity around what the goal is? If yes, then commit to it. Committing means that it will happen and nothing else will get in the way. Commit to the goal to yourself (responsible mindset) and to others who are close to you as accountability partners. At Cisco, your commitment was your word, your identity, and a guarantee that, no matter what, you would make it happen. Commitment should be part of your identity; keep your word to yourself and others. This includes commitment to having the inner drive and resilience to push through difficulties, stay on track, and overcome obstacles in achieving your goal. But it also involves commitment to adaptability and a willingness to experiment with new approaches and learn from both successes and failures to find whatever works best along the journey of your unique situation.

In *The Power of Your Subconscious Mind*, Joseph Murphy explains that if you have a commitment or an intention, there is a way to fix it in your brain and wire your subconscious to focus on it:[20]

- First, you take a pencil and you write down your intention. You are actually doing something physical and tactile.
- Then you read it silently to yourself.
- Then you read it aloud.
- Then you visualize achieving that intention or commitment (the power of positive visualization), and you do that over and over and over again.

---

20 Joseph Murphy, *The Power of Your Subconscious Mind: Complete and Unabridged* (Start Classics, 2024).

These actions will embed that intention into your subconscious as several types of cognitive brain networks get activated.

## 2. PLANNING

This starts with clarity around your goal and objectives, responsibility, desired results, resources, actions, timeline, and alignment. You need a plan. Thinking through how to achieve your goal makes it achievable and lets you think about enablers and boulders to your success.

At Cisco, we spent a lot of time investing in planning collaboratively so that we could all understand what we were going to do together and get aligned. Once we were aligned, we committed to the outcome and the plan to achieve it. This meant execution was much shorter because we had discussed the steps, our risks, and the resources involved and had broken our journey into short-term goals.

We have talked a lot about planning, with the reason being that the clearer your thinking about what you have to do, the better the planning and the faster and easier the execution. Once you are clear, just do it.

## 3. DELIVERY

Just do it. Preparing to do the thing isn't doing the thing. Scheduling time to do the thing isn't doing the thing. Making a to-do list for the thing isn't doing the thing. Telling people you're going to do the thing isn't doing the thing. Hating on yourself for not doing the thing isn't doing the thing. Hating on other people who have done the thing isn't doing the thing. Fantasizing about all of the adoration you'll receive once you do the thing isn't doing the thing. Reading about how to do the thing isn't doing the thing. Reading about how other people did the thing isn't doing the thing.

The only thing that is doing the thing is doing the thing. At Cisco, there were no excuses; the culture held you absolutely accountable for your actions.

## THINKING IS NOT DOING: WASHING THE DISHES

During college, my bedroom was at the far end of the hall in a student house, which meant I had to walk through the kitchen to get anywhere. This meant I had to pass dirty dishes in the sink and on the counters. Day after day, the pile of dishes got bigger and bigger and smellier and smellier. And every time I walked past them, morning or night, I'd think about how I would tackle washing them. I'd mentally plan, *OK, should I take everything out first? Maybe fill the basin with soapy water first? Should I start with the forks or the plates?*

All that planning and debating in my head did absolutely nothing to get those dishes clean. The real key was simply to start. It didn't matter how I would start the cleaning; I just had to do it.

As you think about executing your plan, the only strategy that truly matters is that you just start. Break it down into pieces if that feels doable—seriously small pieces if you want, such as washing only the forks first. The point is that doing even just one bit of your plan is what's important. Those thoughts that stop us, such as believing we need to do it all at once, or perfectly, or superfast, are what keep us from starting.

And if someone else is there to help you get started and keep going, such as an accountability partner, you'll have an even easier go at it. Back in that dorm kitchen, if I had a friend next to me drying the dishes I washed, I was sure to finish the job. So, you don't need the perfect plan; you just need to put your hands in the water, so to speak.

## THE FIVE-SECOND RULE

I learned an execution skill that everybody in life needs to know and that anybody in life can learn. That skill is learning how to take purposeful action, no matter how you feel, because your life doesn't change by thinking about it. Your life changes by doing something about it.

The science of human development tells us there is a five-second window between knowing what you need to do and actually doing it.[21] This window defines your whole life. It determines how much money you make and how healthy you are. It determines what kind of relationships you have with your kids, with your parents, and with your loved ones. There's this moment of hesitation that we all have in the small moments in life in which you have this instinct that you should pick up the phone, or start the conversation, or get off the couch and go to the gym, and instead of actually doing those things, we make this fatal mistake in which we hesitate, and then we stop and *think about how we feel about doing it* rather than just doing it. I started just doing things rather than stopping to think about how I felt about that action. I became much, much more successful.

## 4. LEAVE THE COMFORT ZONE FOR THE LEARNING ZONE

Our brains are wired for safety. Early on, we learn habits from parents and peers that keep us within familiar boundaries, within our comfort zone, as you can see in the innermost circle of figure 23. This is where we feel secure and in control. This wiring can trap us in stagnation, preventing us from tackling the challenges that foster growth.

---

21 Mel Robbins, *The 5 Second Rule: Transform Your Life, Work, and Confidence with Everyday Courage* (Savio Republic, 2017), 7–9.

## GETTING THINGS DONE WITH A BEGINNER'S MIND

From Zen Buddhism, the concept of ***Shoshin*** (beginner's mind) invites us to approach any task, especially a new or intimidating one, with the openness and curiosity of a beginner. By setting aside assumptions and expectations, we make space for fresh insights, creativity, and deeper learning. This mindset not only helps us work toward goals, but it also keeps us engaged and present in the process of growth.

The psychology of inertia is such that we are often hesitant to try new things out of fear of failure. We worry about getting it wrong, and so we stay put. We need low-stakes opportunities to experiment (those stepping stones) in order to grow.[22] The curse of competency is at play again. As we become adept at familiar tasks, we cling to them, even when they no longer stretch us, because competence feels safer than risk. Both tendencies keep us stuck. Yet, when we step into the learning zone, that flutter of uncertainty is actually a sign we're pushing our limits, moving to our learning edges.

You're not on a direct flight to Paris. You'll remain open and adaptable to experiences you have at the stops along the way, and you'll do so consciously. Decide: *Do I need to work on my serve or backhand or to become a better marketing operations professional?* Identify that stepping stone, then ask, *What two or three things can I do every day or every week to improve?*

You'll create a chain of conscious, observable, measurable competencies, and with consistency and persistence, you'll develop and exercise habits that move you steadily forward. Stay in the learning zone and grow—that's progress, not just progression.[23]

---

22 Adam Grant, *Think Again: The Power of Knowing What You Don't Know* (Viking, 2021)

23 Adam Grant, "The Surprising Habits of Original Thinkers," TED talk, February 2016, https://www.ted.com/talks/adam_grant_the_surprising_habits_of_original_thinkers.

## Figure 23: Leaving the Comfort Zone for the Growth Zone, Where Success Happens

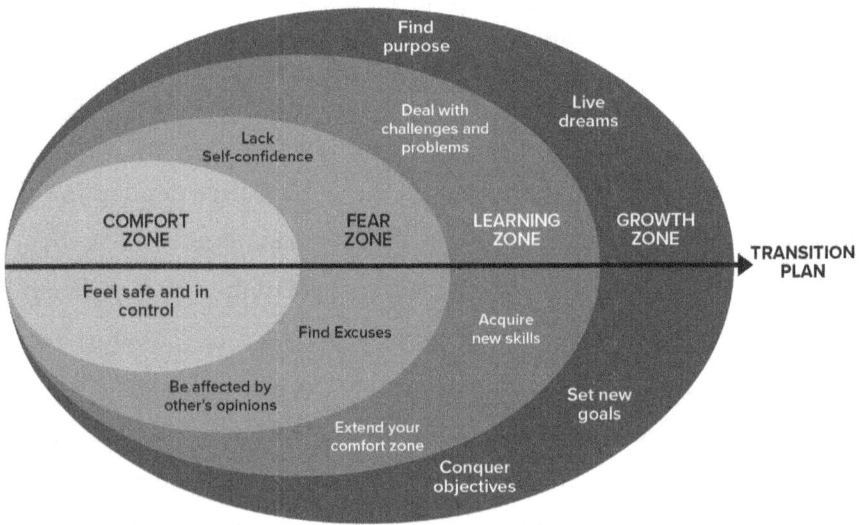


*To make things happen and reach your Next, it's essential to overcome your fears and move to a place of growth. Source: Moo Pie Advisors, Inc., 2025.*

## YOU HAVE 168 HOURS. WHAT ARE YOU DOING WITH THEM?

There are 168 hours in every week. Subtract 56 hours for sleep (if you're lucky enough to get 8 hours a night), 60 for work, 10 for traveling around (such as commuting, running errands, transporting kids), 7 for exercise (if you're that disciplined), and 10 for family meals or quality time. You still have 25 hours left.

> You have twenty-five hours—***every week***. Radical focus means knowing exactly what matters and ruthlessly eliminating what doesn't. Ruthless execution means using those hours with intention, not just activity. Stop telling yourself you don't have time. You do. What you may lack is focus, commitment, and a plan. The time is already there, just waiting to be owned by you.

## THE POSSIBILITY GAP

In the planning stage, you can get stuck because when you think of an idea, you think of all the possibilities and the different outcomes, often focusing on finding the perfect one. And so, we want to wait until everything's perfect. This possibility gap is that space between your starting point (not knowing what to do or how to do it) and the place we all want to get to because it feels good (the place of knowing what to do or how to do it). When in the gap, we all have the urge, and unfortunately there's a lot of reinforcement for that urge, to say things such as, "I can't do this" or "I'm not good at this." None of those things are true.

What you're actually saying when you say those things is "I'm having a really hard time tolerating the space between here and the learning space." You feel frustrated and are likely to give up. Modern education is designed to avoid frustration. When I was in school and college, we were taught to struggle, to have frustration, and so to be in the learning space. When I think about teenagers and college students, I want them to become experts—not experts at knowing but experts at staying in the learning space. Simply put: What do you think you're supposed to feel when you're in the learning space? Frustration!

The goal in life is to have a razor-thin gap between your awareness and the action associated with that awareness. This is the problem with all self-help content, with self-improvement in general; it's just dopamine from information. But there is no action associated with that awareness. You go to the therapy session, and you feel good about the awareness, but what are you doing about it? Where is the action you need to shrink the gap that exists? That's how you change your life. That's where you convince yourself, in the moment of frustration, that you can take that tiny action and something will happen.

The first thing I say to any person in their twenties who comes to me and says they're feeling lost in life is to wake up early and work out for thirty days straight. This has nothing to do with making money. It has nothing to do with your career. It has nothing to do with any of those other areas. What it has everything to do with is rewiring your brain to recognize that you can do a thing and create an outcome. And when you do that, when you convince yourself of that, you become completely invincible, unstoppable.

## MEASUREMENT

"What is not measured is not managed," goes the management dictum. This is particularly true in the case of understanding your personal progress (notice: not progression). In order to be effective in understanding progress, you need to have a baseline that you can measure from to understand whether you are succeeding or failing.

At Cisco, and in my career afterward, I have always sought longitudinal measurements of personal success (over time)—whether daily, weekly, monthly, or quarterly—toward a goal (100 percent achievement of the goal) and a stretch goal (110 percent or more of the goal). Measurement brings reality into your plan and allows for feedback that tells you about successful experimentation, progress, and failure. Remember, we learn as much, or more, from failure than we do from success. When we fail to achieve a goal, we can ask why and decide to do something different. This is learning and making meaning out of metrics.

Committing to these four core principles of the how will enable you to be successful. Now, let's get going with the action!

## What to Do in Step 5: Strategic Actions of Your Plan

To make and implement a plan effectively, you now move into two iterative phases, as you saw in figure 22:

- **Phase 1: Mapping and planning:** from mapping your destination to the channels that can help you get there, the individual people and ways to access them, your messaging, and the conversations
- **Phase 2: Execution:** from outreach to the targeted individuals, interviewing (formally or informally), measuring the success of those conversations, refining your approach, and repeating

Obviously, you should apply the four core principles to each of these phases as you go (the how). The combination of what and how makes you much more likely to achieve your goals and enjoy the journey—a truly critical combination. In getting what you want, you build competency and confidence that you can use over and over again in your life and share with others.

## Mapping and Planning—First: Map Your Destination

First, when planning a journey, it's not enough to say, "I want to go to Paris." You also need to know how you're going to get there. In life and career, there is no direct flight to your Next. You may need to fly, take a train, cycle, or even walk to get to where you're going. You'll need a responsible mindset and to be committed. And you'll need to be flexible and adaptable in taking small steps, such as connecting flights or other modes of transport, that add up to big wins. Think of this as being a hitchhiker trying to get somewhere specific. You've already decided where you're going. Now you need to plan the actual route: What are the towns (goals), the roads (opportunities), and the steps (actions) you'll take to get there?

## Prioritizing and Sequencing

In Step 2, you were introduced to the importance of prioritizing and sequencing your aspirations/goals within the framework of the three horizons (horizon one, horizon two, and horizon three), which generally represent year one, year two, and year three. You took a look at your goals (current goals at that time) and decided what you would need to do first, second, and so on. In Step 3, you brought a degree of specificity to the goals, defining your Next—who you want to become, what you want to do, whom you want to do it with, where you want to be.

Now, you want to view your Next through a bifocal lens because you are not going to take action on everything all at once. Ask yourself the following:

- What purposeful actions can I take now (the short-term view—action I can take daily, weekly, and/or monthly over the next twelve months or so)?
- What are the actions, or steps, that will lead me closer to the thing I ultimately want (the long-term view)?

This requires real clarity of goals and focus, plus a healthy dose of discipline in looking at the steps required to get there. The career transition you want to make might not take three years, so you can adjust the horizons you identified earlier to reflect what is realistic for your current goal.

## Specificity Matters

Excellence starts with specificity. The clearer your goal, the sharper your internal radar becomes for recognizing the opportunities and actions that matter. Now that the time has come to activate a plan to get to your Next, it's important to restate and refine what you are going after. This is not about starting over in defining what you want or about hemming and hawing regarding whether you want it. You've already been there and done that, and it is essential to trust that the work you've done up to now is on point (while leaving room for modifying your goals as conditions change or new information comes your way—adaptability is key).

Specificity is key because the people you're competing with are going all-in with 100 percent of their time, energy, and effort. You can't expect to succeed with a scattered approach when your competitors are doing one thing with absolute focus. That's a recipe for mediocrity. So, be honest with yourself: Do you want to be average, or do you want to be excellent?

Too often, I have seen people get vague at this stage. They want to keep options open, hedge bets, or blend multiple aspirations together. But vague plans lead to vague outcomes. Do you really believe you can compete with the best of the best in a particular competency when you are trying to be good at three or more things rather than just one? Stay focused on your aspirations and goals. You are getting exceptionally precise around that Next. I call this "building your radar."

## EXERCISE: BUILD YOUR RADAR

Identify your target in four dimensions. This should be the same as your Probables/Final Wants list from Step 3 but described as below:

- **Target industry/segment/location:** What field are you aiming for, and where?
- **Target firms:** Which organizations do you want to be part of?
- **Target roles:** What's the specific position or function you're aiming for?
- **Target role models:** Who's doing this well already? Whom can you study or reach out to?

Once you've got this clear, write it down. Be exact. Don't let things get fuzzy. If you've said you want to be a master violinist, don't pivot halfway to "Maybe I'll teach guitar." Stay focused. Be clear about what this means for your time working and commuting and what it means for you financially and socially. Being committed to the reality of a lived experience is not just a concept. You have to want the life you are choosing. It will be your identity. Describe it to yourself as much as you can, and make sure you can live it.

## Stepping Stones in Your Plan

Now that you know where you're going, map out the stepping stones. Each one should mark a meaningful milestone on the path to your aspirational goal. Think of your destination as the one-hundred-meter finish line, with the race itself broken into smaller segments, starting with getting out of the blocks. This approach works from right to left, backward from your goal to where you are now. This forces you to consider scope, resources, and time in reverse, grounding your dreams in actionable reality.

Each stepping stone should break down into smaller, purposeful actions that you can take or practice. These aren't abstract hopes—they're things you can do today. When you write down three actions you can take right now, you take away your excuses.

So, what are the three things you need to do today to get out of the blocks?

### ATOMIC HABITS FOR LASTING CHANGE

In his book ***Atomic Habits***, James Clear argues that lasting behavior change comes not from setting grand goals but from making tiny, incremental improvements.[24] By focusing on improving 1 percent at a time, those little improvements compound over time until you find that you've built positive routines and dismantled unproductive or unhelpful ones.

Clear proposes four "laws" for habit formation: Make it obvious, make it attractive, make it easy, and make it satisfying. He emphasizes designing your environment to support these laws, measuring progress through habit tracking and recognizing that identity change (seeing yourself as "the type of person who exercises" or "eats healthily") underlies sustainable habit shifts. This systems-oriented approach shifts attention away from outcomes and toward the processes that produce them.

24 James Clear, *Atomic Habits: An Easy & Proven Way to Build Good Habits & Break Bad Ones* (New York: Avery, 2018).

Don't overthink it. Resist the urge to say, "I could do it better" or "I could do it differently." No, you're just going to run the race. And in running the race, running becomes the thing. You're not a runner unless you're actually running—you're just someone thinking about it. Doing is the thing.

If you're not doing the work, it's not because it's too hard; it's because you're in your own way. You've chosen inaction over action. And that's on you. Want to be a runner? Then run. Don't obsess over the mechanics. Don't worry about whether you'll win. Just get in the blocks and start. Execution is the only thing that matters now.

## Second: Map Your Channels

Every career change is a team sport—you don't go it alone. In this section, you'll take inventory of the different channels (circles, groups, etc.) you already have and then envision how you can expand those circles to accelerate to your Next. We'll start by finding the right associations, circles, and groups that can open doors for you before moving on to building genuine relationships through mutual value and trust. Finally, you'll discover how to leverage the "third door" mindset—unconventional tactics for meeting high-impact people when the main entrances seem blocked. Together, these tools will help you cultivate the network you need to make your vision a reality.

During all my career moves since leaving McKinsey & Company twenty-five years ago, I have created a spreadsheet to help me focus and manage my search for my Next. This allows me to think about and track my progress. Here is my methodology, but you may invent or adopt your own:

1. Take the information from the Build Your Radar section above and start with the role you are interested in. Put that in a row in column A.
2. Map the companies you are interested in for that role in column B.
3. Tag and group the companies in column B in a new column, C, by industry.
4. Tag and group the companies in column C in a new column, D, by location.
5. Identify for each company the head of recruiting and any contacts or department heads you need to know, with their email, telephone number, and any social media (LinkedIn) that is relevant. Tag each of these individuals in both a social group you can use to approach them and using a method or channel of approach (mail, email, social media, telephone, in person, etc.)
6. Once you commence your campaign of outreach, capture in further columns:
   - When you contacted each person
   - When they replied and the nature of the reply (yes/no, etc.)
   - Next steps for you (send a resume, fill out a form, contact another person, etc.)

This will let you manage at a glance where you are in your campaign and what you should be working on as next steps.

7. Rinse and repeat!

## Find the Right Tribe

Activating your plan does not happen in isolation. You are shaped by the company you keep, and so, by consciously choosing your circle, you will move closer to your Next. Harvard research studies show that the five people you spend the most time with exert an outsized influence on your habits, mindset, and ultimately, your success.[25] They are your reference group. Here's the thing: Your significant other isn't just part of that group. They dominate it. They're the one person who has the most influence over your mindset, your habits, and ultimately, your trajectory in life. If you and your partner are not aligned, you're actively working against each other's goals. You might think that you're building something, but your efforts are quietly being dismantled by competing priorities. You can't operate at peak performance when the foundation of your life is not at peak.

So, whom should you be around? Think of them in four broad groups.

### FRIENDS AND FAMILY

These are your emotional anchors. When they understand and champion your goals, they become powerful cheerleaders and honest sounding boards. Share your Next with them so they can encourage your progress, hold you accountable, and help you celebrate micro-wins.

### ACADEMICS AND PEERS

Classmates, mentors, or fellow learners who are tackling the same challenges help normalize your struggles and amplify your wins. Whether

25 Nicholas A. Christakis and James H. Fowler, *Connected: The Surprising Power of Our Social Networks and How They Shape Our Lives* (Little, Brown and Company, 2009).

it's a study group, a workshop cohort, or an industry association, these peers provide guidance, feedback, and camaraderie. Also, don't forget to reconnect with professors and advisors who are part of the worlds you want to move into or up in.

### INTERMEDIARIES

Lawyers, accountants, bankers, headhunters, and journalists sit at the gateways to opportunity. They know the rules, the pitfalls, and the key decision-makers. Cultivate genuine relationships with these professionals, not by cold-calling but by offering value, asking intelligent questions, and demonstrating your commitment to your field.

### INVESTORS AND INFLUENCERS

These are the people who can fund, amplify, or legitimize your efforts: venture capitalists, angel investors, community leaders, or thought leaders in your domain. Engage them with a clear story of your vision, your progress metrics, and how they can participate in your journey.

## Third: Map to the Right Individuals and Open Doors

Start by defining exactly what "doing the thing" looks like in your field, whether that's building tables, coding software, or creating content. Then identify the individuals and groups already living that reality. Who is doing it the best? What habits do they share? What mindsets drive their decisions? Where and how do they connect? Think of who is doing what you want to be doing three to five years down the line. Identify them. Your goal is to join their world: Attend the meetups, enroll in the courses, subscribe to their newsletters, or simply reach out on social media with thoughtful questions. You are essentially answering the question "Who are they?" Who are the individuals who can help you, and where will you find them?

## Spend Time with Your Tribe

Once you've mapped your tribe, invest time with them. Apprenticeship and mentorship are age-old paths to mastery. By observing your tribe's routines, asking for feedback, and collaborating on small projects, you absorb not just skills but also the unspoken norms and attitudes that distinguish true practitioners from dabblers. This isn't superficial networking; it's about becoming part of a community in which your identity, your brand, and your story all align with the work you're committed to.

## The Cycle of Growth Through Connection

As you engage with each circle—friends and family, peers, intermediaries, and influencers—you'll notice a flow emerge. Confidence builds, clarity sharpens, and new opportunities appear almost organically. Each conversation, each shared insight, and each collaboration propels you closer to your Next. Over time, the steps you once had to force become second nature, and your team becomes both your mirror and your engine for continuous progress.

## Getting Promoted: Internal Tribes and Leaders

What if you're looking to get promoted or move to another role in your existing organization? This type of Next is likely to come up frequently in your journey unless you are an entrepreneur. Here are a few pointers based on my experience of being promoted and of sponsoring and mentoring others toward getting promoted:

1. **Be clear about what you want and why:** In order to get what you want, you will have to ask for it and explain how it relates to your story. There's that "Why you?" again. Which role do you want, why are you a fit, and why do you want it? Answers on how to do this are earlier in this chapter and book, including mapping the right mentors, sponsors, and influencers and how to talk to them. Also, in Step 7, you'll learn about how to influence others and how to manage perceptions of yourself as a leader.
2. **Be clear about your brand and identity, i.e., your competencies:** You will need to be able to show credibility and relevance for the role you want, including a track record of both generalist and specialist skills. The more senior the role, the more developed generalist skills (managing and leading) you will need to have successfully demonstrated to qualify and be selected.
3. **Plan a path:** In moving forward and upward within an organization, you will need to plan a path, typically within a function. Most organizations are organized in a cube-like form around function, geography, and business unit, with functional designations dominating, and then on up to the C-suite. Moving up within a function will require that your brand and identity are associated with both operations (running day-to-day operations and teams) and transformation (delivering successfully on projects and driving teams charged with change and innovation).

4. **Peacock:** Make sure you regularly share your accomplishments with your supervisor, peers, and other interest groups so that they update their mental models of you and share in your aspirations. If going after a promotion, this is a good time to revisit The Why of Your Value Proposition section of Step 4, in which we discussed Harvey Coleman's PIE Model theory of success—that work performance accounts for 10 percent of your career advancement, while the other 90 percent is driven by how people perceive your professional competence and how much they are aware of you.
5. **Collaborate:** Put your team first. The C-Suite in any company wants to build a culture in which there is balance between what the individual wants and what the organization needs. The organization needs the team and the "team of teams" to win. Be a team player and credit others for your accomplishments and success. Humility looks good on leaders. Also, cheer for others' success. Support your peers and their successes. Get to know your colleagues well and make a genuine effort to like them. This is not a null sum game; the pie grows over time, and there is more than enough to go around.

## CONTACT BEFORE CONTRACT

If you're aiming for a promotion within your organization, don't treat it like a transaction. Before others back you for a bigger role, they need to know who you are and how you engage.

The principle of *contact before contract*, popularized by executive coach John Timperley,[26] reminds us that relationships come first. In

26 John Timperley, "Contact Before Contract," *The Results Consultancy*, https://www.timberley.co.uk/blog/contact-before-contract.

practical terms, this means showing interest in others before expecting support. Be curious. Be kind. Know your colleagues beyond the task at hand.

If you want to be seen as ready to lead, invest in people. Build the relationship before you ask for the role.

6. **Be kind and be liked:** Building on point 5, caring about others will take you far. Be curious about them; be kind to them. You *can* succeed as a difficult, unpleasant, and dislikable person, but it is much harder than you think. Organizations are tribal, and they tend to police themselves to isolate or force out difficult personalities. Popularity is reciprocal; the more you like and are kind to other people, the more that will be returned to you. (Remember, this is a key characteristic of success mentioned in the Six Superpower Character Traits in Step 1.) People remember your kindness much more than your achievements.
7. **Build relationships:** Want to be promoted? Build great relationships. As you will see in Step 7, relationships are the foundation of success in executing your goals, building a team, and being a leader. They account for 90 percent of effectiveness in capitalizing on an opportunity or solving a problem, with the plan for doing so accounting for only 10 percent. I learned this the hard way at Cisco. Without close, supportive relationships, you will fail.
8. **Seek feedback:** If relationships are 90 percent of your focus, you should use them to get feedback so that you can progress toward a promotion. What is working? What do you need to work on? One thing I have learned is that getting promoted

without being ready, without having worked on yourself based on feedback, is no fun. You have to put in twice as much work, and with doubters instead of supporters.

Do these things, and you will be on the fast track.

## Gain Access to the Right People

What if the paths to your Next seem out of your reach? Consider Alex Banayan's concept of the third door, the idea that every person who's ever achieved extraordinary success has found a way in beyond both the obvious front entrance and the privileged back entrance.[27]

The front door is the one most people use. It's the main entrance, the big line to get past the bouncer into the club. Think resumes submitted to job postings through the standard application process or trying to be admitted to graduate school with only good grades and test scores and a decent application essay. It's the heads of recruiting I sent my resume to when I wanted to relocate from London to San Francisco. The front door leads you to the same recruiters everyone else is contacting "cold" or the same admissions committee all applicants are appealing to. Many undergraduates or graduates are pursuing the same investment banks, management consultancies, tech companies, etc. There is a lot of competition, and it's hard to stand out. This door is open to about 99 percent of people, but it's a very competitive, slow, and bureaucratic entrance.

Then there is the VIP entrance. It's for the 1 percent. This one's open to you if you already have connections, wealth, or power. You gain access through family ties, influential colleagues, legacy admissions,

27 Alex Banayan, *The Third Door: The Wild Quest to Uncover How the World's Most Successful People Launched Their Careers* (Crown, 2018).

monetary contributions, or insider networks that bypass the usual gates. Congratulations if you have the golden ticket. Most of us do not.

The third door is the scrappy, improvisational route. This is the side entrance, through the kitchens. It's about creating your own way in. And it's for the people who are brave and curious enough, and have enough know-how to find or talk their way in.

Banayan illustrates this with stories ranging from sneaking backstage to interview Bill Gates at his billionaire conference to cold-calling advisors on college campuses or turning chance encounters into lifelong mentors. Many times in my own life, through sheer force of will and a bit of cunning, I've managed to get to what I wanted by opening up the third door. You, too, can often get to almost anyone or anything you really want if you have a great story, are willing to tell it, and show bravery and persistence. The world can be a strangely resource-rich place if you're willing to find a way.

## Fourth: Map to the Messaging

I learned while working at McKinsey & Company that you make things happen through conversations, by understanding people and ensuring that they understand you. Success happens one dialogue at a time. You introduce yourself, share who you are and what you want, listen with genuine curiosity, and offer your unique strengths in return. Every conversation, whether with a peer, a mentor, or a future collaborator or employer, becomes an opportunity to deepen understanding, build trust, and demonstrate value.

## Execution: Outreach

Most of the people I work with in career transitions overthink outreach. This is what I hear all the time: "I don't know what to say," or "I saw a role I love, but I'm terrible at selling myself," or "I opened my email inbox and froze; it's so intimidating to reach out to people I don't know." Let's work on that! Here are tried and tested approaches for three different audiences and that have worked for hundreds of people I have coached.

### TO RECRUITERS/HEADHUNTERS

*Hello [Name], I came across your profile and saw you recruit in [industry segment/function/type of role]. I've got [# of years of experience and x competency] as a [job title], and feel I would be a good fit should your clients need someone with [x competency and y relevant skill set]. Would it be worthwhile setting up a [Zoom/coffee/meeting] to get to know one another and explore how I could be helpful?*

### TO HIRING MANAGERS

*Hello [Name], I noticed you are recruiting for a [role or job title], and I believe I would be a great fit. I have [insert # years of experience] in [detail the specific competency required for the role and mention a specific relevant achievement] as highlighted in the professional summary of my attached resume (see attached). I am motivated to join your company by [x intrinsic or y extrinsic motivations and values] and believe I would be successful in your team environment. Would you be open to a face-to-face introduction to talk further [by Zoom, in person, etc.]?*

### TO A PEER AT YOUR DREAM COMPANY

*Hello [Name], I saw you work at [z company] and have heard it's a great place to work, with terrific values and personal development. I would love to confirm what I have heard and learn more to see if [z company] would be for me. Would you be open to meeting [by Zoom, in person] for a quick chat? I really appreciate your time.*

## Research and Personalization

In the Mapping and Planning section above, you identified whom you want to have conversations with. But what do you know about them? In order to have both a higher success rate in outreach and also in interviews (formal or informal conversations), you need to learn as much about these individuals as possible and tailor your approach.

Twenty or thirty years ago, this was a much more difficult process—there was no Google (or other search engines) and far less data on people online, and there was no social media. Now, of course, most people are very discoverable: What jobs do they have? Where did they go to school? Do they have children? What sports or hobbies do they like? With careful and thorough research, you can build a picture of whom you want to meet and what they are interested in. This lets you not only see which groups or channels you should use to contact them but also what to include in your messaging to them, either in the outreach or the interview.

Personalization is key; it lets you signal affinity and common interest very quickly ("How 'bout them Bears!" or "I see we went to the same school," or "I have children of the same age").

## Using the Tools of Connection

At its core, social media isn't about chasing likes or mastering every feature. It's about telling your story in a way that draws the right people to you. Think of each platform as a different kind of megaphone: LinkedIn offers a more professional, relationship-oriented channel, while X (formerly Twitter), Instagram, or niche communities let you broadcast short, high-impact updates and showcase the journey you're on. Whichever platform you choose, lead with why you're doing what you're doing (or want to start doing), whom you're becoming, and what you hope to learn.

On LinkedIn, you've already crafted a profile that tells your story (see Step 4). Now shift into outreach mode. Identify the people who occupy the roles or industries you aspire to join, and then send them a concise, value-packed message that connects your narrative to their world. Frame it not as a cold ask, but as an invitation: "I'm on a mission to master X. I've been [brief achievement or insight], and I'd love to hear how you approached [specific challenge]." If you send out enough of these and tailor them to each recipient, someone will reply—certainly not everyone, and maybe not a high percentage, but some will. And even those you never hear back from will have taken note of your name and might have glanced at your profile, so you'll be planting seeds of curiosity and opening doors for the future.

Across all channels, break your overarching message into a handful of subthemes—your key milestones, lessons learned, and questions you're exploring. Use short posts or threads to shine a spotlight on one subtheme at a time: a quick case study, a lesson from a recent failure, or a micro-win worth celebrating. Ask for feedback, invite people to follow your progress, or even experiment with "sponsored" content as a way to monetize your learning journey. These aren't tricks; they're strategic ways to keep your narrative top of mind and to signal to your network that you're serious about your Next.

### RESOURCES FOR GETTING VISIBLE AND CONNECTING ON LINKEDIN

- *LinkedIn Unlocked* by Melonie Dodaro—a comprehensive book that guides you in building authority, expanding your network, and engaging with decision-makers.
- *Linked: Conquer LinkedIn. Get Your Dream Job. Own Your Future.* by Omar Garriott and Jeremy Schifeling—a book with insider strategies from former LinkedIn employees for profile optimization, networking, and mastering the modern job search[28]
- "Rock Your LinkedIn Profile," LinkedIn Learning course—offers practical video tutorials on networking etiquette, message templates, and leveraging advanced search. [29]

## LinkedIn's Third Door

In your parents' or grandparents' day (or maybe even early in your own career if you've been at this for a while), the way to access the people you needed to talk with was to ring them up on the phone or go sit in the lobby of their office with your best determined look and a whole lot of patience. Now, you can do all that virtually by finding the right people on LinkedIn and initiating conversations there.

You won't hear back from every stranger or close second-degree connection you reach out to on LinkedIn, but just as it only took a

28 Omar Garriott and Jeremy Schifeling, *Linked: Conquer LinkedIn. Get Your Dream Job. Own Your Future.*, (Workman Publishing Company, 2022).

29 Lauren Jolda, "Rock Your LinkedIn Profile," LinkedIn Learning, October 28, 2019, video, https://www.linkedin.com/learning/rock-your-linkedin-profile-28032639/connect-to-opportunity-with-linkedin.

handful of responses to my large mailing to get me from London to San Francisco, all you need is a few interested folks willing to help. Consider these specific moves to make on LinkedIn.

## FROM COMPANY PAGE TO PEOPLE PROFILES

- Look up the LinkedIn company pages of organizations that interest you, either because you want to work there or because you believe that people who work there can help you break into their industry.
- While on the People tab of the company's page, use the search field to find people relevant to your targets. You might type in a title such as "product manager" or keywords such as "training and development." To find those who sound like they'd be the hiring managers, you may have to manually sift through some profiles, but the search is worth your time.

## FINDING PEOPLE CLOSER TO YOU

- Your own LinkedIn network, of course, is an obvious place to find potential hiring managers, but you'd be surprised how many people forget, or don't know how, to search their own network.
- Click on the My Network icon on the main navigation menu. Then click on Connections.
- Within the Connections area, use the search field and filters. Enter "[your target position] manager," and then filter for first- or second-degree connections and your target geographic location. You might also choose to filter by your past

employers and school(s) attended to find people you have things in common with.

### TAP INTO THE "SECRET" JOB MARKET ON LINKEDIN

- On the main page of LinkedIn, enter "Hiring + [your target position]" in the main search bar.
- You'll get a sampling of posts and people who might be hiring for your desired position.

When you focus on the connections and conversations you want to spark, rather than just having a static profile, social media can amplify your story and enable you to forge relationships that will help you learn, grow, and move confidently toward your Next.

## Execution: Interviews

Any conversation that helps you get to your goal should be thought of in three parts: preparation, conversation (informal or formal), and follow-up. All three are crucial for success and require practice. Building the correct behaviors and habits will help you be more successful and confident over time.

I was reminded by a very successful actor friend of mine, when talking to him about my experiences interviewing, that actors have to audition all the time and that those who are successful look at auditions as part of the job, not as some separate hurdle. You have to be good at showing your craft and building rapport rapidly. Similarly, interviewing is a core skill that you need to learn and practice.

## Preparation

Whom are you going to meet, and what do you want out of the interaction? Do not just show up and wing it. Although you may be charismatic and entertaining, your lack of preparedness will show. Do your research on the person, company, opportunity, competition, etc. Think through the following:

- **Why do I want to meet this person?** What is the purpose of the meeting, and do they know this?
- **What is my core story/value proposition**? Do I have my elevator pitch down?
- What will they mean to me on an ongoing basis (relationship, not transaction—boss, mentor, associate, etc.)?
- **What do I know about them, their organization, their career, or their expertise?** What do we have in common and can talk about? Do we know people in common?
- What icebreakers can I use to create affinity? How can I be curious about them?
- **Where am I meeting them?** Is it loud or busy? Will there be interruptions?
- **What should I wear?** (Match what they are wearing to be appropriate to the time and space, and make them feel comfortable.)
- **Do we have enough time together to achieve my goals?** If not, how do I summarize or break up the conversation to achieve my priorities?

- **How can I be helpful to them?** What problems do they have, and how can I help?

Prepare with your friends, family, and trusted colleagues. The more comfortable, confident, and curious you are, the more successful you will be.

## Informal Conversations

The US Central Intelligence Agency has a famous saying: Everyone is worth a cup of coffee. And I cannot tell you how many opportunities this mindset has opened up for me. And it's not just about business. You never know who someone is. You never know who they're going to be. You never know when you're going to cross paths with them again. So, the next time that you hesitate to reach out, just remember that everyone is worth a cup of coffee and that cup might change everything. By the way, the same applies when you're on the receiving end of an invitation. You might operate in a culture in which it's customary to be skeptical of an informal invitation if there's not a clear purpose, or you might be on the introverted side, but it's just about always worth giving it a go.

Informal interviews are for you to gain visibility, become discoverable, collect intelligence, and build your network. Networking is about building a web of relationships with people who have an interest in the same area as you and hopefully an interest in your story. There is a famous adage: It's not what you know, but whom you know. My experience tells me that it's both, but your network, if you invest in building it and in keeping it informed and updated about your progress, will be a source of more opportunity over time than any reactive opportunities publicly sourced.

## FOUR SETS IN YOUR NETWORK AND HOW TO KEEP TRACK OF THEM

As you consider the ways you'll communicate with people in your network and how often you'll do so, it can be helpful to think of your network as consisting of four interlocking sets. Contacts can be members of multiple sets:

1. **Operational**: people who help you execute—individuals whom you would have on your team that specialize in competencies that augment you or fill gaps
2. **Strategic**: people who help you think—mentors, coaches, thought partners
3. **Aspirational**: people who help you grow—individuals who are your idols or are five to ten years ahead of you in their careers and who are modeling competencies and mindsets you aspire to
4. **Access**: people who are gatekeepers—individuals who control access to forums, other people or assets you need

Wherever you keep your contacts, whether in a simple spreadsheet or a fancy database, tag or label each person according to the set(s) they belong in. Then, put thought into how and when to contact people in the various sets. For example, the aspirational folks don't need to hear from you very often—maybe once a year or even less often, while strategic network members and those in the access category expect and deserve much more frequent communication if you expect them to open doors for you and provide support. This helps you avoid the trap of falling out of touch and then showing up out of the blue, needing something from the other person. Instead, you sustain contact at an appropriate level and keep the relationships growing.

Your network is your source of third-door access. Get to know people, be interested, and be kind. We are all fellow travelers on the road, and it can add a lot of joy to your journey to your Next by having more people to hang out with, not just to access roles.

When you enter a networking conversation or an exploratory interview, bring genuine curiosity about the person you are meeting. Apply kindness paired with flexibility and adaptability. Consider how you can help them, not just how they can help you. Personal development and leadership expert Zig Ziglar said, "You can have everything in life you want, if you will just help enough other people get what they want."[30]

Do not be transactional in these encounters. You are trying to build a relationship and have someone be interested in you. For instance, if you insist you're "only looking for a full-time role," you might walk away from the very project that could launch you to your Next. Instead, ask, "How can I help you solve a problem today?" and remain open to whatever form that help takes. Many of the best opportunities arrive disguised, such as a short-term contract that turns into a permanent position. It's like when a five-minute open-mic slot at two in the morning becomes the stage for an aspiring stand-up comic's breakthrough performance.

> **"It takes 20 years to build a reputation and five minutes to ruin it. If you think about that, you'll do things differently."**
>
> **—Warren Buffett**

By seeing each invitation as a stepping stone rather than dismissing it because it doesn't match your checklist, you position yourself to capitalize on unexpected doors—perhaps that third door we've talked about. This is a mindset of taking your shot wherever you can, doing the work, and trusting that the experience you build today will lead you to the opportunity you truly want tomorrow.

---

30 Zig Ziglar, *See You at the Top* (Gretna, LA: Pelican Publishing, 1975), 161.

One of the best books on this subject of creating, leveraging and maintaining networks is *Your Invisible Network* by Michael Urtuzuástegui Melcher.[31]

My network, built over thirty years, has been responsible for all but one of the roles I have won since I left McKinsey & Company. Invest in yours; it will pay you back many times over.

## Formal Conversations

Your informal conversations were about relationship building so that you can build your network and gather intel regarding what roles, companies, or strategies might be right for you. Then, if your Next involves looking for another job, you will move into formal conversations, i.e., job interviews. This unfolds in several stages: screening interviews, investigative interviews, and interviews for fit and motivation. In a formal interview process, you need to focus even more on preparedness.

### SCREENING INTERVIEWS

These are typically one or two meetings with human resources or the recruiting function of a company. The focus is on your resume, your education and experience, and why you have moved between roles or made the choices that you have in your career. This is where the Four Axis Framework comes back into play. Employers are looking for a match of competency, which includes your credibility and relevance, against the job description. Can you do the job? Do you have the

31 Michael Urtuzuástegui Melcher, *Your Invisible Network: How to Create, Maintain, and Leverage the Relationships That Will Transform Your Career* (Dallas: Matt Holt Books, 2023).

skills, experience, and track record they need? The tighter the match, the more likely you are to progress to the next round.

To succeed at screening interviews, do the following:

- Study the job description before the interviews and map your competencies directly to what the role requires. You'll show not only that you're qualified but also that you bring something distinct—your value proposition.
    - Research the industry—trends, news, competition, critical success factors, etc.
    - Research the company—latest reports, key personnel, history, etc.
    - Research the people you are going to meet—how long have they been at the company? Where were they before? Have they published any articles? What do they like?
    - Research the role—how are you differentiated or especially relevant?
- Perform well during the interviews:
    - Articulate clearly how you fit the role description precisely (competency).
    - Be clear about why you want the role (your story).
    - Be clear about your relevance—your value proposition/differentiation.
    - Try to exhibit and illustrate the character traits that we discussed early on in this book—positivity, curiosity, persistence and consistency, flexibility and adaptability, and lastly, kindness.

## INVESTIGATIVE INTERVIEWS

These are typically with the line manager who will supervise you and a couple of subject matter experts whom you are likely to work with. They will focus their questions not on what you have done but on what you will do—the role's responsibilities. They are testing for your competence again but are likely using a series of prompts rather than discussing your resume. They may ask questions about how you manage or lead, they may ask questions about successes or failures, or they might even ask you to perform a "case study" with them—walking through a hypothetical example of something that could happen in their business and how you would go about thinking through and solving the problem.

Here are some common questions you should prepare and practice for:

- "What has been your biggest failure, and what did you learn from it?" or "Tell me about a mistake you made and what you learned from it."
- "What has been your biggest success, and how did you learn from it?"
- "Tell me about yourself."
- "Why do you want this job?"
- "What are your strengths?"
- "What is your greatest weakness?"
- "Why should we hire you?"
- "How do you lead or inspire others?"

- "Give me an example of how you multitask and deal with different priorities?"
- "Tell me about a time when you have had to manage personal conflict. What did you do to resolve it?"
- "Where do you see yourself in five years?"
- "Why are you leaving your current job?"

Every answer is an opportunity for you to showcase your expertise and align yourself with the role and the interviewer. Always remember that interviewing is about exploring your ability to build relationships quickly and friction-free by demonstrating your credibility, relevance, and the character traits laid out above. These interviews are testing whether you can do the job standing on your feet.

## FOLLOW-ON INTERVIEWS

These later-stage interviews focus on *fit* and *motivation*. How well would you align with the team, culture, and role? Will you mesh well here? What drives you, and does that align with the company's mission and pace? Will you thrive here? Do you want to be here?

Typically, these interviews will be with the hiring manager again but can also be with other sponsors or critical touchpoints that you may have in other functions, geographies, or business units. Or if you are very senior at, chief officer level, they will be with the board or shareholders of a company. You'll still touch on competencies, but they will likely be generalist competencies (problem-solving, communication, collaboration, and so forth) rather than the specialist competencies that you were dealing with in investigative interviewing. Your main focus should be on demonstrating your understanding of the values and culture of the people interviewing you, the teams you would be working with, and the company as a whole, and explaining why you'll be successful within that culture.

Finally, consider what you should ask throughout the process. Smart questions show engagement, insight, and that you've done your homework. They also help you assess if the job is truly right for you. Here are some effective examples:

- Ask about the role:
    - "What does success look like in this role? How will performance in the role be measured (metrics of success)?"
    - "What are the immediate challenges (first six months) that I would have to focus on in this position?"
    - "How does this role contribute to the company's goals (what value drivers does it touch and what KPIs does it have)?"
    - "What are the most important relationships I would have to develop to be successful in this role?"
    - "Can you share a story about how you manage your team?"
    - "Can you give me an example of how you have effectively managed conflict in your team?"
- Ask about the company:
    - "What are the company's top priorities (goals) this year?"
    - "What values are most important to the company (and you)?"
    - "How does the company support professional growth (generally and specifically in this role)?"

- "What excites you about the company's future and why?"
- "What three personality traits or values thrive here? Why?"
- "What challenges is the company facing in this current moment?"

- Ask closing questions:
    - "What are the next steps in the hiring process?"
    - "What is the timeline for making a decision?"
    - "What are the decision criteria for making a decision? Do you need anything else from me regarding these?"

Also, remember that more than 80 percent of the way we communicate with each other is nonverbal, so-called somatics. Be aware of how you sit, smile, and gesture. In fact, recent research has shown that over 80 percent of our impressions of interviewees are based on just two traits: warmth (kindness) and competence.[32] It's not how tall, how rich, or how attractive you are. It's how quickly you can signal warmth: *I'm a friend. Trust me. You can rely on me.* And how you can convey competence: *I'm capable. You can count on me to do the job.*

> **"If people like you they will listen to you, but if they trust you, they'll do business with you."**
>
> **—Zig Ziglar** [33]

32 Susan T. Fiske et al., "Universal Dimensions of Social Cognition: Warmth and Competence," *Trends in Cognitive Sciences* 11, no. 2 (2007): 77–83.

33 Zig Ziglar, *See You at the Top*.

The faster you can signal these two things, especially in a virtual setting or first interaction, the more people will like and respect you. There's a kind of recipe of nonverbal cues that help you do this:

- **Warmth (kindness) cues** include:
    - Authentic smiling and repeated nodding in agreement with their statements, which can cause someone to speak longer and explain more. It's an authentic signal that says, *I hear you. I see you. Tell me more.*
    - Looking the person you are talking to directly in the eyes—*I hear you. I see you. Tell me more.*
- **Competence cues** include:
    - Gestures such as the steeple—hands together with pointer fingers forming a "steeple" in front of you while speaking. This signals *thoughtfulness and command.*
    - Using your hands to emphasize conversation points or draw virtual diagrams as you explain how you would do something. This signals *expressiveness and conceptual skills.*
    - Repeating what you heard—"So, what I heard you say is . . ."—shows *summarization skills and listening skills.*

Keep these in mind when your interview goal is to build rapport, establish trust, and get people to engage with you quickly and meaningfully.

Building on this, there are also certain types of phrases used by confident people that signal competence and trust and make them instantly stand out in interviews:

- "Here's my perspective". This phrase doesn't seek permission and doesn't apologize. It simply says, "I have a valid opinion and you should listen to it."
- "That's a great point. I have something to add to it." Warm/kind people do not compete. They collaborate, so they acknowledge your opinion and add value to it.
- "I see things a little differently, and here's why." Warm/kind people do not say, "I disagree," because that sounds confrontational. Instead, they build a constructive conversation.
- "I don't know the answer, but I'll figure it out and get back to you." Competence is not about knowing everything. It's about owning what you don't know and not being insecure about it.

## Closing the Deal with a Follow-Up

Some people assume thank-you notes after networking meetings or job interviews are unnecessary or old-fashioned. Will they even get read? Most likely, yes. Will a note make a difference at all? It can!

Thank-you notes are more than expressions of thanks. They are not just about courtesy or etiquette—they're about strategy. A well-crafted follow-up note shows professionalism, reinforces your value, and keeps you top of mind. It's your chance to remind the person who you are, what you bring to the table, and why the conversation or interview mattered—both to you and to them. You're also keeping the relationship warm for the future.

### MODES OF SENDING

Email is the most common method and usually the best. If your communication has been happening via LinkedIn, a message there might be fine. If you've been texting back and forth, a short, thoughtful text can be appropriate. And in rare cases, if you believe a personal, more formal, and timeless touch would be valued, a handwritten card sent by mail can leave a lasting impression.

## ANATOMY OF A THANK-YOU NOTE: NETWORKING MEETING

After each networking conversation, take a moment to reflect on what was discussed. Think about which aspects of your background seemed to resonate most with the person and what they said that struck a chord with you. Did they light up when talking about a particular career path you're exploring, saying why it could be a good fit for you? Did they offer a specific piece of advice or a contact that felt especially useful? These insights should guide your thank-you note and make it feel specific and sincere.

While you can start with a general outline or template, such as the five points below, always tailor the message to the individual and the conversation. A thank-you note should have:

1. Greeting and warm thanks for the time
2. Quick reminder of your conversation
3. Highlight of a key insight or takeaway
4. Brief reminder of your background/goals
5. Next steps or invitation to stay in touch

Keep the note brief. Make every word count, and avoid filler. Phrases such as "just wanted to say" or "touching base to follow up" take up space without adding value. Instead, be direct and warm.

Your goal is to be memorable, thoughtful, and have the note be an easy, quick read.

### SAMPLE NOTE: NETWORKING FOLLOW-UP

Hi Jordan,

Thank you again for taking the time to meet with me yesterday. Our conversation about careers in social impact strategy gave me a clearer sense of how I might pivot my experience in product marketing into work that aligns with my values.

Your insight taking on a contract role to bridge into the nonprofit world was especially helpful. I've already started looking into the organizations you mentioned.

As a reminder, I bring more than ten years in go-to-market planning and a passion for storytelling that connects people to mission-driven brands. I hope you'll keep me in mind when you hear of any need for what I have to offer. Also, don't hesitate to let me know how I can help you in any way.

I'll stay in touch as I navigate this next phase to let you know how it's going and to see how you're doing. I want to hear how that Q4 initiative turns out for you and your team!

Warm regards,

Natalie

## ANATOMY OF A THANK-YOU NOTE: JOB INTERVIEW

After every interview, reflect on what was covered. Consider which parts of the conversation seemed to excite or interest your interviewer—perhaps a discussion about how your experience in launching product lines matches a current challenge they mentioned.

Also think about what excited you. Was it the team's energy? A project they're about to kick off? These elements are your opportunity to personalize your thank-you and to reinforce your fit. Like your resume or cover letter, your thank-you note should feel specific and intentional, not boilerplate, though you can start with these five elements to make the writing easier for you:

1. Greeting and appreciation
2. Reference to the specific job/interview
3. Emphasis on a key topic discussed
4. Reaffirmation of fit and enthusiasm
5. Closing thanks and next steps

Be concise. Say enough to reiterate your value without rehashing your resume and to express your interest in the position without sounding desperate. Steer clear of clichés such as "It was a pleasure to meet you" or "I look forward to hearing from you" unless those phrases are backed up with specifics. Instead, use vivid, memorable language that aligns with your voice and underscores why you're a great fit.

### SAMPLE NOTE: INTERVIEW FOLLOW-UP

---

Dear Ms. Thomas,

Thank you for the engaging conversation earlier this week about the marketing director role at Luma Health. I appreciated the chance to learn more about your vision for growth and the team's collaborative culture.

Our discussion about leading go-to-market strategies for new verticals resonated with my experience at Helix, where I drove that 35 percent lift in qualified pipeline over two quarters, as we discussed.

I remain very enthusiastic about the opportunity to contribute to Luma Health's next phase of expansion. Please don't hesitate to reach out if I can provide additional information.

Warm regards,

Daniel Klein

## Negotiations

Negotiation is a specialty of mine. Originally as a lawyer, and then as a consultant, general manager, corporate development executive, and coach, I have negotiated company deals, contracts, memoranda of understanding, letters of intent, alliances, partnerships, and my own employment. Negotiating effectively has been one of the longstanding secrets of my success. You, too, will need to build and invest in this competency over the years to ensure that you get what you want in any working relationship, exchange, or job.

Here are some basics to focus on and practice for employment-related negotiations.

### 1. DO YOUR RESEARCH—INFORMATION IS POWER

Gather information (both primary data through informational sessions and secondary research, such as from Glassdoor) on the compensation and benefits for comparable positions.

I always used to call the headhunters in my network at the "SHREK" search firms (Spencer Stuart, Heidrick & Struggles, Russell Reynolds Associates, Egon Zehnder, and Korn Ferry) and ask them to provide me with comparables for the role I was seeking by industry segment and geography.

Assess market forces. How high is the demand for your unique combination of competencies and experiences? The more demand, the more leverage in the negotiation you have.

## 2. WHAT DO YOU WANT (PRIORITIZE HARD), AND WHAT IS YOUR WALK-AWAY?

There are many factors to balance around what you want in a role and what your priorities are, such as compensation (base salary, bonuses, stock-based compensation, signing bonus, pensions or 401(k), etc.), location, title, paid time off, benefits (health insurance, life insurance, and the like), start date, car, and club memberships.

You will not get everything you want, so be very clear about your priorities. Which elements are you willing to give up or compromise on, and which are you fixed on?

Your best alternative to a negotiated agreement (BATNA) represents the most advantageous course of action a party can take if a negotiation fails to produce a satisfactory outcome. Essentially, it's your backup plan, your Plan B, if you can't reach an agreement with the other party in a negotiation. So, what is your alternative to accepting the offer? Having a strong BATNA provides you with leverage and confidence during negotiations. It allows you to assess the value of a potential agreement and decide whether to accept it or walk away. If you reach that point, consider the following:

- **Identify your alternatives:** List all possible actions you can take if you don't reach an agreement.
- **Evaluate the alternatives:** Assess the potential value of each alternative, considering factors such as cost, time, and resources.

- **Choose the best alternative:** Select the alternative that appears most favorable.

Your walk-away is the number or set of circumstances that triggers your rejecting the offer during the negotiation and going with your BATNA. What is your walk-away?

Be clear; be explicit. Communicate what is most important to you in getting a deal done and what is nonnegotiable (e.g., location) versus moveable (e.g., start date). Make sure not to budge if it really is nonnegotiable; don't negotiate against yourself!

## 3. UNDERSTAND YOUR LEVERAGE

Early in the interview process, the employer has maximum leverage and intends to use it. There are usually multiple candidates, and one easy way to reduce the list is to eliminate the expensive merchandise. If you price yourself out of the job or create too much complexity at this point, the job is lost to you. It is therefore critical to keep away from any discussion of compensation history or requirements in the early stage.

Leverage continues to favor the employer through the remainder of the interview process. Getting into compensation negotiations in the third, fourth, or fifth interview is risky because the employer isn't committed to you. If, all of a sudden, you look too pricey, they will focus on finding a more "suitable" (read: less expensive) candidate. You should continue to defer salary discussions.

You have maximum leverage at the time an offer is made. They have decided they want you and are actively fantasizing about the work you will take off their hands. The employer will be prepared to do whatever is feasible to get you to say yes. Negotiate only when you are in that driver's seat.

Your leverage drops back to nearly zero once you accept the offer. If something is important to you, get it during the negotiation. Once you are on the job, there is little incentive for your employer to make big changes for you. The employer's assessment is that you won't quit even if they don't meet your demands. Sadly, this is based on long experience that employees will stick with a company, even when denied requested raises or adjustments.

### 4. AVOID TALKING ABOUT COMPENSATION UNTIL YOU HAVE AN OFFER

Since you have no leverage, avoid discussing compensation during interviews. Be prepared to deflect or defer questions about salary requirements or salary history.

If you get asked about your compensation history, try to give a general response: "I have been fortunate to work for organizations that paid very competitively. Based on my research, your organization also pays competitively." Then, ask a question.

If you sense that your interviewer is concerned that they can't afford you, answer the question behind the question: "If your concern is that you won't be able to meet my compensation requirements, let me assure you, based on my research, I don't expect compensation will be a problem."

Without offering a fixed figure, you should peg expectations appropriately based on your talents and market demand, such as "I have done my research, and for a candidate with my qualifications, if I should be so lucky as to get an offer, I would be expecting that offer to be in the top quartile of the range for this position."

## 5. ALWAYS NEGOTIATE THE OFFER

Most companies have significant ranges in compensation and many other levers they can pull. Make sure you explore what these are and their degree of flexibility. Human resources representatives and hiring managers expect you to negotiate.

But before you do that, always get the offer in writing. Do not rely on verbal offers and assurances. If the company is not willing to put the offer in writing, ask why. You just want time to review it, and having it in writing avoids any misunderstanding. Be very suspicious of any offer that an employer won't even put in an email.

## 6. ALWAYS ASK FOR SOME TIME TO REVIEW THE OFFER

Forty-eight hours is about the minimum. For senior level positions, you may reasonably ask for up to a week. Never accept a job immediately, as this will preclude any type of negotiation. If you really want the job, make lots of positive sounds, be excited, give the right signals, but hold out on your final answer until the adrenaline rush subsides.

## 7. PUSH ON THE BASE COMPENSATION

A gentle push is "Can you do any better on the base?" or "Do you have any flexibility on the base?" If the offer is way out of line with what you need or expect, then express surprise. Say, "Based on my research, I would have expected a position with this level of responsibility to pay between X and Y." Stop there and see if they squirm. Don't say anything further until you see whether they are prepared to up the base. If they need to discuss this with someone else, agree, but ask to review the whole offer first.

Ask, "Do you offer signing bonuses?" Wait for a response. If no, move on. If yes, ask what they can offer you. Whatever is offered, ask,

"Is that the maximum bonus you offer?" Stop, see if more money hits the table. You don't want to spend a lot of time on this, but you do want to push for the maximum. Signing bonuses are often a good way for companies to make you happy without messing up their internal pay scale, as they don't add to your base.

Next, ask about performance bonuses. Do they offer them? What percentage of the base is usually offered? Will you be eligible for the maximum percentage? If not, that's something you would like. Again, this is a way for the employer to open the door to a higher level of compensation without affecting your base pay.

Explore the possibility of moving up your first compensation and level review to six months. "I think you'll be really pleased with my work, and I would expect to see that in my compensation review." This opens up the possibility of more money within six months.

If stock options or profit sharing are part of a company's compensation package, explore whether you are getting the maximum. Make sure you know what the company's stock price is so that you can evaluate the value of this component.

In discussing salary, signing/performance bonuses, and stock options, you are letting the employer know that there are multiple ways to sweeten the pot for you.

## 8. DON'T OVERLOOK THE NONMONETARY ITEMS

Nonmonetary items can be very valuable. Consider these points, as relevant:

- If the company offers flextime or telecommuting (which you should know from your research), ask about the possibility of an alternative work schedule.

- Do you like the title you've been offered? If you'd prefer something different, ask for it.
- Will the company pay your association memberships or cover part of a club membership?
- Will the company promise to send you to the annual convention for your profession?
- Will the company provide a company car, computer, home phone and/or fax line, or cell phone?
- Will the company cover tuition costs for further education?

All of these are questions you can ask to determine where the company has flexibility.

### 9. WRAP UP THE NEGOTIATIONS

Always review your understanding of the offer. If you need more time to weigh the offer, review the details to ensure you have them written down correctly, and then ask for a day to consider.

Are you in a Zone of Possible Agreement? Essentially, do the terms that the company has laid out match or exceed what you are looking for? If yes, accept. If no, keep negotiating if you think they have more to give and are flexible; if not, tell them they have reached your walk-away and reject the offer. Maintain an open stance; several times, companies have come back to me after making offers I refused. Be prepared to compromise on some things to get a deal done.

## Execution: Measure

So, you've mapped and mapped and mapped to put your plan together and activate it. Congratulations! But having a plan and taking action are only half the battle. You can outline every step and check every box, but unless you track how those steps are unfolding, you risk drifting off course, or worse, burning out without realizing how far you've come.

My advice is to track everything in the spreadsheet we discussed earlier in this chapter. The best thing I did in terms of awareness and progress during this time period as I was navigating roles was track every single job application I sent out and every single introduction that I attempted. If I had an interview, I tracked whether or not I felt confident or if I could solve the problem they gave me. If the answer was no, I would come back at a later time and figure out my best answer. What gets measured gets improved.

Remember what we talked about earlier in this chapter around "what's not measured is not managed" as part of ruthless execution, as well as the differences between progress and progression? All that kicks into gear now. It's essential to measure your progress, not just your progression; celebrate the small victories that fuel your momentum; and then rinse and repeat, using what you've learned to refine your plan and propel you toward your next milestone.

## Execution: Repeat

As you repeat and iterate your action plan, following the four core principles, you still might get stuck. So, I want to offer you some thoughts on sticking with this for when that happens.

Repetition is like training for a sport. It follows a path of measurable progress. When I was going through this on my own journey, my mind went to five characteristics of great athletes I knew who trained and progressed well.

Number one is that they learn from their failures and do not identify with them. Failure is just an event—as opposed to a person with a fixed mindset who, when they fail, it's "I'm a failure." For them, failure is an identity, not an event.

As an illustration, here is what Roger Federer, possibly the greatest tennis player of all time, has to say on this matter: "In the 1,526 singles matches I played in my career, I won almost 80% of those matches. Now, I have a question for you. What percentage of the POINTS do you think I won in those matches? Only 54%. In other words, even top ranked tennis players win barely more than half of the points they play. When you lose every second point, on average, you learn not to dwell on every shot. You teach yourself to think: OK, I double faulted. It's only a point. … When you're playing a point, it is the most important thing in the world. But when it's behind you, it's behind you … This mindset is really crucial, because it frees you to fully commit to the next point … and the next one after that … with intensity, clarity and focus. The truth is, whatever game you play in life … sometimes you're going to lose. A point, a match, a season, a job …"[34]

Number two is obstacles. The successful athlete embraces obstacles. They look for them as challenges and ways to learn. They don't duck from the hard things. The fixed-mindset athletes don't want to do the hard thing because the probability of failure is higher, and they don't want anything to do with that.

Number three is effort level. The successful athlete gives their best regardless of how they feel. As we have discussed previously, they have discipline, and practice as hard as they play. The fixed-mindset athlete only gives their best when things are going well.

---

34 Roger Federer, "2024 Commencement Address by Roger Federer," *Dartmouth College*, June 9, 2024, https://home.dartmouth.edu/news/2024/06/2024-commencement-address-roger-federer.

## THE DISCIPLINE OF MAINTAINING RELATIONSHIPS: STAY IN TOUCH AND STAY REAL

A lot of people drop the ball after the first coffee chat. But real opportunity lives in what happens days, months, and years after that. The best relationships are compounded over time, built through check-ins, updates, gratitude, and genuine care.

Staying in touch doesn't mean pestering or self-promoting. It means keeping people informed of your progress, showing appreciation, and looking for ways to help. A quick note to say "I tried your advice—thank you again" or sharing a helpful article with a brief "Thought of you" can keep the door open and the relationship alive.

Think of your network not as a transaction log but as a balance sheet of trust—one that grows with every authentic interaction. As you evolve in your career, the people who helped you, and those you've helped, form the fabric of your story. After all, you're not building a contact list. You're building a life.

Number four is that they seek critical feedback. Successful athletes don't just embrace feedback. They want it. It helps them get better. They want as much measurement and tracking data as they can get.

And, last but not least, they learn from the success of others. They observe and ask others about how they do things.

Motivation is a feeling that comes and goes, and in that five-second moment, it doesn't matter whether it's there or not. Discipline is infinitely more important. So, no matter how you feel, get up and do what you're supposed to do. You need discipline.

Discipline in repetition isn't restriction; it's remembrance. Every time you choose the discipline of sticking with it, of showing up, you're not depriving yourself. You're reminding yourself who you said you wanted to become. And it's not about being perfect. It's about showing up for the future you, even when today's version feels tired, distracted, or triggered. Discipline is another way in which you stop abandoning yourself. You break your own trust every time you say you're going to do something and you don't follow through. As we have shown earlier in this chapter, that's not a time management issue; that's a self-worth issue about prioritizing yourself. Real confidence doesn't come from hype. It comes from keeping promises to yourself when no one's watching. Lastly, discipline is a love language for your future. You don't need more motivation. You need a higher standard because when you really respect yourself, laziness stops being OK. When you love who you're becoming, discipline becomes obvious. You're not forcing it anymore. You're just literally done betraying yourself. Discipline is nothing but self-respect at the highest level.

Removing your own obstacles is the final, and often toughest, barrier to action. But the solution is simpler than you might think. Stop watching cooking shows—get off the couch and cook. Doing beats planning every time. So, make sure you are not sabotaging yourself before you even start. These are common culprits:

- **Unclear goals:** Do you need to revisit Step 3 to better define your Next? It's hard to muster up the effort to work toward a goal when it is fuzzy.
- **Unclear value proposition:** Do you need to do more work around articulating your unique strengths? You might need to revisit Step 4 to strengthen your resume, pitches, or conversation strategies.
- **Doing too much at once:** Have you broken your plan down into executable steps?

- **Starting at the wrong place:** Have you possibly made the mistake of choosing the hardest path first, making everything needlessly difficult?
- **Fear and excuses:** Are you making excuses such as "I don't have the right connections" or "It's too risky"? What is holding you back from making the first (or second or third) move, and are those valid reasons?

## THE WEEKLY SYSTEM

In the spirit of developing habits that sustain you in execution and improvement, here is a weekly system "regime" that I developed in my mid-forties that led to a significant part of my career success. I used to think there was never enough time, but I learned you don't need to do more; you need to do what matters on repeat. Remember, you have 168 hours each week. How will *you* use them? The shift from other people's agendas to my own really helped me, and the detailed planning, reflection, and accountability of this system drove my ability to stick with it.

Start with three layers, from top to bottom in granularity, to plan and activate your weekly time allocation and activities:

1. **Life pillars:** your goals
2. **Weekly rhythms:** your rhythm to focus on these life pillars
3. **Daily focus blocks:** your execution engine—how you spend your time each day and in what order

Let's walk through my system:

1. **Life pillars:** Go through this book's exercises in Steps 1 through 4 and figure out what you really want. What you

desire. That will give you the key to the first layer. Remember the Rule of Three!

- What is most important to you in the short term (this week) and in the long term?
    - Write them down.
    - Make them nonnegotiable and create boundaries (how will you feel if you do not do this?).
    - Define what success looks like for you. What is good performance for you?

2. **Weekly rhythms:** Design a weekly default map of how you are currently spending time. Look at your calendar. What patterns do you notice? How does this map to your priority pillars?
    - What is the amount and weighting of time by day and throughout the week?
        - work/meetings
        - thinking/problem-solving
        - exercise
        - eating
        - family
    - What existing routines do you have? Do they work for you?
    - How are you using downtime/weekends/evenings—the approximately twenty-five hours you have free each week?
3. **Daily focus blocks:** Each day, divide the times as follows:

- Core blocks: blocks of 90 to 120 minutes when you are most effective at working your current priority (solving a problem and collaborating, not processing emails or watching videos!)
    - What times are you most awake, attuned to the activity, or productive? Do you do your best thinking in the morning?
- Support blocks: blocks of an hour at a time to focus on calls, administration
    - Are these best first thing in the morning, at lunch, or at the end of the day?
- Life blocks: blocks of an hour at a time to focus on family, exercise, relaxation
    - What's the best time to be present with family or friends?

I completely changed the way I organized my days and spent my time. I noticed my biorhythms and tried to map my work to them. Every week, I spent thirty minutes looking at what worked, what drained me, and what I had missed that week that I needed to focus on the next week. And, crucially, I stayed aligned with my life pillars.

This quote from Roger Federer about doubt and relentlessness says it all: " … it's a roller coaster, with many ups and downs. And it's natural, when you're down, to doubt yourself. To feel sorry for yourself. And by the way, your opponents have self-doubt, too. Don't ever forget that. But negative energy is wasted energy. You want to become a master at overcoming hard moments. That to me is the sign of a champion. The best in the world are not the best because they win every point … It's because they know they'll lose … again and again … and have learned how to deal with it. You accept it, cry it out if you need to … then force a smile. You move on. Be relentless. Adapt and grow. Work harder. Work smarter. Remember: work smarter."[35]

One of the most common questions my coachees ask me as they go through this process and it starts getting hard is "I'm stuck in a rut. What do I do?" My answer is that it's likely due to one of four things. And it could be a combination of these:

- **Number one**: What are you avoiding? You need to go right at it. Sit down and take a long, hard look at what you are avoiding and why. Very often, the five-second rule will help here.
- **Number two**: Where do you need to start again? Translate your goal into something very simple that you can do today. What is your top priority? Think about Steve Jobs and Jonny Ive and radical focus.
- **Number three**: How do I win today? Just write down three things you can move forward on today, and then get up and repeat that tomorrow.
- **Number four**: What are the habits that are interfering with where I want to go? Reflect. What needs to change for you to be successful? Make the decision to do it differently.

The bottom line is this acid test: Do you truly want this? If you do, there's no legitimate reason not to act. Remember that responsibility mindset? Identify three steps you will take today, and pursue them relentlessly.

Get up, get moving, and get out of your own way.

---

35 Federer, "2024 Commencement Address."

## You're in the Homestretch: From Step 5 to 6

There are things that change the course of your life. For me, the most pivotal points were getting into Oxford University, joining McKinsey & Company, and spending time at Cisco. These experiences created whole new trees of opportunity for me. Because of them, I've built networks, gained confidence, acquired skills, and accomplished a great deal. As you build your network and implement your plan, you are changing the course of your life.

In Step 5, you've focused on constructing and implementing your plan to reach your Next, and we wrapped up the step with measuring your success to that point. Step 6 will focus on what happens after you get to your Next. You'll celebrate success at a whole other level than just slogging through the steps to get there. You'll acknowledge all your hard work and put some serious thought into what this means for you on a professional level and also a deep, personal level. So, head on into that homestretch!

## CHAPTER WAYPOINTS

Define your Next with absolute specificity—know exactly where you're headed.

Break that destination into stepping stones, working backward from goal to today.

Map your contacts—identify your tribe, cultivate relationships, and use the third door when necessary.

Enter every conversation with genuine curiosity, kindness, and flexibility, ready to solve problems.

Apply radical focus—choose a few critical targets and say no to distractions—and execute with a responsibility mindset.

Live by "doing is becoming"—take daily purposeful actions that shape your identity.

# PART 3

# Living Your Next

# STEP 6

## Increase: Know Your Success

> **"Success is liking yourself, liking what you do, and liking how you do it."**
>
> **—Maya Angelou**

"Am I successful?" I have often asked myself. I am sure you have too. How would I know? Can I establish a quantitative absolute measure, or is it all qualitative and comparative? My answers have varied by the stage of life I was in, the people I spent time with, and through the process of research and reflection. These answers have shaped my opinion of myself, my identity, and a good deal of my happiness. If you are going to spend a third of your life on something, shouldn't you know what success looks like? Shouldn't it feel like success?

Figure 24: Focus on Step 6

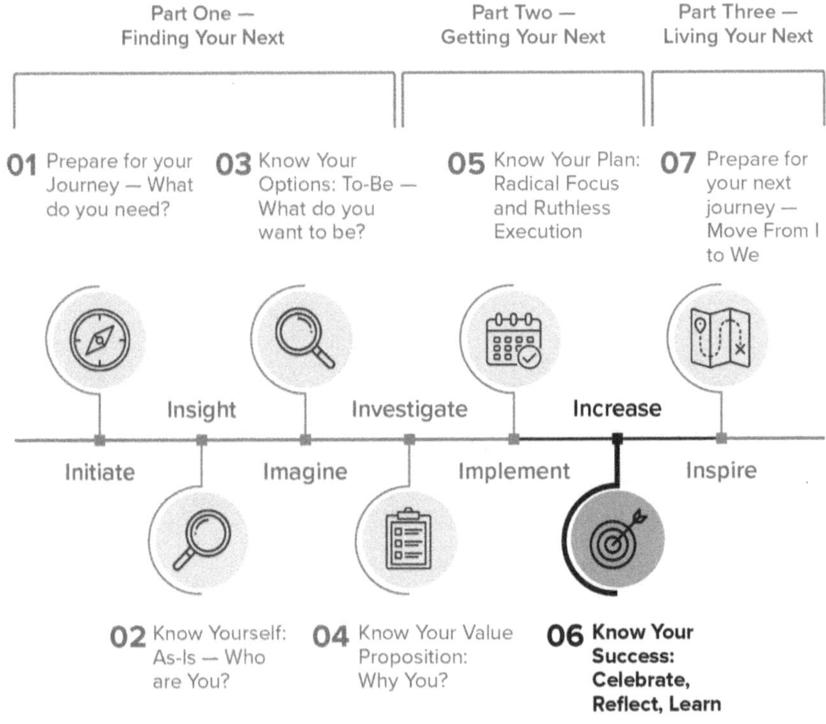


*In this chapter, we focus on Step 6—Increase: Know Your Success. Source: Moo Pie Advisors, Inc., 2025.*

Over the years, I've watched many of my Oxford University classmates come to reunions and alumni dinners disillusioned, burned out, unhappy, divorced or separated, and alienated from themselves and their friends and families. I can guarantee you that not a single one of them graduated with the deliberate strategy of getting to this stage of their careers unfulfilled. Yet a shocking number of them unwittingly implemented that strategy. Many had become enormously successful in monetary terms or in fame, such as wealthy bankers, lawyers, entrepreneurs, famous writers and producers, or powerful politicians, but very few seemed happy and fulfilled with their careers and lives. I have talked with many of them about the reasons for this. I have also spent years in inquiry with successful people in technology, healthcare, retail, and education and with academics and researchers on this condition of success without fulfillment. I have also turned the mirror on myself and pondered why I so often got the thing that I wanted, but it did not provide the satisfaction that I craved.

All this has led to introspection, reflection, and reading, resulting in my take on the *what* and *how* of success that you will learn about in this sixth step of your journey. For my own sake, I found that no matter how much *progression* I achieved, no matter the extrinsic rewards, my success felt empty. I had earned it without *progress* toward my own growth, competency, and purpose. I felt like an imposter and could not settle. Not until my forties, when I learned to have enough gratitude for what I had and started to turn my attention to helping others, did I feel truly satisfied and happy. As for my university friends, I found that, first, they had not known—and still did not know—what they really wanted in their careers, and they didn't hold front-and-center critical life pillars (shown again in figure 25) as they decided how to spend their time, talents, and energy. Second, they did not understand how to measure success—in many individual cases, they did not see themselves as actually successful in their careers or as compared to their expectations or their reference peer group.

It seems that success in your career is a matter of perspective, and being happy with what you have achieved is a choice.

Figure 25: Life Pillars

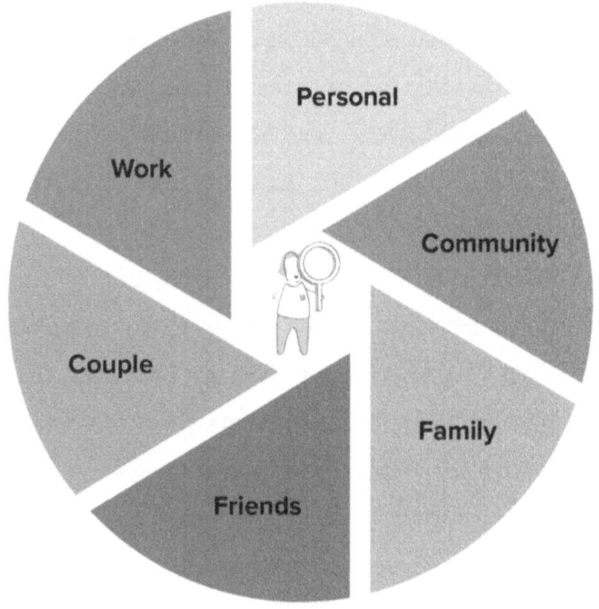


*How will you measure success in each slice of life? Source: Moo Pie Advisors, Inc., 2025.*

## The What and How of Step 6

The experience of success without realization, satisfaction, or fulfillment requires diagnosis—an honest reckoning with the reasons many outwardly accomplished people still feel unfulfilled. I want to see if this is the case for you and suggest ways of avoiding it. My experience tells me success is often paradoxical. You can feel successful from the size of your bank account, the title after your name, or the way others laud you, but you can also feel empty, sad, and full of regrets. This paradox of success seems to depend on perspective.

I've diagnosed six traps or "symptoms" commonly associated with the downside of this success paradox:

1. **Deferring happiness:** putting off being happy until some future milestone is reached
2. **Not knowing what you want:** not truly knowing what you want from your life and career, getting fixated on success in one area of your life and having no balance, or just choosing the wrong thing to succeed in
3. **Living someone else's dream:** chasing what others want for you, not what you want
4. **Losing sight of "enough":** tying identity to achievements and never achieving the mirage of "enough"
5. **Achieving loneliness:** reaching the top only to find you're alone there
6. **Not experiencing gratitude:** failing to pause and feel grateful for what you have and what you've been able to do, and not taking time to express your appreciation to those who have helped

These are the common signs of *what* to avoid in becoming successful. We will examine them in more detail below.

The *how* of success is twofold: the active practice of measuring your success with meaningful metrics that matter from your own perspective and of celebrating it in ways that reinforce connection, purpose, and joy. Together, these will help you not only get what you want but also know it when you do.

Let's look at the *what* and *how* in more detail as you work through Step 6, beginning with those six common traps of what to avoid.

## Deferred Happiness

Many of my classmates, the successful people I have worked with and studied—and me for a long time—put off happiness, constantly saying to ourselves: *Once I get my degree, then life will begin. Once I buy that house, or once I get the promotion or pay this off, then we can start being happy.* This is a very transactional, outcome-based view of life in which you don't enjoy the journey. Achievements, although impressive, become mere preludes to some idyllic future. But that future is often a mirage that fades as you approach it.

I have learned that this is called Deferred Happiness Syndrome (DHS),[36] which refers to the tendency to postpone happiness and fulfillment to a future point, often tied to achieving a specific goal or circumstance. It's the belief that "When I get X, I'll be happy," but the X constantly moves further away, leading to a perpetual state of waiting for happiness rather than experiencing it in the present.

DHS often manifests in behaviors and attitudes such as:

- Neglecting relationships, hobbies, or personal well-being in pursuit of future goals, often believing one can make up for it later
- Missing out on the opportunities for happiness and fulfillment that exist in the present moment, which can lead to anxiety about not achieving the desired future, further reinforcing the postponement of happiness

36 Raj Raghunathan, *If You're So Smart, Why Aren't You Happy?* (Portfolio/Penguin, 2016).

- Downplaying or overlooking past successes as the focus remains on what still needs to be achieved

A way to avoid and defeat this syndrome is practicing something called episodic future thinking (EFT), which refers to the capacity to mentally simulate or "pre-experience" specific future events, envisioning what it would feel like to go through them.[37] Research shows that EFT relies on the same brain networks used for autobiographical memory and plays a critical role in shaping our decisions, emotions, and behaviors. EFT helps avoid bad choices and actions by thinking about what you would *feel* like after you have done the thing.

A good example is thinking about how you would feel if you were discovered doing something unethical at work to get your way or to get a promotion. Thinking about shame can prevent bad actions or decisions. Another example is using EFT to think about missing out on your son's or daughter's play or concert because you are going to work instead. The basis is that the determinant is how you feel, not what you have done, and that your future self is wiser than your present self.[38]

## Not Knowing What You Want

As you've moved through the earlier steps of this journey—clarifying who you are, what you want, and how you'll get there—you've focused primarily on your career and professional self. But real success in life isn't confined to career achievements. If you neglect the other life pillars, such as family, friends, health, community, and personal life, you may

37 Donna R. Addis and Daniel L. Schacter, "The Cognitive Neuroscience of Constructive Memory: Remembering the Past and Imagining the Future," *Philosophical Transactions of the Royal Society B: Biological Sciences* 362, no. 1481 (2007): 773–86, https://royalsocietypublishing.org/doi/10.1098/rstb.2007.2087.

38 Ibid.

end up with external accomplishments but internal emptiness or a complete imbalance with success in one area but failures in others. The image in figure 26 is a reminder that career is just one slice of the whole, although a very big slice (remember those ninety thousand hours!).

Figure 26: What Do You Want: Identifying and Understanding Intrinsic Motivation

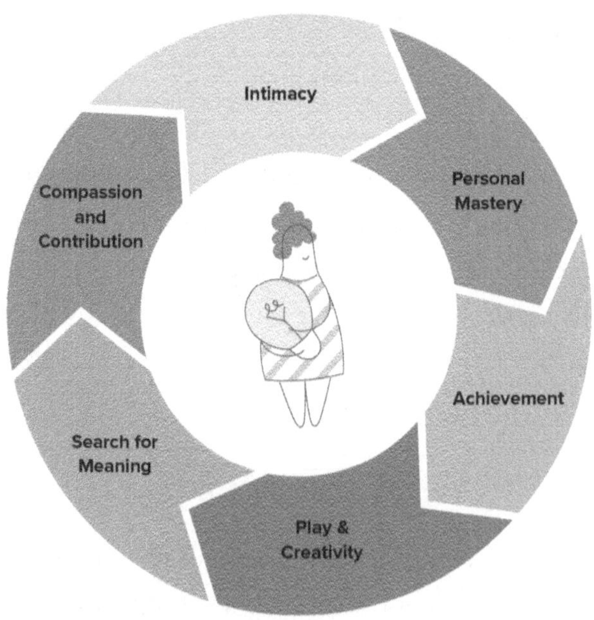


*Are you living in alignment with your motivations or with what someone else thinks they should be? Source: Moo Pie Advisors, Inc., 2025.*

You *can* be successful in your life and career without carefully defining what you want. However, you're essentially stumbling into success through a combination of talent, luck, and effort. Also, that success is likely to lack meaning and purpose if you have built success in one domain at the expense of all the others. We discussed the dangers of this in Steps 2 and 3 as you took stock of your current (at that time) reality and how you wanted that to change based on who you wanted to become. And you saw the examples of Caroline, Rachel, and Pierre as they factored family lives, their own well-being, and their geographic locations into their career choices and goals.

So, what we are looking for is picking the right kind of success in your career and looking to have some balance between your life pillars, particularly as you grow older.

In your twenties, if you are career oriented, being out of balance and prioritizing work seems like a no-brainer. Building competency and brand, dedicating yourself to getting in the repetitions, and building the right habits and practices will no doubt pay off and help you get ahead. You will most likely succeed, but when you hit thirty, will you be happy? Many of my coachees in their twenties tend to focus on extrinsic factors (money, title, power and control, status) and have not sufficiently explored their intrinsic or creative motivations.

As an example, I spent much of my twenties focused on having a blast, being very social, going out every night, doing what my friends wanted, and pursuing very extrinsic goals. Then I woke up in my late twenties and figured out what I wanted for myself. I wanted to get rid of my imposter syndrome. I wanted to feel that I was really good at something. I prioritized putting effort into building some real competency, walking away from spending every night out and having a broad set of friendships to becoming much more selective and much more focused on my fulfillment. But, from my perspective, success still eluded me.

In your thirties, overly focusing on work to the exclusion of other life pillars is likely to start to have some significant downsides and result in missed life opportunities and a sense of something missing. This lack of balance can lead to burnout. This happened to a significant number of my colleagues in Silicon Valley. And many of the people I have coached over the last five years reprioritize at this stage in their careers and look for more balance and a new perspective on the definition of success, much more driven by relationships, family (aging parents or siblings that have moved away), health, and other nonwork-related priorities (intrinsic and creative motivations).

I did the opposite and really doubled down on work to the exclusion of other factors in my thirties, still chasing that success. I felt I had to catch up with the progression of my classmates (keeping up with the Joneses!) and that I was really interested in pursuing my growing competency mastery and brand. This led to a lot of distance between my friends and me, lost personal relationships, and a growing sense of loneliness. I compensated by building some fantastic lifelong work relationships, particularly at Cisco. This time also led to the beginnings of a health crisis—too much eating and drinking, too many late nights, and too little self-care. Thank goodness I am still here!

In your forties and fifties, not knowing what you want or having misidentified it can cause extreme pain, as we have seen with my Oxford colleagues. A sense of time running out and of time and life force wasted can bring severe consequences in other areas of life—partner, family, health, etc. I have also seen many clients and colleagues in Silicon Valley become rich through luck (right idea, right time, but no development of mastery—progression without progress). They suffer significant imposter syndrome because they could not repeat their success and so felt undeserving and shallow. Many then go to enormous lengths and expense to "find themselves," never having defined what they were looking for in the first place.

I went through some serious consequences myself, including a divorce and a quadruple bypass. Career takes its toll. Luckily, I found a new sense of purpose and a new family, experienced some terrific career highlights, and launched my coaching career. So, there is hope for all of us!

Time is our one irreplaceable asset. Make sure you understand what you want and with what balance, or you will certainly waste it and live to regret it.

## Living Someone Else's Dream

I had dinner with one of my coachees one night, a woman who was a senior executive and who had made tens of millions of dollars in investment banking. She had a penthouse overlooking Manhattan, several super luxury cars, two ex-husbands, two personal trainers, and two children in expensive US private schools, but she said something to me that changed my perspective on success: "I did everything right. I went to college. I climbed the ladder. I got the job title. I married a handsome guy. Then, one day, I looked around and I realized, *Hey, wait, I'm living somebody else's dream*. First, I lived my mother's dream. Then my friends'. Then my husband's, and finally my children's, but never mine".

> **Time is our one irreplaceable asset. Make sure you understand what you want and with what balance, or you will certainly waste it and live to regret it.**

She thought she was happy because everyone else was happy for her: her parents, her partners, her friends, her children. The praise and applause felt like progress, but it wasn't purposeful; it was not hers. She realized true happiness doesn't come from following what others want you to do. It comes from doing what makes you excited every single day. She gave up her successful career, got divorced, moved to the Hudson Valley, and started writing detective novels, and she now has five dogs, six cats, and a very loud and rude parrot! Her view on success now is celebrating every day with a glass of champagne.

As discussed in Steps 2 and 3, understanding your intrinsic motivation is crucial to building a life that truly aligns with who you are, not just what others expect of you. These motivations go beyond titles, wealth, or status and include things such as personal mastery, play and creativity, intimacy, the search for meaning, compassion, and contribution. Too many people get stuck chasing extrinsic outcomes that lack soul. Compassion and contribution, in particular, are often missing from externally defined success paths, yet they are central to feeling fulfilled. The woman with the penthouse and accolades had achieved enormous progression but not purposeful progress. She was living someone else's dream, not her own.

I also suffered from this source of regret. For much of my adult life, I tried to do what my mother and father would have wanted of me. From my parents' point of view, I spent a lot of my twenties burning the candle at both ends, spending far too much time in "da club" and not enough focused on work and on my family. I was disapproved of. This reactive motivation was a significant factor in my getting on a plane at twenty-seven years old to go to San Francisco, and it unfortunately characterized my relationship with my father all the way to his death (he never came to see me in California). It was also a significant factor in eventually sorting myself out (the twists and turns of our inner workings), getting me to really focus on my career and, later on, prioritizing stability in my personal relationships and building a strong relationship with my mother after age forty. I lived my dream, then theirs, and then finally, my own.

Are you living your dream or someone else's dream for you? Think about the exercise on motivation in Step 2 and what you discovered about your own motivations and goals.

**Are you living your dream or someone else's dream for you?**

## Losing Sight of Enough

One of the most common issues I've seen among high-achieving professionals is the inability to know when enough is enough. They didn't know how to measure their success, so they simply carried on chasing more money, power, prestige, influence. But even with all of that, they never seemed to "arrive." They could not switch off the pursuit, could never rest, could never settle. Why? Because their identity had become so tightly bound to achievement that any pause in striving felt like a threat to the self.

This is the identity trap. You start to believe you are your job title, your income, your corner office. You achieve one milestone and immediately raise the bar again. I have a friend who is a serial startup CEO. He is nearly sixty and constantly frets about whether he has enough money to retire. He has millions of dollars and has successfully built and sold multiple companies but cannot rest to feel comfortable or safe. In a commencement address at Dartmouth College, Roger Federer, someone who could have easily defined himself by trophies and rankings, put it this way:

> *Life is bigger than the court. A tennis court is a small space. 2,106 square feet, to be exact. I worked a lot, learned a lot, and ran a lot of miles in that small space … but the world is a whole lot bigger than that … even when I was in the top five, it was important to me to have a life … a rewarding life full of travel, culture, friendships, and especially family.*[39]

Federer understood that success is not just about performance and identity tied to that performance but about perspective. It's about grounding your achievements in a meaningful, broader life. The work is important, but it is not the whole "you" or your whole world.

## Achieving Loneliness

Another consequence of success without fulfillment is loneliness. Many high achievers climb the ladder only to find themselves isolated at the top. Some never stopped to build deep relationships along the way. Others arrive only to realize they have no one with whom to celebrate, no one who understands the cost of what they've achieved. As described earlier, some are simply lonely—they don't have others to share their success with or don't know how to connect with others to celebrate. The result is a life with little integration or appreciation for what's been accomplished.

This kind of loneliness often stems from an achievement-driven life that lacks relational intention. If you've spent years optimizing every moment for performance and progress, you may have inadvertently deprioritized the people who give your success meaning. It's a common regret: getting to the top and realizing you didn't bring anyone with you. Real success doesn't happen in isolation.

---

39 Federer, "2024 Commencement Address."

## Not Experiencing Gratitude

Another contributing factor to feeling unsettled with your success is failing to feel grateful for what you have and what you've been able to do and not taking time to express your appreciation to those who have helped.

In Japanese culture, the concept of gratitude and shared appreciation is described by the collective term *kansha*, which encompasses a deep appreciation for everything, including both positive and challenging experiences. Kansha is rooted in Buddhist philosophy and involves cultivating a sincere and mindful attitude of thankfulness. It encourages a shift in perspective to see the positive aspects of life and appreciate the journey, including its ups and downs.

This umbrella concept covers other related important types of gratitude that are relevant for us in measuring and celebrating success, including *mottainai*, which embodies the idea of not wasting but cherishing the resources that you have and ikigai, which, as you well know by now, emphasizes finding purpose and meaning in life and our journey of experience.

At this juncture, it is particularly important to reflect on whether your success is "whole," taking in all of the ikigai elements, or is unbalanced, focusing on just one or more. There are two elements to reflect on: first, feeling real gratitude for the journey, what you have become, and the reward of the destination for you and your loved ones; and second, sharing that gratitude and appreciation with them. Without both of these, I have found many people feel emptiness, dissatisfaction with understanding their existing success and their progress, and a sense of being unmoored in not having shared their story with others.

## A "Cure" for Success Paradox Symptoms

"There is nothing better in life than being a late bloomer. I believe that success can happen at any time and at any age."—Salma Hayek

## It May Not Be Too Late

If you're reading this in your twenties or thirties and feel behind, you're not. You're early! The data tell a story that differs from the one culture (or our own sense of ticking clock) often shouts at us. For example, the average self-made millionaire in the US reaches that milestone around age fifty-seven, and most small business founders start their ventures in their mid-to-late forties. Even the average billionaire is closer to sixty-seven, not the twenty-seven-year-old in a hoodie you might picture. And if you're thinking of changing careers? The typical American does so around age thirty-nine. Monetary success, in other words, is rarely early. It's built over time through pivots, experiments, setbacks, and course corrections.[40]

By the end of 2024, there were more than three thousand billionaires worldwide, and the vast majority—nearly three-quarters—got there not by inheritance or employment but by building something of their own.[41] Among US millionaires, 45 percent are entrepreneurs, while another 30 percent are senior corporate leaders,

40 Andrei Kurtuy, "60+ Career Change Statistics for 2024 [That You Didn't Know!]," *Novoresume*, updated September 15, 2025, https://novoresume.com/career-blog/career-change-statistics; Pierre Azoulay et al., "Age and High-Growth Entrepreneurship," working paper no. 24489 (National Bureau of Economic Research, April 2018), https://www.nber.org/papers/w24489; Paul Sullivan, "The Average Age When People Become Millionaires," *The New York Times*, May 23, 2014.

41 "The World's Billionaires List," *Forbes*, April 2024; *The 2024 Global Wealth Report* (Credit Suisse Research Institute).

most of whom advanced through decades of work.[42] These numbers aren't meant to glorify wealth but to normalize later success. They show that it's not too late to start something new or to grow into the person you want to become.

## The Power of Regret Redux

When my classmates expressed significant regrets, they were over things they had done and things they had not done and regrets about the way they had spent time. As you know from the initial discussion of the power of regret in Step 3, this is a very common experience for people, particularly late in their careers or at the end of their lives.

In Step 3, you used the power of regret as a way to future-proof your decisions. You had the chance to choose directions that would stave off future regret. In Step 5, you were reminded that taking action to execute those decisions was also buoyed by the power of regret. Adopting a mindset that was based, in part, on not wanting to regret in the future your past action or inaction was a way of helping you move forward. Now, as you measure your success, bring the power of regret back into the mix.

You're now looking at regret in a more reflective way. You were introduced earlier to Pink's classification of regrets as foundational (doing things), boldness (taking chances), moral (doing the right thing), and connection (making time for those who matter). As you reflect on your current level of success in reaching your Next, think

---

42 Melissa Houston, "Why Most Millionaires Own Businesses and How You Can Join Them," *Forbes*, October 27, 2024, https://www.forbes.com/sites/melissahouston/2024/10/27/why-most-millionaires-own-businesses-and-how-you-can-join-them/; Jack Kelly, "The Making of a Millionaire, and Why $100K Is No Longer the Benchmark Salary for Wealth in America," *Forbes*, May 23, 2023, https://www.forbes.com/sites/jackkelly/2023/05/23/the-making-of-a-millionaire-and-why-100k-is-no-longer-the-benchmark-salary-for-wealth-in-america/.

about which of these categories, if any, you feel some degree of regret in and complete the following Regrets Reflection exercise.

## EXERCISE: REGRETS REFLECTION

**Reflecting on foundational regrets:** Making career decisions with what feels like so many opportunities available to us can be paralyzing. However, letting career opportunities pass you by can be just as harmful as making the wrong decision. Consider these questions and jot down your thoughts:

- What could you have done differently or even just done at all?
- What can you still take action on?
- Do you need to remind yourself to "just do it"?

**Reflecting on boldness regrets:** This category was the most prevalent and powerful among all respondents in Daniel Pink's study, so be sure to take enough time to think about the chances you could have taken. Write down your thoughts on these questions:

Have you gotten stuck in your comfort zone, not able to tolerate the discomfort (fear, doubt) of being in the learning zone?

What chances have passed you by, and how can you avoid that happening again?

Is there something you can still take bold action on? Take a chance on?

**Reflecting on moral regrets:** Think about missteps you've made, perhaps when your inner compass malfunctioned or because you had not matured enough. Consider the following questions:

- Do you need to revisit your values and get back in alignment with them?
- Which wrongs can you correct?
- Have you been relating to people who share your internal compass (as you explored in Steps 2 and 3)? If not, do you need to find a new tribe?

**Reflecting on connection regrets:** Spending time connecting with people and activities you care about can easily slip through the cracks without intentional effort to balance all the pillars of your life. As an example, I have a daughter who has just graduated college and whom I am very proud of. I did not see her enough when she was younger, or even when she was in high school, as I spent too much time working rather than sitting on the sofa watching endless repeats of the film *Spy* with her. I am told that 80 percent of the time we spend with our children over our lives is before they are eighteen and leave the house.[43] I will regret my decisions for the rest of my life. Ask yourself:

- Can you renew a meaningful connection with someone important to you?
- How could you adjust the time you spend with those who matter to you?

## My Own Success Paradox

Let me be quite honest: I have had a winding road to finding real career purpose and fulfillment, and I have had to learn hard lessons from many failures throughout my career.

For the longest time, I did not feel as though I was successful. Not until celebrating my fortieth birthday did it really strike me: I had succeeded in achieving my teenage dreams. My perspective on success snapped into place, and I decided to be happy.

As a teen in semirural England, I wanted to escape my small-town existence. My friends and I grew up watching TV with lots of American shows such as *The Rockford Files*, *Falcon Crest*, and *CHiPs*, and I, in particular, dreamt of California. This was especially so

---

43 "80% of the Time We Ever Spend with Our Kids Is Over by the Time They Are 18 Years," *The Fit Dad Lifestyle* (blog), https://www.thefitdadlifestyle.com/blogs/news/80-of-the-time-we-ever-spend-with-our-kids-is-over-by-the-time-they-are-18-years.

during the summer before I went to college. I watched the video of "Everybody Wants to Rule the World" by the band Tears for Fears and longed to drive down the spectacular California Highway One in an old MG sports car, just as they had done. In the mid-1980s these images and sounds were very compelling to a young man from Maidenhead in Berkshire.

So, there I was on my fortieth birthday, sitting on my deck in the glorious California sunshine, surrounded by my wife, close friends, work colleagues, and two very large, hairy dogs. All the hard work and struggle had paid off. I had done what I had set out to achieve (via a very roundabout route). As I reflected on my life up to that point, I realized that I had meaningful work that I loved, a meaningful set of relationships (remember that reference group concept in Step 5?), security, wealth, and something to look forward to. I was in the adventure, enjoying the journey, not being a resentful bystander or waiting for some abstract arrival or achievement. The journey, the living that I had constructed, was the thing. As John Lennon said, referencing Jean-Paul Sartre's book *Nausea*, "Life is what happens while we're making other plans." I was not just existing or planning; I was living my dream.

By virtually any metric, I was successful; however, I had actualized by a series of very fortunate accidents and opportunistic behaviors rather than a purposeful plan. So, I felt like an imposter. Also, in my case, career and job comparison with others was my particular thief of joy. I still had to learn to slow down, be grateful, and realize how lucky I was—and that enough was enough. I still had questions about balance, about meaning (work and relationships), about identity.

My journey was far from complete. I spent the next fifteen years of my life understanding my success and how I measured it, changing my perspective, and deciding to vote for my own happiness. Let's now look at how *you* will measure and celebrate your success.

## How Do You Measure Success?

> **"Too many people overestimate what they lack, but underestimate what they have, and lose the chance to become a winner."**
>
> **—John D. Rockefeller**

Now that you've been faithfully showing up, taking purposeful actions each day, and holding yourself accountable along the way, it's time to pause and look back on how far you've come. The goal here is to recognize your success and let yourself be satisfied with it rather than being restless, jumping to the next thing.

### MEASURING AND MANAGING

Management guru Peter F. Drucker, in his seminal 1954 book *The Practice of Management*,[44] was one of the first to talk about the importance of measuring results. He makes the point that when you track specific metrics, you bring focus and discipline to your efforts. This principle has become a cornerstone of modern management practice, reminding leaders that without clear, measurable indicators, even the best-laid plans can drift off course.

So how do you recognize that you've gotten to where you wanted to be (gotten the right perspective)? How do you enjoy it, both along the way and once you're there? Let's have a look.

44 Peter F. Drucker, *The Practice of Management* (Harper & Brothers, 1954).

## Framing Your Success: The Success Thermostat

We all have an inner thermostat for different aspects of our lives, such as:

- career success
- personal health
- relationship with partner
- relationship with friends

This concept, originally developed decades ago by Dr. Maxwell Maltz,[45] compares the human tendency to return to a baseline level of success to a home thermostat regulating temperature.

This thermostat regulates our view of our life experience. It is adjustable, but only with awareness and internal work to adjust our view of reality.

### FOR FURTHER READING: IMAGINED THERMOSTATS

Interested in a modern take on how internal "set points" for success are maintained? Yuval Noah Harari, bestselling author of ***Sapiens***,[46] describes how humans live within "imagined realities" that regulate how we define ourselves and what we believe we can achieve. Harari's insights offer a compelling parallel to the idea of inner "thermostats" by saying that our internal measures of worth are shaped not just by personal history but by the cultural stories we collectively uphold.

45 Maxwell Maltz, *Psycho-Cybernetics: A New Way to Get More Living Out of Life* (Prentice-Hall, 1960).

46 Harari, *Sapiens*.

In my experience, many people get stuck at a certain level of their thermostat of success. This is because of several reasons, including fear of failure, thus keeping them where they are, or fear of success, stopping them from exceeding a range on the thermostat. This is self-sabotage. Instead of working to adjust their cognitive and emotional (internal) view of the thermostat level or make it more flexible, they look to external or extrinsic stimuli or results that they believe will solve their issues surrounding success. Classic examples of this are recording artists, actors, or lottery winners. Outwardly, they are successful, but their inner thermostat does not move, leaving them feeling unsatisfied.

Success does not erase or solve insecurities; it amplifies them. When we gain success, recognition, fame, or money beyond our conception of self (thermostat), inner conflict emerges, such as imposter syndrome and shame. I see this with founders or executives in Silicon Valley who are in the right place at the right time but who are not especially good leaders, yet they become overnight successes. As a former boss of mine used to say, even a frozen turkey can fly in a hurricane!

We all desire alignment between our external reality and our internal self-image. If these are unaligned, we get confused, feel "emotionally hijacked," and begin to react badly, as you learned about in the Clarity Versus Confusion section of Step 1.

## EXERCISE: YOUR SUCCESS THERMOSTAT

Where is your success thermostat set? Think of the life pillar categories or others you want to focus on:

- work/career
- personal/health
- relationships—couple

- relationships—friends
- relationships—family
- relationships—community

Think of a range between zero and one hundred, with one hundred being the most successful and self-fulfilled. Where are you now? Why? What is driving this? What would more success look like, and how different would you feel?

## Framing Your Success: It's About the Journey, Not the Destination

If you don't know how to measure your success, you won't be happy. How do you know how much success is enough? You'll recall that some of my classmates and a number of my colleagues could not switch off the pursuit, could never rest, and could never settle. They always wanted more. They had failed to connect with their intrinsic motivation and with goals around their life pillars, not just their career. Extrinsic motivation had proved unsatisfying and impermanent.

And never mind measuring success; they had not actually defined it in the first place. What does success look like for them? Money? Power? Influence? Insight and wisdom? Mastery? Freedom? Something else?

So, the first step is to know what success is and how you are measuring it. You have to frame it up, which means thinking in terms of progress rather than progression. Progress is about the small, consistent steps that move you forward. It's the "1 percent better" mindset—a stoic, patient commitment to the craft, not just the goal. Progress says, "I am doing. I am learning. I am becoming." Progress, the journey, also becomes your identity (doing is becoming) and so allows you to accept success. Be an astronaut. Be a better astronaut. Walk on the moon.

Progression is a sequence of milestones—a checklist of external validations. Progression is fine. But it's limited. Roger Federer didn't become great because he won every match. He became great by improving his points, by choosing the right metric, which was his ability to show up and play each point with excellence.

Ask yourself: What are you measuring? Accolades? Or mastery? If you're measuring the doing—not just the outcomes—you're building something sustainable. This isn't about ignoring your goals. It's about tracking the right things: your effort, discipline, mindset, and habits.

## EXERCISE: PROOF OF PROGRESS

Write down three specific things you did in the last week that felt like real steps forward:

"I showed up and ..."

"I practiced by ..."

"I learned how to ..."

If you get into the habit of doing the Proof of Progress exercise regularly, you won't just progress through a checklist, and you won't be bragging about how much you've gotten done. You'll be making genuine progress, showing how you improved at core tasks, deepened your relationships, and reinforced your identity as someone who does the work. As you look back, you'll see that each of those micro-wins has carried you to your next waypoint. So, find what works for you to make this stocktaking a habit. For me, this means my long walk to the beach, which is long enough to quiet the noise in my head so I can begin to reflect on what I'm taking stock of.

## YOU CONTROL PROGRESS; YOU DO NOT CONTROL PROGRESSION

You are always in control of your own progress—what you learn, how you grow, the effort you put in. But you do not control progression. That's up to other people—that second-degree contact you're trying to nail down a networking appointment with or that hiring committee with their own agenda for filling the role. You are, to some extent, at the mercy of others when it comes to your progression along the waypoints of your journey. So, focus where you have agency: Make progress every day, and progression will fall into place.

What I've discovered in listening, doing it myself, and reading, is that it's the old Buddhist *Zen and the Art of Motorcycle Maintenance* story. It's the road less traveled. It's the journey, not the destination. You don't need to win every race. Not everyone gets the trophy. But everyone can get better, and that's the deeper reward: becoming the kind of person who is consistently improving, who is committed to the work, who finds joy in the making of the thing, whether that's a table, a project, or a career.

In my own life, I often had the feeling that I needed to achieve something, and I was hyperaware of the risks and problems around me. I am obsessive about solving problems! This made me a very effective strategist and executive but a miserable person. I had to learn to stop worrying, to stop looking at the world negatively as a series of risks and problems to be solved and instead to enjoy the ride and enjoy the now. After thirty years of cognitive behavioral therapy, I will tell you my best recipe for avoiding this problem is to get a dog, or in my case, four dogs! Happiness is a choice, not an outcome. It is how you see reality. It is internal, not external, and in my opinion, it is best seen through the eyes of a dog.

Your journey is a marathon, not a sprint. And in that marathon, your stepping stones, those small purposeful actions, those "I showed up" moments, are not just milestones. They are *evidence* of who you are becoming. As Clayton Christensen put it, the most important question isn't "What did I achieve?" but "How did I measure my life?" You can apply that same wisdom at the career level. Ask not just, "What have I achieved?" but "How have I grown?" and "Who have I become in the process?" Being, and enjoying who you are, is a pretty good measure of success. Validating that through your circle of friends and family will embed and reinforce this more. Is there still something missing? Remember ikigai? Is it rewards? Is it competency? Is it passion? Is it mission?

Some people build that identity in ten years. For others, it takes thirty. Either way, the question is the same: How are you measuring success? If you measure only the end, you're missing what shaped you. When you measure the doing and becoming, not just the outcomes, you become far more accountable and more honest with yourself.

## The Company You Keep—Who Came on the Journey with You?

> **"No one who achieves success does so without acknowledging the help of others. The wise and confident acknowledge this help with gratitude."**
> **—Alfred North Whitehead**

Whether you landed the role, closed the deal, finished the program, or started your venture, who helped get you there? And whom did you enjoy it with? Just as tennis players run into the stands after a match to celebrate with their team or fans, so, too, should you recognize that success is more meaningful when shared with mentors, friends, family, colleagues, clients, or community. Celebration is happiness shared.

**Celebration is happiness shared.**

## LET OTHERS SEE THE NEW YOU

Now that you've reached your Next, it isn't enough simply for you to know how you've reshaped your identity at your current stage of life. Others need to recognize and understand this new version of you as well. That might mean sharing the news directly in conversations, clarifying your role or focus with colleagues, updating your social media presence, or refreshing your personal brand. In doing so, you make sure your success isn't just something you celebrate privately but is a visible, shared reality that helps align others' perceptions with who you are today and what you currently do (and don't do).

In one of the longest-running studies in history, the Harvard Study of Adult Development—often referred to as the Harvard Longitudinal Happiness Study—began in 1938 and is still ongoing as of 2025, tracking 724 men and their families. They've looked at factors such as careers, personal physical health, mental health, and relationships with their spouse, children, and friends (social connection). They found that the last group, friends and social connections, was the single largest contributor to men's happiness. Those with deeper, longer-lasting (a core group), and more numerous friends had greater motivation, less stress and anxiety, and less brain function decline over a seventy-year period.

Success is rarely solitary. Who came with you on your journey? Which five people were in your core group? What roles did they play in your success, and have you thanked them explicitly and celebrated with them? I have found, through hundreds of iterations, that successful people often have a significant blind spot in this regard. This both robs them of shared joy and memories and puts distance between themselves and their closest allies.

When people over seventy are interviewed, they emphasize the journey and experiences they have had, not their prizes or achievements, and in particular, they cite the teams and friends that they went on those journeys with. In my own life, the teams that I was part of at Cisco stand out as more than colleagues—especially the team that built Emerging Markets into a five-billion-dollar juggernaut over five years (bigger than Amazon at the time). I still try to stay in close touch with many of these remarkable and diverse leaders.

Take stock of how your network has

- grown in numbers and breadth, and
- increased in quality and depth of relationships.

Write that down, and then answer these two questions:

1. Who are the core five or so people who have helped the most? Have you thanked them? When was the last time you did so?
2. And how have you learned to be better at relationship building (earning trust, conveying warmth, understanding others) with them and others? What could you do differently here?

What does this tell you?

## The Kind of Company You've Been to Others

After taking stock of the relationships you've built along your journey and the role that others have played in your success, flip the tables and consider who and how you've been in the eyes of others. How people feel after working with you is a key element in measuring success. Are you the kind of person others will want to collaborate with again?

Yes, there are people who burn hot and fast, delivering results but leaving scorched earth behind. Over time, though, it's the decent ones, the curious, kind, and supportive folks, who get invited back into the room. Being good company is about the tone you set, the energy you bring, and the small but meaningful moments of respect and encouragement you offer. When you help others succeed and root for your teammates, when you lead with generosity, people notice. The kind of company you are to others will shape the company you keep. *That* is meaningful success!

## Making Meaning of Success

If you don't stop to measure success, you won't know when you've won. You'll keep reaching, striving, chasing. But if you make the key shift from asking "What did I achieve?" to "What did it mean?" and "What did I learn?" you'll be closer to enjoying true success and feeling fulfilled.

Clear your mind. Sitting, walking or drifting and reflecting should alert you to your intuition about making meaning of your success. It's in the quiet moments alone that you can see what you have learned and what it has meant. I build a week a year into my calendar to go to the mountains or the sea or sit by a river and just read and reflect. This really works for me and has added immeasurably to my life and satisfaction. I recommend it to you.

In my opinion, experience, and studies, close consideration of what you want in each area of life and in which order of priority (remember the Rule of Three in prioritizing and sequencing) is a critical activity in deciding what you want and avoiding regret later. This means defining both success and balance for yourself. I am not a life coach, and this book is not about overall advice in life. However, many of my colleagues and coachees have found that focusing on success in other segments of life beyond "work"—the quandary of parenthood versus career or where to live in relation to family and friends, for instance—was enormously fruitful and much more satisfying than simply pursuing more or larger career goals. One thing is for certain: Your priorities will change as you move through life's transitions, as we discussed in the reflections on motivations in Step 2.

### EXERCISE: MEANING MAKING AND SUCCESS

Take time to reflect on these questions about your success. Write down your answers.

- Has it brought you closer to being the person you want to be?
- Does it reflect your values?
- Has it connected you with others?
- Would your twelve-year-old self be proud of what you have become?
- What would your seventy-five-year-old future self say about where you are?

As Christensen and others have emphasized, the real question isn't whether you earned a title or made more money. It's: How did you spend your time? Did it matter? It's not about owning the yacht; it's about how you came to be able to own it.

## How Can You Celebrate Success?

Even when people reach extraordinary heights, they often don't stop to celebrate—to enjoy the view. Many high achievers climb the ladder without looking up, and when they finally arrive, they feel more relief than joy, if they feel anything at all. Celebrating success requires presence, self-trust, and a connection to something deeper than performance metrics. But these are often underdeveloped muscles in success-driven cultures. My CEO at Cisco, John Chambers, used to regularly ask in meetings, "Whom will I congratulate when this is complete?" to emphasize the celebration of commitment and team effort.

Some never celebrate because they're already focused on the next goal. Others worry that pausing to enjoy the moment might slow their momentum or make them seem weak. Some are simply lonely—they don't have others to share their success with or don't know how to connect with others to celebrate. The result is a life with little integration or appreciation for what's been accomplished.

Celebrating doesn't mean throwing a big party, unless that's your thing, in which case, have a blast! It does mean marking the moment in a way that sustains you. You don't want your life to be only early mornings and hard sprints. It can't just be discipline and struggle. You not only need to win, but you need to enjoy the win. My mother taught me to treat myself whenever I achieved something I was proud of, to signify an event and memorialize it. I would celebrate with a good meal with friends and buy myself a gift that was symbolic.

Ask yourself:

- What reward motivates you?
- What symbol would you use to mark your progress?
- Whom do you want to share this with?

- What's a small but meaningful ritual you could adopt for finishing a goal?

Some people take a walk and reflect on these questions. Others write a letter to themselves or send an update to their mentor or coach. Some book a weekend away or buy something symbolic. Just don't skip the celebration. It's part of the system. If you don't pause to enjoy it, your progress will start to feel like punishment. Let's take a closer look at the elements of celebrating success.

### CELEBRATING SUCCESS BREEDS MORE SUCCESS

Celebrating small wins along the way isn't just a feel-good moment—it's neuroscience. When you pause to recognize progress, your brain forms positive synaptic connections that reinforce the behavior. This builds momentum. Daily and weekly celebrations create a feedback loop, and success becomes a habit. The more you acknowledge what's working, the more likely you are to keep doing it. Rinse and repeat—this is how lasting change and sustainable growth take root.

## Stepping Stones Versus Destinations

As you already know from measuring your success, the steps we take to get to our Next are just as important as reaching the destination. Real growth, meaningful identity transformation, and the deeper reward lie in the stepping stones of the journey. But too often we celebrate only the destination—the promotion or new job, the launch, the big win.

When you focus only on crossing the finish line, you miss the identity that is forged along the way. Your true identity doesn't come from the final victory; it comes from how you showed up again and again, when things were uncertain, slow, or difficult. That's where pride, resilience, and self-trust are built. So, be sure to celebrate the process, not just the prize. Each stepping stone represents a new capability unlocked in your skill tree, a new relationship for your network, a new experience and lesson learned. All are worthy of celebration and reflection.

## Celebrating Defeats and Failures

> **"It's not what you achieve, it's what you overcome. That's what defines your career."**
>
> **—Carlton Fisk**

It's easy to celebrate wins, but often, the bigger growth comes from celebrating how you handled the losses. Did you persist? Did you learn? Did you show up again?

Federer lost hundreds of matches. Michael Jordan has famously talked about how he missed more than nine thousand shots in his career and lost nearly three hundred games. And, twenty-six times, Jordan was trusted to take the game-winning shot and missed. He attributes his success to failing over and over and over in his life.[47]

Knowing how to fail, being uncomfortable with failure, and understanding that failure is a way of learning—these mindsets breed success.

How can you celebrate your own failures? Don't let the fear of failure block your willingness to take bold steps next time.

---

47 Chuck Swoboda, "Why 'The Last Dance' Is Must-See TV for Business Leaders," *Forbes*, May 29, 2020, https://www.forbes.com/sites/chuckswoboda/2020/05/29/why-the-last-dance-is-must-see-tv-for-business-leaders/.

### KINTSUGI: FINDING STRENGTH IN IMPERFECTION

The Japanese art of ***kintsugi***—mending broken pottery with gold—reminds us that setbacks and disappointments aren't signs of failure but part of our personal craftsmanship. When the path toward a goal leaves us with cracks, whether that's missed opportunities, detours, or mistakes, we can choose to see them not as flaws to hide but as marks of resilience and growth. Like pottery repaired with gold, our experiences make us more unique and valuable, and often more capable than we were before. In this way, kintsugi offers a powerful truth: Your journey's imperfections are part of its beauty.

In my thirty-plus years of striving, I have lost more than I have won. I have been fired, I have missed deadlines, and I have failed to grow businesses. I have not gotten roles or jobs I really wanted. But like a kintsugi piece, I am now better for it. I learned, adapted, got back up, got better, and got what I wanted.

## What Did Success Look Like for Caroline, Pierre, and Rachel?

Let's revisit our three friends. Each took a different path, and the outcomes of their journeys highlight some of the most important lessons from Step 6.

Pierre took the time to clarify what he wanted, aligned his motivations with his values and desired context, and pursued a path that matched his definition of success. He transitioned out of consulting and into a leadership role with a multinational insurer back in Paris, closer to his family. He now finds himself content in his family life, in a supportive context, and professionally fulfilled. Pierre's story is a case study in knowing what you want and going after it with intention—and being able to celebrate once you've arrived!

Rachel, by contrast, stayed where she was. Despite articulating a strong desire to pivot into interior design, she ultimately chose safety and stability. She remained at the large consultancy, prioritizing family and financial security over career reinvention. Her decision reflects both reactive and creative motivations, but it also illustrates the challenge of deferred happiness. She did not pursue the dream she had expressed, and while she has found peace in leading and supporting her family, she may one day look back with a sense of regret over the opportunity not taken. Let's hope she also abides by the "it's probably not too late" philosophy.

Caroline achieved her initial goal: She became general counsel and earned a prestigious board seat. But she found the rewards hollow, and her identity was defined more by titles than meaning. She realized she had been chasing a success metric that didn't reflect who she truly was or what she wanted her impact to be. So, she pivoted. Drawing on her background in international law, she took on a leadership role in a nonprofit in Eastern Europe. Caroline's path reminds us that it's almost never too late to redefine success and take a new direction. Her journey also reflects the power of stepping stones and relationships—that the people and experiences we encounter along the way can change our destination.

Clearly, success is not a singular concept. It is personal, evolving, and, when defined and pursued with care, deeply rewarding.

## Closing Thoughts on Step 6

This book is a huge milestone for me. It represents a life goal—one I didn't reach by accident but by choice, habit, and hard work. If you focus on the big, meaningful things that align with your values and that bring you into deeper service, you will have lived a life that matters. You'll have worked on things worth working on.

And remember: What's not measured is not managed. But you get to choose how you perceive, measure, and celebrate your growth and success. Progress or progression? Journey or destination? "I am doing it" or "I did it"?

## CHAPTER WAYPOINTS

Most people fail to experience fulfillment not because they aren't successful but because they haven't stopped to define what success means to them.

Success is largely perception. It is internal first before being external. If you believe you are successful, then you have created the conditions for progress.

Progress is the consistent, daily effort you put in. You control your progress. Progression is the sequence of milestones that are influenced, in part, by factors outside your control. Focus on what you can control.

Measuring success requires you to choose the right metrics: effort, presence, learning, alignment with values, and connection with others.

Celebrating success keeps the journey sustainable. Mark the stepping stones, not just the summits, and keep track of the failures, not just the wins.

Make meaning of your success: Did it connect to who you are and who you want to be?

Contentment may be simpler than you expect: meaningful work, meaningful relationships, and something to look forward to. A simple and effective formula to remember and live by.

Happiness is a choice, not an outcome. It is how you see reality. It is internal, not external.

Stay in the learning zone, measure progress with the right metrics, celebrate small wins, and then rinse and repeat.

# STEP 7

## Inspire: Move from I to We

**"Alone we can do so little; together we can do so much."**

**—Helen Keller**

If you've worked through the steps of this book so far, you've clarified what you want, activated a plan to get it, and paused to measure and celebrate what success looks like for you. So, what is next? Unless your goal is to be an individual contributor or solo professional practitioner, you'll have to work through and with others to get what you want. Whether you're trying to launch a new initiative, grow a business, or simply solve a problem, your success will depend on your ability to work in teams. That means leadership of people, and that means moving your skill set and mindset from "I" to "we." So here in Step 7, I help you shift from how *you* get what *you* want to how *we* get what *we* want.

I have spent more than thirty years practicing and perfecting my approach to successful relationship-focused leadership as a management consultant, general manager, functional leader, C-suite member, board advisor, board member, and coach. This chapter is a high-level walk-through of the proven, successful methodology that I use in coaching for business leadership and that I'll explore in depth in my next book.

Figure 27: Focus on Step 7

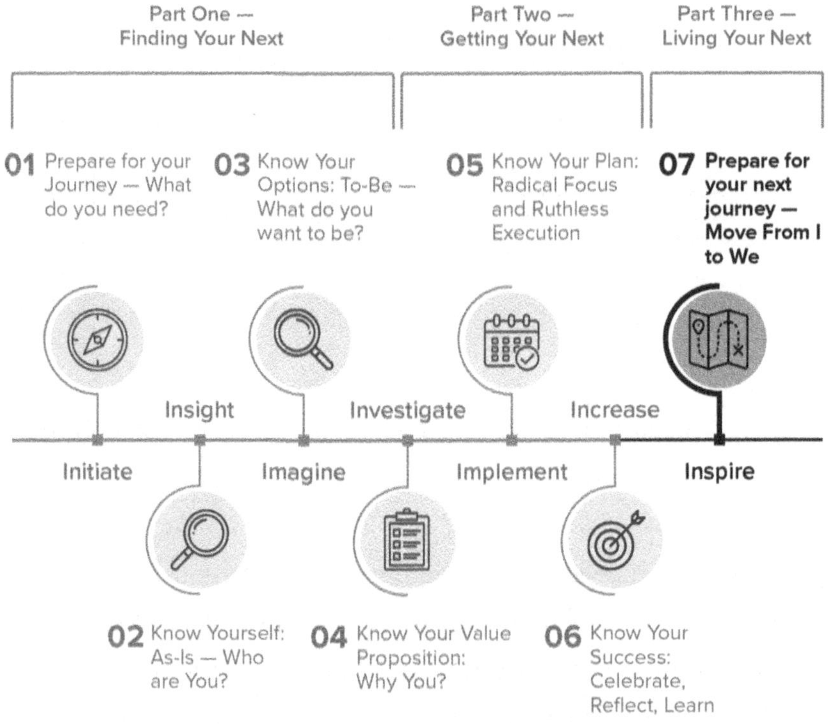


*In this chapter, we focus on Step 7—Inspire: Move from I to We. Source: Moo Pie Advisors, Inc., 2025.*

Think of this chapter as your launchpad for scaling the impact and success of the hard work you've done on understanding what you want and how to get it. This step builds on the same principles and processes as in Steps 1 through 6, now with a pivot toward the *how* and the *what* of team leadership. We are going to cover three primary things:

1. The mindset shift from I to we in assuming the role of a leader
2. The role of relationships in your success
3. Your focus in the first one hundred days of your new role or job as a leader

You can also go to my website for descriptions of how you can further develop as a team leader through the courses, live master classes, coaching with me, and other resources.

Welcome to navigating your team!

## Challenge: The Woolly Mammoth Problem

Let's step into a time machine and go back ten thousand years to just after the last ice age. You are in a cave. Winter is coming; it's cold and you can hear the rain coming down outside. You're hungry. Your family is also hungry and looking at you. You need to source a lot of food. You want a woolly mammoth. But you can't capture a mammoth alone. That would be far too complex, onerous, and dangerous. To succeed, you need other people's skills and resourcefulness. And so, you must lead others in the quest for a mammoth! You need to move from what *you* want to what *we* want.

So, what do you do? You gather fellow hunters in your tribe and explain your vision. You want the mammoth. You and your family want to eat. The other hunters must also want the mammoth and be willing to follow you to get it, perhaps through great danger. You sketch the mammoth on the cave wall to help visualize the goal. You discuss how you will achieve your goal, and you assign and agree to roles: chasers, spear throwers, attackers, etc. You prepare your weapons, coordinate movements, and plan the return. The hunt requires trust, timing, commitment, shared understanding and alignment, and shared rewards and risks. This is a very human process of collaboration to achieve collective success. You get what you want. We get what we want.

Today's "mammoths" in the workplace are no different. Maybe you're launching a new company or new product, solving a social problem, educating a group of students, or navigating a merger. Maybe you're building a grassroots movement. Whatever it is, you can't do it alone!

The mammoth is the metaphor, but the real challenge is getting a team to believe in your vision, organize around it, and move together toward it. The workplace challenge is this: You want what *you* want, but to get it, you have to persuade others to want it too. Leadership is not coercion or control but collective service in pursuit of a goal.

As soon as you shift from "What do *I* want?" to "What do *we* want?" the game changes. You're no longer navigating alone for your career Next. You're mapping a path for others and through others. The competencies that you used to get what you want are different from those that you will need to lead others. The context to develop them is different and, crucially, so is the mindset. Let's take a high-level look at that path here—the one that I will explore in greater depth in my forthcoming book.

## The Big Idea: Leadership as Relationships

Here's the core reality of achieving a team goal: The plan is 10 percent, and the people are 90 percent. You can achieve nothing with a plan alone. I spent the first ten years of my career as a management consultant crafting meticulous strategies and plans at Andersen Consulting, Cambridge Technology Partners, and McKinsey & Company. But once I stepped into operating roles at Hitachi and Cisco, in which I was responsible for the business outcome as well as the plan, I realized not only that my best plans would fail if people didn't trust each other or didn't care enough about the goal but also that teams were uneven and needed to develop in order to achieve goals. In the last fifteen years of working closely with private equity firms, it has been drummed into me even more that 90 percent of the risk in an investment's success or failure is in the team executing the plan (typically the top thirty to fifty people). So, how do you get teams to succeed? How do you lead people?

It is important to understand that we are talking about leading and not managing people. You can use the authority invested in you by title, position, or seniority to get others to do things for you, but that is transactional in nature. You are managing them as an organizational asset to achieve an outcome. Your use of motivation is forced. Your relationship with them individually is transactional, and you are managing them, not leading them.

Effective, lasting organizations are built on trust, not just transactions. In transactional systems, people trade short-term value with each other quid pro quo, without thought and consideration for the long term. In trust-based systems, people invest in more than just the transaction; they want the collective team or organization to be successful, not just themselves. They build relationships based on mutual engagement, and they show up for each other, especially when it's hard. We want the mammoth *together*, and *we* believe in our hunting team, rather than being a manager-led group of individuals. In the hunting team, our relationships are peer-to-peer and based on shared vision, trust, and engagement created by a leader. In a managed team, the relationships are individual to the manager and dependent on transactional control and payment. Trust-based systems build equity that helps in crises. Transactional systems fail because of a lack of loyalty under duress.

**Trust-based systems build equity that helps in crises. Transactional systems fail because of a lack of loyalty under duress.**

This is why I align with the great Bill Campbell's business coaching philosophy—the *Trillion Dollar Coach* mindset. Leadership is relationship work. It's about ensuring that you and the team both *know why* we're doing this and that we *care why*. It's about shifting your mental model from "How do I solve this?" to "How do we solve this, and what motivates us to do it successfully?" Writing about Campbell's philosophy, former Google chairman and CEO Eric Schmidt says, "Bill didn't work the problem first, he worked the team. We didn't talk about the problem analytically at first. We talked about the people on the team and if and how they would get it done."[48] Bill learned this from coaching the football team at Columbia University and the executive teams at Intuit, Apple, and Google. The reality of leadership as relationship work is particularly evident in dynamic sports teams and creative teams such as orchestras or theater troupes.

Just as with killing the mammoth, as a leader you need to provide your teams with both a *know why* and a *care why.* A leader defines the problem itself, the logical issue or opportunity to be solved, the so-called *know why* that a team needs to understand and apply through individual and collective action. However, the leader also defines and

48 Eric Schmidt et al., *Trillion Dollar Coach: The Leadership Playbook of Silicon Valley's Bill Campbell* (HarperBusiness, 2019), 113.

explains the way the team relates to the problem and the solution, the so-called *care why* (What is the individual and collective motivation? What are the incentives and personal impact for the individuals and, collectively, the team to solve the problem and do something new?).

These concepts are critical foundations of leadership and execution and show the shift from I to we and from merely building a plan to leading other humans in successful action and adaptation. Collaboratively articulating and discussing *know why* and *care why* with your team creates clarity rather than confusion, a shared vision, and a sense of shared purpose. Together, these are the foundations of scalable engagement in the shared purpose and trust in you as a leader.

## LEADERSHIP VERSUS MANAGEMENT

It's important to recognize that leadership and management, though closely related, are two different disciplines. They are both necessary in scaling organizations or programs. Management is about running the machine—process, control, and efficiency—keeping it running smoothly. Leadership, on the other hand, is about designing the machine—vision, direction, and motivation—ensuring it is headed to the right destination.

As Warren Bennis, citing Peter Drucker, put it: "Management is doing things right; leadership is doing the right things."[49] And Stephen R. Covey has characterized the difference as, "Management is efficiency in climbing the ladder of success; leadership determines whether the ladder is leaning against the right wall."[50]

In this chapter, the focus is on leadership—defining the right vision and inspiring others to pursue it.

49 Warren Bennis and Burt Nanus, *Leaders: Strategies for Taking Charge* (Harper & Row, 1985), 21.

50 Stephen R. Covey, *The 7 Habits of Highly Effective People* (Free Press, 1989), 57.

Moving a team, and yourself as a leader, toward achieving the right goals and improving over time requires a simple set of elements:

- *Why*: a way of thinking about teams and relationships in terms of your success—this is my Leadership Lenses model
- *What*: frameworks for understanding how teams work and a set of levers to improve them over time
- *How*: a process to follow that maps your hitchhiking guide to forming and improving teams and your leadership

Instead of our previous steps as an individual trying to get what *you* want in your career, we will be following six steps to get what *we* want as a team.

## Six Steps for Team Navigation in Your First One Hundred Days

So, how do you understand what you want as a leader and translate that to your team? How do you actually apply your own clarity and motivations, which you have spent time and energy working on in the previous chapters, to the world around you: your team, your business, your mission? This takes a structured cycle of attention and action. Figure 28 provides a bird's-eye view of the six-step framework that will guide you in moving from I to we. This framework will be critical to your success as you go through your first one hundred days in joining a company at a new job or your transition to a new leadership role within a company. This crucial time introduces you to your new team and context and lets you establish yourself and your agenda.

Figure 28: Navigating Your Team: Lifecycle Phases

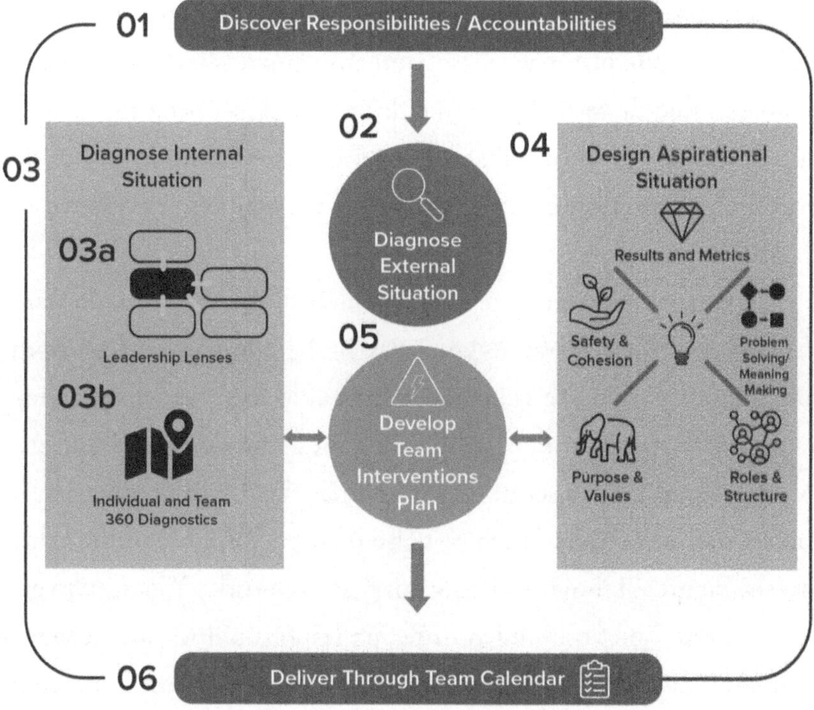


*This chapter introduces the highlights of these six phases of leading teams toward goals.*

*Source: Moo Pie Advisors Inc., 2025.*

## Step 1: Discover Responsibilities and Accountabilities

First, clarify exactly what you are responsible and accountable for as a leader. The way you're going to do this is to understand how your role links to the company's value creation, operating procedures, and leadership metrics. You'll identify the specific outcomes desired and the levers you can pull to achieve them whether you're an entrepreneur building from scratch or inheriting an existing situation.

Let's start with understanding the systemic context you are in. All businesses are just math. The company's financial outputs map to business value drivers, these value drivers map to operating metrics (typically some kind of KPIs), and those map to actions and initiatives that people (leaders) are responsible for (sometimes referred to as OKRs).

Your first question should be "Which bit of that equation am I responsible for?" How do you impact the company math? Both you and your team are generally responsible for a set of operating metrics and a set of leadership metrics. These should be laid out in a role description and a set of responsibilities that tie to the metrics. If you are a C-suite leader, then you also own one or more of the value drivers. Figure 29 shows you how this first step works. You need to get in "hard sync" on your and your team's responsibilities and accountabilities with your boss (supervisor), your immediate peers, and your team (both individually and collectively).

## Figure 29: Discover Responsibilities and Accountabilities: How Does Your Role Link to Company Value Creation, Operating Metrics, and Your Team's Performance?

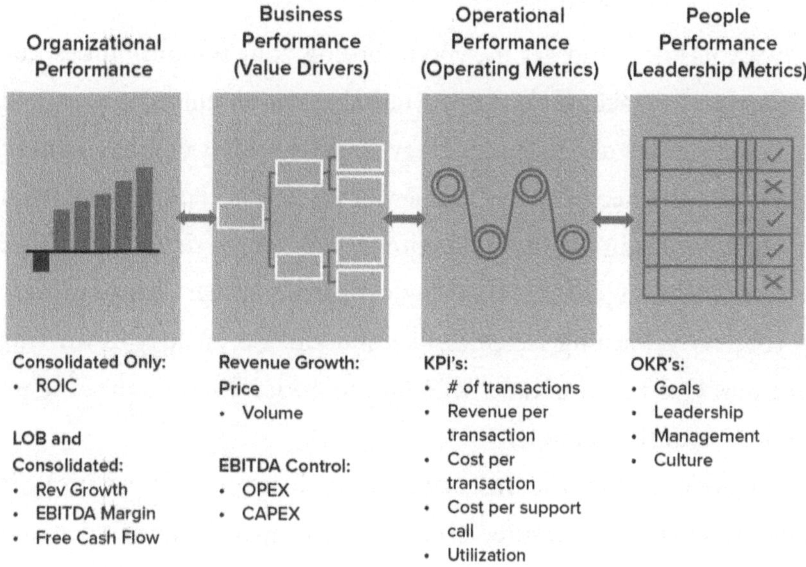


*As a team leader, you are responsible and accountable not only for your team's performance but for contributing to organizational performance and outcomes. Source: Moo Pie Advisors Inc., 2025.*

Mapping yourself and your team in the company value equation tells you which value drivers you need to address, tied to which KPIs. This in turn tells you which competencies you and your team are going to need to be successful, and in what systemic context. Based on understanding this, you can figure out how to be successful in the role. What are the critical roles on the team, and what are the critical relationships you have to focus on both in and surrounding the team? I cannot overemphasize the importance of this activity and of remaining in sync with your boss, peers, and team. This is the *know why* of your and your team's existence. It is your mammoth.

## Step 2: Diagnose the External Situation

Once you know and get in sync regarding your responsibilities, the next step is to take stock of the external environment, to understand the current "lay of the land." Every leader operates within a marketplace, and you need a clear-eyed view of where you stand in it. Are you winning or losing against competitors? How much time do you have before conditions change, and what risks are looming? This assessment is your early-warning system, much like the old analogy of the frog in a pot. Don't be the leader who fails to notice the water heating up to boiling until it's too late.

Understanding the urgency of your situation is also critical. Is this a moment for measured evolutionary change, or does it demand rapid revolutionary action? Your answer shapes not only what you do but also how you do it. A realistic, timely read on the external context equips you to decide which priorities to pursue, how to pace your efforts, and which resources or allies you'll need to bring to the table. In short, it sensitizes you to the realities outside your team's walls so you can lead with both focus and foresight.

## EXERCISE: ASSESSING TEAM RISK

Write down all the risks to your team being successful in achieving its desired outcome (customer, competition, political, economic, product, etc.). Now tag and organize them by impact (low, medium, high, extreme), by time horizon (now, six months, twelve months, eighteen months, etc.), and by likelihood (low, medium, and high).

- How does this affect your sense of purpose and urgency?
- How can you calibrate and sync this view with that of your boss, peers, and team?
- How can you discuss mitigations for these risks?
- What does this do to the resource requirements of your team—skills, resources, incentives, etc.?
- Is your mission possible as a leader, or are you signing up for a suicide mission?

## Step 3: Diagnose the Internal Situation

Once you've clarified your responsibilities (Step 1) and sized up the external landscape (Step 2), it's time to look inward at the reality inside your own organization. This is where you check whether your assumptions and plans match what's actually possible. You'll approach this diagnosis in two ways: first, by running your hypothesis through a set of leadership lenses that give you multiple perspectives on the same reality, and second, by confirming those perspectives with other internal and external voices who can reveal blind spots.

The goal is to make sure you understand the true state of play before committing to a course of action. It is vital you understand the "systemic view" of you and your team, and the system's commitment to your success (particularly that of your sponsors, your boss, and your peers). You also need to understand their view of your competency and starting situation.

## Use the Leadership Lenses to Diagnose

I developed the Leadership Lenses Framework after my experiences at Cisco, particularly in complex, dynamic environments driving teams such as Emerging Markets. I needed to diagnose what I was getting into. I have used it in every role over the last twenty years and now teach it to executives all over the world.

You'll take the roles, responsibilities, and external context you've already defined and test them through four important perspectives, or leadership lenses.

## Figure 30: Leadership Lenses for Diagnosing Your Internal Situation

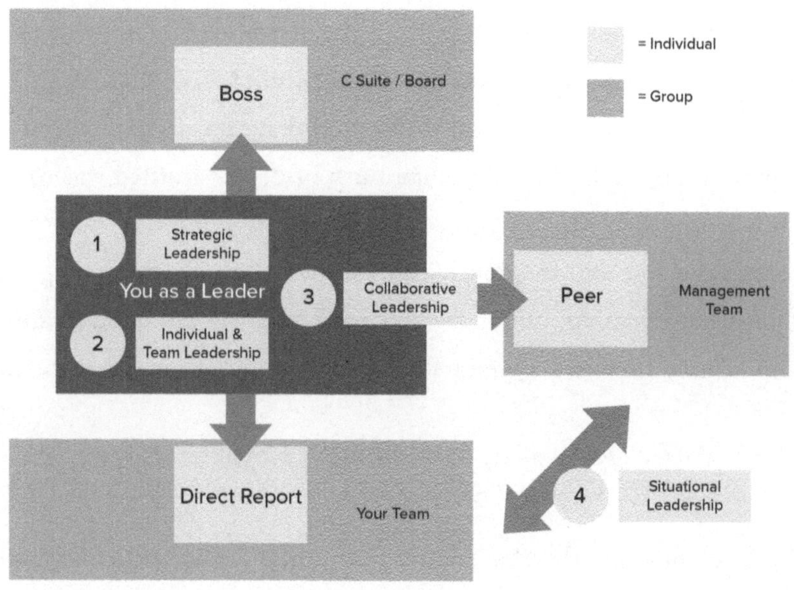


*As a team leader, use each of the four leadership lenses to manage relationships with bosses, peers, direct reports, and stakeholders unique to various situations. Source: Moo Pie Advisors Inc., 2025.*

### LENS: STRATEGIC LEADERSHIP—YOUR BOSS (OR EQUIVALENT)

Start with the person you ultimately answer to. That might be the CEO, a division head or other senior leader, the board chair, or investors. Get into hard sync with them on your accountabilities, the current external situation, your time frame, and your output metrics.

## LENS: COLLABORATIVE LEADERSHIP—YOUR PEERS

Next, check your alignment with peers across the organization. One of the most common leadership mistakes is assuming your peers understand and support what you've been tasked with. In reality, many will disagree with your priorities or simply be unaware of them, which can lead to conflicting agendas or just plain conflict.

Relationships are critical to long-term success in any corporate environment, so build rather than burn bridges. I learned this to my cost in my early years at Cisco. I believed in achieving victory no matter the cost and frequently rubbed my colleagues the wrong way. I got what I wanted, but at a high cost. Luckily, I had good mentors and learned how to succeed with people rather than without them.

## LENS: INDIVIDUAL AND TEAM LEADERSHIP—YOUR DIRECT REPORTS

Then, sit down with your team—both one-on-one and collectively. Confirm that they understand the mission, the constraints, and the urgency. Do they *know why* and *care why*? Are they incentivized to pursue the goal (financially, competency-wise, experientially, etc.)? What are their personal development and career goals, and how do they relate to the team and its success? Ask questions; be curious; be kind. Build relationships.

> **Trust and loyalty are built through a simple equation: Competency + Kindness + Integrity + Consistency × Number of Iterations (instances) = Engagement. Engagement over time creates trust.**

Understanding this formula and asking the right questions ensure the team is aligned, committed, and equipped, rather than assuming they're on board when they may not even agree with the objective. Think of your team as your body. They are your brain and arms and legs. They are your face to the world. Take care of them as you would yourself. Without them, you will fail.

## LENS: SITUATIONAL LEADERSHIP—OTHER KEY STAKEHOLDERS

In the final lens, you broaden the aperture to other influential voices: colleagues in other divisions, partners, customers, analysts, advisors, outside counsel, bankers—anyone whose cooperation or insight could make or break the plan. Here, you're asking practical feasibility questions: Is the opportunity real? Are the necessary resources or targets available and affordable? Can the initiative actually be executed? This step can save you from charging after a goal that turns out to be impossible.

I've experienced the importance of this fourth lens directly. I had the board of a company I worked for tell me to go do something that I subsequently found out was actually impossible. They had a set of assumptions about the availability and executability of a set of merger and acquisition transactions to fuel inorganic growth as part of a strategy that turned out to be not just untrue but impossible. I had some leadership miles behind me, so I went back and said to them, "We can't do this. The strategic growth plan that you've got that says we're going to be $X billion in three to five years is not achievable via acquisitions or mergers. There are no companies available and affordable." This led the company to decide to no longer stay public and to go private.

## From Conversations to More Formal Assessments

Once you've viewed your mission, role, stakeholders, and current situation through the Leadership Lenses Framework, the next action to take in Step 3 is to get an unvarnished view of both yourself as a leader and the team you've got. As a team or organizational leader, you constantly need to be thinking about how to improve personally, as a team, and relative to the system/company. This means gathering honest, often uncomfortable, feedback through 360s, structured interviews, and targeted assessments (for example, the Leadership Circle Profile, the Birkman Method, or the other tools listed in appendix E). Ask your boss, peers, and other executives about your leadership style, track record, and degrees of freedom. Find out what resources you truly have, what skills and mindsets your people bring, and whether they've succeeded at this type of challenge before.

This will help you understand and get clarity on what your priorities should be and what strengths or weaknesses you need to address. As an individual leader, in relation to the system you and your team are part of, you particularly want to understand:

- What are your strengths (competencies and behaviors)? What should you keep doing or do more of?
- What are your weaknesses? What should you do less of or stop doing?
- What should you start doing?
- What should you do differently?

This process is not just about collecting opinions but about establishing a measurable baseline. Alongside the external metrics you're working toward, you now add qualitative insight into your own strengths, gaps, and style, plus the team's current capacity.

I recommend and use two separate, proven frameworks developed by organizational psychologists John Hackman and Bruce Tuckman. These frameworks can help you map this terrain for your team and not just yourself. You will find more information about these frameworks in my forthcoming book and on my website, together with survey-driven diagnostics called You Are Here and the TCS Team Selfie Tool, which are free tools that Fred Walkover, Lynn Thorsell, Karie Brown, and I created. You can use these to collect data from your team and look at where it is against the Tuckman and Hackman frameworks.

## HACKMAN'S TEAM STRUCTURE MATRIX

Where does your team sit today? Are you simply a group of individuals, a leader-led team, a self-managing or self-designing team, or a self-governing one? What is your starting point as a leader in relation to the team? Knowing this helps you choose the right interventions to help the team progress and mature, such as team-building exercises, skills development, facilitation, team training, and so on.

Hackman's matrix, shown in figure 31, focuses on the distribution of authority and work. Who holds different types of authority and performs tasks: the team or you as the leader? Hackman's theory is that more mature and effective teams are distributed and collective decision-makers, rather than leader-driven.[51] My experience has led me to believe this is true, with the proviso that the self-designing or self-governing teams must be able to make both efficient (volume and speed) and effective decisions (successful outcomes). This is a crucial factor for you as a leader in the design of your team, as it

51 J. Richard Hackman, *Leading Teams: Setting the Stage for Great Performances* (Harvard Business School Press, 2002).

requires explicit agreements, behaviors, and competency from the team concerning accepting collective responsibility and adopting specific problem-solving practices.

Figure 31: Diagnose Internal Situation: Use Hackman Diagnostic to Understand Current Team Landscape of Responsibilities

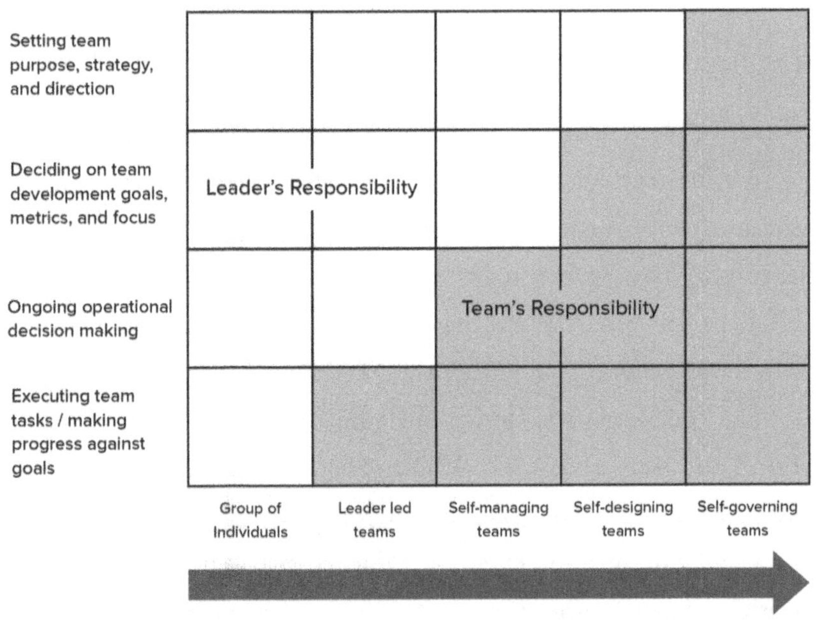


*Based on the work of Richard Hackman, this table illustrates the responsibilities of teams and leaders. Source: Moo Pie Advisors Inc., 2025.*

## TUCKMAN'S TEAM LIFECYCLE

Whether your team is greenfield (newly created) or brownfield (preexisting), your arrival as leader changes its dynamics. Bruce Tuckman developed a model to describe how teams form, develop, mature, and eventually dissolve. Expect your team to evolve through these natural stages as defined by Tuckman: *forming*, *storming*, *norming*, and *performing*.[52] Your role as a leader is to guide the team through these shifts, anticipating the tensions and needs at each phase. Navigating these stages requires both leadership and team interventions: team building, team training, use of facilitators, assessments, etc. Your team will need to become aware of its current state, develop a plan to evolve, and explore skills and mindsets in order to improve.

There is substantial literature surrounding Tuckman's model, which is beyond the scope of this chapter; suffice it to say that moving through the lifecycle is an active pursuit as a leader. In fact, it is the definition of leadership. How you lead teams in forming, storming, norming, and performing, as shown in figure 32, is, to a great extent, who you are as a leader and will determine your long-term success.

---

52 Denise Bonebright, "40 Years of Storming: A Historical Review of Tuckman's Model of Small Group Development," *Human Resource Development International* 13, no. 1 (2010): 111–20, https://doi.org/10.1080/13678861003589099.

Figure 32: Tuckman's Diagnostic for Understanding a Team's State

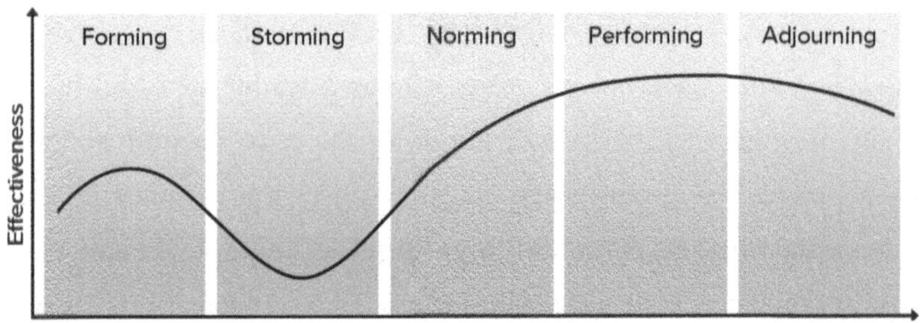


*Based on the work of Bruce Tuckman, this graphic provides an example of the trajectory of a team as they move through forming, storming, norming, and performing. Source: Moo Pie Advisors Inc., 2025.*

By placing your team on both the Hackman and Tuckman axes, you gain a clear "as-is" picture of capability and cohesion, as well as a road map for the developmental moves to make next.

Only when your internal picture matches your external understanding can you move forward with confidence into designing the aspirational future in Step 4.

## Step 4: Design an Aspirational Situation

Once you know where you are, the next move is to define what you want, but unlike defining *your own* Next, you are now making decisions together, as a team.

Figure 33: Five Levers for Team Effectiveness

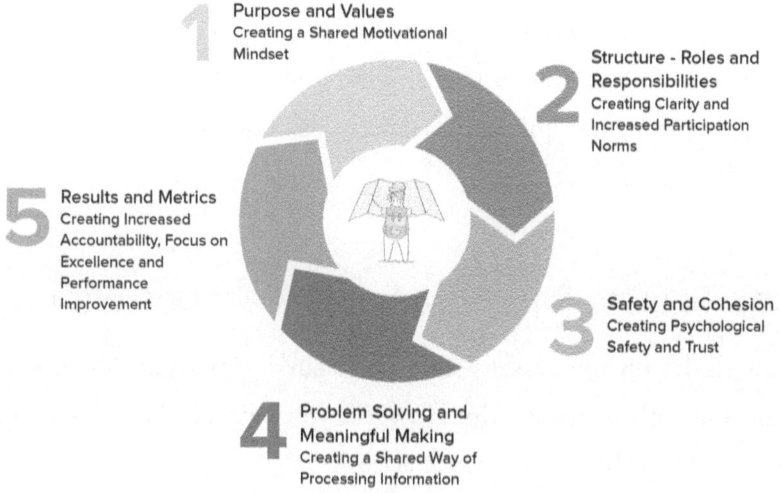


*Creating and sustaining effective and efficient teams requires a leader to ensure that these five levers are in place. Source: Moo Pie Advisors Inc., 2025.*

All teams require five levers to be in place for success, and all effective leaders need to ensure they are present:

1. Purpose and values
2. Structure, roles, and responsibilities
3. Safety and cohesion
4. Problem-solving and meaning making
5. Results and metrics

Without these five levers (shown in figure 33), any team is just a group of individuals. With these five levers, both operational and project-based teams can achieve their goals and develop and mature through Hackman's and Tuckman's models to become high performance.

As a leader, you will work these levers over and over again, bearing in mind both the *know what* and *care why* nature of the team as you go. The process for creating or utilizing the levers is the same. It requires you to organize and host conversations with each team member and with the team collectively.

## Step 5: Develop a Team Interventions Plan

With clarity on the current state and shared aspiration, it's time to build the path. Planning doesn't mean you have all the answers but that you know how to sequence action.

The three-horizon framework you used before for your own aspirations also helps here for the team:

**Horizon 1**: What do we need to do first? (immediate steps, early wins)

**Horizon 2**: What do we do next? (building capacity, evolving systems, examining adjacencies)

**Horizon 3**: What do we aim for in the long run? (vision, transformation)

Map where you want to be on both Tuckman's and Hackman's frameworks with your team across these three horizons. How far is that from your current starting point? Share this plan with them. They have to want to go on the journey and have to understand where they are and what they need to do. Does this make sense to them, and what are their inputs?

This is also where your bifocal vision comes back in: You lead for both what's urgent and what's important. You create feedback loops, priorities, roles, rituals. You prepare people not just for the sprint but for the journey. This is all encapsulated in a series of interventions that you suggest and host, which are designed to develop the team. Interventions fall into two categories: working on the team and working as a team. This is you working as a coach. Let me explain further.

## Working on the Team

How do you build a better container? You work on skills and mindset—essentially, being in training and development. Think of a tennis player working on fitness, drills, and service; examining recordings of opponents; and spending time discussing confidence with their coach, etc. Operating like this allows you to understand each other and to become aware of issues and opportunities and the behaviors, skills, and habits attached to them.

Once you are aware, you can make different decisions, and hopefully, better ones. Examples of ways to do this include:

- **Team building**: storytelling, check-ins, assessments, competitions, group work, etc.
- **Team training**: strategy, planning, problem-solving, decision-making, communications
- **Team discussions**: values, psychological safety, etc.
- **Social events**: team dinners, get-togethers, trips, or outings

## Working as a Team

How do you execute better as a team? This requires practicing the behaviors and habits you examined in the "working on the team" interventions. Think of this as a tennis player getting on the court in actual matches to implement and practice in real terms what they have been taught or decided to do differently. The purpose is to make theory real by practicing as a team the actual business of the team. Examples of ways to do this include all the types of collective meetings the team needs to execute its purpose:

- Blue Ocean brainstorming meetings
- Red Ocean diagnosis meetings
- Competitive or market briefings
- Planning or budgeting meetings
- Decision-making meetings
- Business, product, or customer review meetings
- Project status meetings

This is about using time and space (meetings) in a purposeful way and creating and practicing accountability: Who owns what? How are we tracking and measuring success? How are adjustments being made? Leaders in technology companies can spend upward of 70 percent of their time in meetings. Leading well means engineering this time and these meeting spaces to drive what matters most. That's the strategy that will build bridges from where you and your team are to where you want to go. You've done this for yourself in Steps 1 to 6 of *Navigating Your Next*, so you know you can do it. Now, you're just applying the same logic, but outward. You're creating the environment for your team to do their best thinking and best work.

Create a plan to close the gap between the current and aspirational states. This includes setting priorities, sequencing initiatives, and ensuring that interventions address both performance metrics and team culture. This leads you to Step 6 of the I to we cycle, in which you operationalize all this at the calendar level. A personal example of this approach is presented in figure 34 below. I took a team of fourteen regional sales directors from *forming* to *performing* over six months, using two three-hour interventional meetings per month and practicing as a team in weekly and monthly reviews.

## STRUCTURED VERSUS EMERGENT LEADERSHIP APPROACHES

Structured leadership relies on formal roles, routines, and authority to create clarity and coordination. Emergent leadership arises organically from team interactions, with individuals gaining influence through expertise, communication, and fit with the group's needs. In practice, high-performing organizations blend both: structure for reliability with emergence for agility and innovation. To learn more, I recommend reading *Mastering the Art of Team Coaching: A Comprehensive Guide to Unleashing the Power, Purpose and Potential in Any Team* by Georgina Woudstra.

# Figure 34: Developing a Team Interventions Plan

## Develop Team Interventions Plan

**Session 1: Kick-Off**
Work on the Team
- Check-in/'I'm in'
- Individual origin stories
- What does the company mean to you—values?
- Rules of engagement

Work as a team
- Team Purpose
- Team Structure
- Individual and team roles and responsibilities

**Session 2**
Work on the team
- Check-in
- One thing about me
- Proudest moment at company
- Epic personal failures

Work as a Team
- Team norms for safety and cohesion

**Session 3**
Work on the Team
Check-in
- What is my passion/purpose?
- An object of desire
- Personal communication styles

Work as a Team
- Team norms for safety and cohesion

**Session 4**
Work on the Team
- Check-in
- Decision making styles

Work as a Team
- Understanding, Alignment, Agreement/Action
- Problem solving process

**Session 5**
Work on the Team
- Check-In
- Conflicts and how I resolved them

Work as a Team
- Conflict Management—Kantor playing cards

**Session 6**
Work on the Team
- Check-in
- Best thing I learned this week

Work as a Team
- Making meaning—iterative learning
- How do we capture learning?

**Session 7**
Work on the Team
- Check-in
- Accountability—Moments of shame

Work as a Team
- How to measure what matters—metrics and what good looks like

**Session 8**
Work on the Team
- Check-in
- 'I have never ever...'

Work as a Team
- Decision making game—Resource Prioritization
- Decisions we avoid

**Session 9**
Work on the Team
- Check-in
- Things I avoid and why

Work as a Team
- What decisions do we never discuss - Elephants

**Session 10**
Work on the Team
- Check-in
- What do we do well as a team/what would we change?

Work as a Team
- If we had to only do three things to innovate, what would they be?

**Session 11**
Work on the Team
- Check-in
- Best company celebrations of success

Work as a Team
- Decision making rights—when is a decision a decision
- Systemic consequences

**Session 12**
Work on the Team
- Check-in
- What did we learn/what will we keep?

Work as a Team
- Team Building
- The Deming Method—Iterative improvement

*Here is an example of the flow of meetings and areas of focus when developing a Team Interventions Plan. Source: Moo Pie Advisors Inc., 2025.*

As you see in figure 34, there is a constant balance of working on the team and working as a team, allowing the team to work itself out and then practice the real-life decisions teams have to make.

## Step 6: Deliver Through a Team Calendar

In Step 3: Diagnose the Internal Situation, I suggested you understand and map the corporate calendar (the system that you are part of). As humans, we are all captives of time and space, but even though this is obvious, it is often forgotten. If the reality is that a plan accounts for 10 percent and people are 90 percent of achieving a goal, then as a leader, shouldn't you focus on understanding how those people share time and space (events, meetings, and forums)? How you will get things done is through controlling and influencing processes and events that occur over time—a calendar.

All companies have a calendar that dictates more than dates. It establishes a rhythm and cadence for the work, connecting your team's efforts to the larger system in which you operate. See figure 35 as an example. The calendar forces you to think in terms of time and space—two constants that shape every project and every organization. Are you moving too fast for the system to absorb change or too slowly to seize opportunities? Are you syncing with existing company processes or constantly playing catch-up?

So, once you've designed the interventions and your use of team modes based on your team's needs—who should be involved, which skills or capabilities they need to develop, and how you'll move them from one point in the matrix to another—the next step is to anchor all of this to the company calendar. If you want to influence an outcome or drive a decision, you can't simply show up at the moment of decision; you have to be ahead of the process. That means identifying the key decision points, aligning your team's work to those milestones, and designing interfaces with the people and groups whose support or approval you'll need.

As a personal example, if I wanted to influence my chief revenue officer's annual plan, I had to do work ahead of his annual sales planning process. I had to understand his inputs, his fact base, his influencers, and current hypotheses. Only by doing this could I organize my team to do the work to get him to think about alternative go-to-market models or introduce new customer account coverage designs.

Preparation is key to getting ahead of the game and allowing you to lead proactively. We will use the calendar in figure 35 and my experience as a chief strategy officer as an example. Here is the method I recommend you follow.

Figure 35: Delivering Through a Teams Calendar: Use the Calendar, Both Personal and Company, to Achieve Your Goals.

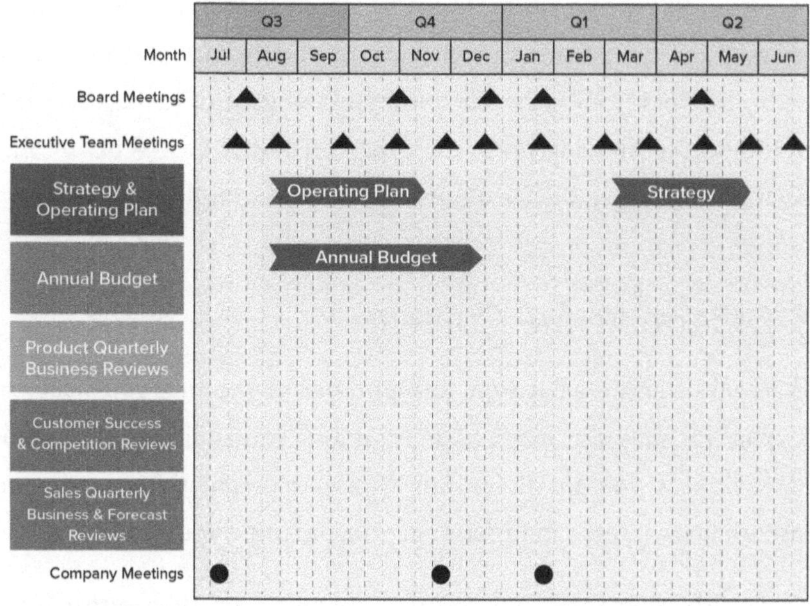


*Here's an example of how a team's calendar can connect to the broader organizational calendar. Source: Moo Pie Advisors Inc., 2025.*

## 1. Determine Your Attachment to Processes and Deliverables

This will calibrate you to the priority and sequencing of deliverables, influence, and decision-making. Based on your responsibilities and accountabilities, understand what needs to happen and when. Do you need to produce results, provide a review/report on status, or get a decision on investment, etc.?

## 2. Determine the Participants

This will calibrate you as to whom to influence and how. Remember, we used the Four Lenses Framework to understand your interfaces with your boss, your peers, etc. Now you can use this to map yourself to the people showing up in the processes and events. Who are the decision-makers and what inputs are required to influence them?

## 3. Determine the Context

This will calibrate what type and purpose of meeting you need to prepare for that will move your team and your objectives forward. Based on this, you can direct your team as to preparation, creation of input materials, etc., in order to get the outcome you need.

- **Meeting type**: one-to-ones, executive meetings, cross-functional reviews, leadership offsites, company all-hands, board meetings, etc.
- **Meeting purpose**: briefing, status or review, decision-making, planning, etc.

## 4. Determine Your Style

Based on points 1, 2, and 3, you can calibrate what type of leadership presence—your style—is required to be most effective given the participants, the purpose, and the stage of the process. We have covered the six leadership styles previously. What style is appropriate to influence the participants in the particular context?

This method is also how you establish and track clear measures of success and pair operational outcomes (quality, timeliness, efficiency) with leadership impact metrics (alignment, engagement, capability growth). Use the calendar to build in review points during which you celebrate wins, learn from setbacks, and adapt the plan to sustain progress.

This might appear burdensome and overly complicated to some of you and too rigid to others. However, one of the most frequent problems in high-tech firms, as they move out of startup mode into scaling the company, is that they are so used to running informally based on constantly changing priorities and the agenda of the founders that they struggle to adopt using the calendar, events, and forums in a more organized manner for discipline and a more regular cadence. Startups work informally because there are a small number of people who can flex easily, but this does not scale and allow for collaboration, communication, and learning. One of the primary rules of organization is that for every 20 percent of new resources you add (one in five people), you break the norms of that team and have to reset/restart Tuckman's process back to forming.

In short, this final step in navigating your team is about making sure great intentions and well-designed interventions don't get lost in the chaos of day-to-day demands. By embedding them in a disciplined, system-aware calendar, you give your team the structure, visibility, and momentum to deliver.

## The Leadership Choice

You either want to be a leader, or you don't. You have a choice. Leaders are not just custodians of operations; they are catalysts for transformation. Your role goes beyond managing tasks; you are being compensated to empower your team members and elevate their potential. By investing in their development, you not only enhance individual skills but also foster a culture of continuous growth and innovation. This is where you find true significance as a leader—creating meaningful change that resonates throughout your organization. Embrace your responsibility to uplift others and watch as your team flourishes.

If you do want to be a leader, then what we've covered in Step 7—and that I will lead you through in much more detail in my next book—is the price of admission. I view leadership as an honor and the most fun I have had in my career. This chapter has given you a preview of what it means to shift from individual growth to team leadership. If *Navigating Your Next* has helped you clarify and claim what you want, then I'll be honored to help you build the vehicle to get to your team's Next.

Let's continue our journey!

# CHAPTER WAYPOINTS

You can't achieve your goals alone. If you want to achieve more than personal goals, then the next stage of your development will be less about you and more about the relationships you build with your boss, peers, and team and how you show up as a leader.

Making things happen as a leader is 10 percent the plan and 90 percent the relationships.

There is a repeatable process to leading well: Gain awareness of current reality, define aspirations and desired outcomes, map a strategy, and then execute and adapt.

Leading means managing across multiple lenses: strategic, collaborative, team, and situational.

# CONCLUSION

You started this journey because you were curious about where you might go next in your professional life. Or maybe you were more than curious—perhaps you were committed to making a change but just weren't sure what that would look like or how to do it. As you've seen, the answer doesn't come all at once. It comes through a deliberate process that involves purposeful action and a determined mindset.

As I walked you through my *Navigating Your Next* process, I hope you gained clarity and confidence around two fundamental questions:

- What do I want?
- How will I get it?

To answer those questions, you've got to step out of confusion and into clarity. You have to see yourself clearly—your competencies, your contexts, your motivations, your values—and then make a decision. Not a perfect decision. An informed, mindful one. Then you act. And reflect. Then iterate. And iterate again.

Those who succeed are not the ones with the most credentials or the best resumes. They're the ones who take purposeful action. They own their calendar. They work their relationships. They focus. They know when to say no. They understand that career success isn't a onetime leap but a series of deliberate moves. And most of all, they take responsibility.

If there's one thing I hope you take away from this process, it's this: You are responsible, not just for your actions but for your trajectory. You define what a "good" job, "good" career, or "good" life looks like for you, and you take responsibility to make that happen. You control your progress toward that "good."

We've covered a lot, and you might be wondering, *So, where do I actually go from here?* Whether you're still working on Step 2 or have already popped the champagne to celebrate in Step 6, the answer is the same:

- Keep being the defining force of your life. The only thing worse than failing is succeeding at the wrong thing. Continually define what you want, not what others think you should want.
- Keep practicing purposeful action. Work the plan; do the reps.
- Remember that success isn't linear. Use feedback loops. Set up ways to know when you're off course and then course correct.
- Continue to build strong relationships. Nothing worth doing is done alone. Cultivate trust, in others and in yourself. Other people make your life and journey fun; let them in and enjoy them.
- Measure success now, not later. Understand both what good looks like and how you are getting better every day, week, month, etc.

- Enjoy the journey. It may zig and zag, but no matter what, it is doing it every day and enjoying it that will turn it from stress and strain to freedom and expression.

And one more thing: Celebrate. Don't wait for permission or aim for perfection. If you've reached a waypoint, mark it. Acknowledge your effort and share it with others. Meaning is not found in achievement alone; it's found in how we make sense of the path. Never miss an opportunity to celebrate!

I am a Stoic, so let me leave you with two quotes from Marcus Aurelius that have anchored me again and again, and I hope they will both anchor and inspire you.

> **"Our life is what our thoughts make it" and "Begin—to begin is half the work, yet half still remains; again begin this, and you will have finished."**
>
> **—Marcus Aurelius**

You've made it through this book. Now, keep moving forward. Whether your Next is around the corner or years away, you have the tools and the insight. You know what you want. You know what to do.

You've got this. Just do it.

# APPENDIX A

## Generalist Competency Examples

This appendix provides a sample list of generalist competencies to help you complete the Step 2 exercise "My Generalist Competencies." These are skills that are highly transferable across various roles and industries, and they tend to be especially useful for roles that require leadership, project management, communication, and teamwork. Use this appendix to reflect on which generalist competencies you already possess and which you may want to develop or emphasize in your career journey.

This list is not mutually exclusive or collectively exhaustive. The list here is intended as a springboard to spark further ideas. If you possess generalist competencies that are not included below, feel free to add those to your worksheet.

Adaptability
Active listening
Analytical reasoning
Change management
Collaboration and teamwork

Conflict resolution
Coordinating
Cross-functional collaboration
Critical thinking
Customer service
Data skills
Decision-making
Delegation
Emotional intelligence
Facilitation
Influence and persuasion
Interpersonal communication
Leading meetings
Mentoring and coaching
Negotiation
Organization and planning
People management
Presentation skills
Problem-solving
Project management
Resilience and stress tolerance
Reporting
Scheduling
Stakeholder management
Strategic thinking
Team leadership
Time management
Verbal communication
Written communication

# APPENDIX B

## Specialist Competency Examples

This appendix presents examples of specialist competencies to help you complete the Step 2 exercise "My Specialist Competencies." These are skills that are typically tied to specific fields, industries, or technical areas. They are developed through education, training, self-directed learning and practice, or on-the-job experience.

If your career field, functional area, or industry is not reflected here, or if the listings in each category do not cover all of your skills, simply use these as examples for ideas of your own specialized skills in your domain(s).

**Business leadership:** board reporting and governance, budget ownership and forecasting, business development strategy, capital allocation, competitive positioning, crisis management, culture shaping, executive decision-making, financial statement analysis, organizational design, P&L management, performance management systems, pricing and margin optimization, product life cycle oversight, strategic planning, team building and talent development, vision setting

**Consulting:** hypothesis-driven problem-solving, benchmarking and best practices synthesis, business model evaluation, change management planning, client relationship management, cost reduction and efficiency optimization, cross-functional team coordination, executive presentation development, market and competitor analysis, operational improvement analysis, root cause analysis, slide deck creation (e.g., PowerPoint storytelling), stakeholder interviewing and facilitation, strategic road map design, structured communication (MECE principle, pyramid principle), workshop design and delivery

**Education:** curriculum design, instructional strategy, classroom management, academic advising, student performance tracking, learning assessment, online education tools (e.g., Canvas, Moodle), educational technology implementation, policy development, faculty coordination

**Engineering:** CAD software operation, materials testing, mechanical system design, fluid dynamics modeling, product prototyping, regulatory certification (ISO, ANSI), process engineering, circuit board design, thermodynamics simulation, engineering cost estimation

**Finance:** financial modeling, equity analysis, investment strategy, risk assessment, portfolio management, budgeting and forecasting, internal auditing, mergers and acquisitions analysis, regulatory compliance, tax planning

**Healthcare:** clinical diagnostics, medical coding, patient care planning, EHR system navigation, healthcare analytics, clinical research protocols, telemedicine platform use, pharmaceutical sales, hospital operations, HIPAA compliance

**Law:** legal research, contract drafting, litigation strategy, compliance auditing, case law analysis, employment law, intellectual property management, regulatory filings, international law negotiation, corporate governance

**Marketing:** SEO strategy, email campaign automation, customer segmentation analysis, content development, social media analytics, brand positioning, product launch planning, marketing funnel optimization, CRM management, event coordination

**Nonprofit and public sector:** grant writing, stakeholder outreach, program evaluation, advocacy strategy, community organizing, policy analysis, donor stewardship, government reporting, nonprofit accounting, volunteer management, due diligence, prospect research, fundraising (face-to-face relationship building and mass communication fundraising), working with CRM databases

**Technology:** software development (Python, Java, JavaScript), cloud infrastructure (AWS, Azure), cybersecurity threat analysis, machine learning algorithms, data engineering, systems architecture, UI/UX design, agile project delivery, database management (SQL, NoSQL), DevOps and CI/CD pipelines

# APPENDIX C

## Values Examples

This appendix provides a sample list of values to help you complete the Step 2 exercise "Values and Culture." The values listed here are examples of what might be important to you. They are qualities, conditions, or organizational culture characteristics that you might prioritize—things that can help you feel aligned with a role, an employer, or a career field as a whole.

Some of these values are likely to focus on you (perhaps you strive for achievement, want autonomy in how you do your work, or prioritize job security). Others might be qualities you value in others as they interact with you or that you value in the organizational culture you're a part of, such as consistency, respect, or support.

This list is not exhaustive but is provided as a springboard to spark further ideas unique to you and what matters to you. Feel free to add values not listed here to your worksheet.

Achievement
Adventure
Altruism

Ambition
Authenticity
Autonomy
Challenge
Clarity
Collaboration
Compassion
Competence
Competitiveness
Connection
Consistency
Contribution
Craftsmanship
Creative expression
Curiosity
Dependability
Discipline
Diversity
Drive
Efficiency
Empathy
Empowerment
Equity
Excellence
Exploration
Fairness
Financial stability
Focus
Freedom
Fun

Growth
Harmony
Helping others
Honesty
Humility
Impact
Inclusion
Independence
Influence
Innovation
Integrity
Intellectual stimulation
Job security
Joy
Leadership
Learning
Legacy
Loyalty
Mastery
Mentorship
Mindfulness
Openness
Order
Ownership
Passion
Pragmatism
Precision
Prestige
Professionalism
Purpose

Recognition
Respect
Resilience
Responsibility
Risk-taking
Routine
Security
Service
Spirituality
Stability
Stimulation
Strategy
Structure
Support
Sustainability
Synergy
Teamwork
Tradition
Transparency
Trust
Variety
Wisdom
Work-life balance

# APPENDIX D

## Examples of Motivations

This appendix presents examples of motivations to help you complete the Step 2 exercise "My Motivations." These motivations are grouped into four types—intrinsic, extrinsic, creative, and reactive—and reflect the underlying drivers of decisions, goals, and behaviors. Understanding your motivations can help clarify what truly matters to you and how those priorities shape your career path and create a sense of purpose.

### INTRINSIC MOTIVATIONS

Mastery (pursuit of excellence)
Learning
Autonomy/freedom
Creativity
Curiosity (how things work)
Personal growth (sense of challenge)
Helping others
Intellectual stimulation/problem-solving
Aesthetic appreciation

Physical well-being
Spiritual fulfillment

## EXTRINSIC MOTIVATIONS

Progression—career advancement, status (job title)
Wealth
Awards—academic honors, certifications
Prestige—fame and reputation
Material rewards—comforts
Bonuses and incentives
Recognition/public approval/applause and attention
Power/influence
Social comparison

## CREATIVE MOTIVATIONS

Social impact
Family well-being
Family security
Family wealth
Environmental responsibility
Innovation
Legacy
Serving a cause
Creating change
Empowering others
Community betterment
Cultural contribution
Education and advocacy

## REACTIVE MOTIVATIONS

Fear of failure

Shame

Guilt

Peer pressure

Family expectations

Social norms

Avoidance of judgment

Compliance

Jealousy

Competition

Obligation

Sense of duty

Need for approval

Fear of missing out (FOMO)

Desire to fit in

Insecurity

# APPENDIX E

## Assessments

Below are assessments you might consider taking at any point in your journey, but particularly during Steps 2 or 3.

These tools are designed to measure dimensions of your profile, such as interests, values, personality, motivations, abilities, and decision-making style. The advantage of standardized instruments is that they often yield results more objective than your own reflections alone.

Some of these are entirely self-administered; others require a licensed professional (such as an executive coach or career counselor) to access. Most offer free or low-cost versions, though engaging an independent coach or counselor to curate, administer, and interpret assessments (which can cost hundreds or thousands of dollars) can be a worthwhile investment. Links and information on how to take each assessment are provided below.

I particularly recommend taking the Birkman and Leadership Circle assessments and doing so through a coach. Coaches can be found at the links provided under each of those listings below.

### BIG FIVE (FIVE-FACTOR MODEL)

Measures personality across five trait domains—openness, conscientiousness, extraversion, agreeableness, and neuroticism—and is widely considered to be scientifically robust. Truity offers a free preview and a paid full report at https://www.truity.com/test/big-five-personality-test?utm_source.

## Birkman Method

A personality and career assessment framework for insights about motivations, behaviors, and occupational preferences. Birkman assessments available for purchase directly by consumers include the following:

BirkmaND—a brief snapshot of your strengths and motivations

Birkman Basics Report—a concise overview of personality traits and work preferences

Career Typing—helps match your personality to potential career paths

For a more in-depth look into your personality and career direction, you can invest in a signature coaching package that includes personalized guidance from a Birkman-certified coach.

Access all options at https://direct.birkman.com/sales.

### CLIFTON STRENGTHSFINDER (GALLUP STRENGTHS)

Assesses thirty-four talent themes or strengths and identifies where you naturally excel. Access at https://www.gallup.com/cliftonstrengths/en/252137/home.aspx.

## DISC

Profiles behavioral style and communication preferences. Often used in business and leadership contexts, but you can purchase it on your own at https://www.thediscpersonalitytest.com/?view=Assessments_disc&gad.

## HOGAN ASSESSMENTS

Measures personality, leadership potential, values, and risks, with a focus on workplace behavior. Typically administered by a certified practitioner. Learn more at https://www.hoganassessments.com/.

## THE LEADERSHIP CIRCLE PROFILE

A comprehensive and highly research-backed 360-degree leadership assessment that provides a comparison of leadership competencies with internal assumptions and behaviors. Designed for leaders seeking deep insight into how their inner world drives their outer effectiveness.

Available at https://leadershipcircle.com/en/products/leadership-circle-profile/.

## MYERS–BRIGGS TYPE INDICATOR

Assesses personality preferences across four dichotomies to assign one of sixteen types. Although the Myers–Briggs Type Indicator's scientific validation is widely disputed, it remains a popular tool for sparking self-reflection and conversations about personality differences. Often administered with interpretive feedback by a certified provider, but you can pay for a self-administered version at https://www.mbtionline.com/en-US/Products/For-you.

## O*NET INTEREST PROFILER (US DEPARTMENT OF LABOR)

Free, self-directed tools that assess your work-related interests and suggest occupations that align. Access them at https://www.mynextmove.org/explore/ip.

## PRINCIPLES YOU

A personality assessment grounded in the Five-Factor Model (Big Five) for self-awareness, career discovery, and team development. A detailed report includes twenty-eight archetypes across domains, including cognitive orientation, values, and interpersonal style. Available at https://principlesyou.com/.

## YOUSCIENCE APTITUDE & CAREER DISCOVERY

Uses timed brain-game exercises to uncover aptitudes and align them with career matches. Also includes a personality and interest assessment. Find the DIY version at https://www.youscience.com/buy-now/.

# APPENDIX F

## Recommended Resources

> **"Those who can reach the pinnacle in business, writing, acting, or other pursuits of achievement are all because they can steadily and persistently pursue a plan of self-development and growth."**
>
> **—John D. Rockefeller**

If you'd like to go deeper on some of the concepts, strategies, and frameworks shared in this book—or if you're looking for more tools and exercises to help you along your journey—these books, thinkers, and online resources can help. The resources are arranged in categories that follow an order mirroring the steps you'll go through on the way to finding and reaching your Next.

At the end, you'll also find a QR code for additional free tools and worksheets on my own Moo Pie Advisors site.

## Understanding Yourself and Your Career Options

*Designing Your Life* by Bill Burnett and Dave Evans
Uses design thinking to explore and test different life and career paths through experiments.

*Designing Your Work Life* by Bill Burnett and Dave Evans
A follow-up to *Designing Your Life*, this book focuses on how to make your current job more enjoyable and meaningful or how to identify better career options through design thinking principles.

*Drive: The Surprising Truth About What Motivates Us* by Daniel H. Pink
Explains intrinsic versus extrinsic motivation and how to apply the concepts in work and life.

*Ikigai: The Japanese Secret to a Long and Happy Life* by Héctor García and Francesc Miralles
A beautiful introduction to the concept of ikigai, which is central to this book's approach.

*What Color Is Your Parachute? Your Guide to a Lifetime of Meaningful Work and Career Success* by Richard Bolles
The classic guide to discovering your strengths, values, and interests and for exploring your best-fit career options.

*What Color Is Your Parachute? For College: Pave Your Path from Major to Meaningful Work* by Katharine Brooks
A spin-off of the seminal Bolles book, this one focuses on students and recent grads carving out their careers and seeking entry-level jobs.

### OTHER RESOURCES

*Barbara Sher's Idea Party Method*
Great for brainstorming life and career directions with others.
https://barbarasclub.com

Justin Wright's *Brilliance Brief*
Source of the cognitive bias framework shown in Step 2 for emerging leaders, growth-minded professionals, and anyone ready to lead with clarity and purpose and to achieve real-world results.
https://brilliancebrief.com

## Decision-Making

*Decision Making Under Deep Uncertainty: From Theory to Practice* by Vincent A. W. J. Marchau, Warren E. Walker, Pieter J. T. M. Bloemen, and Steven W. Popper
Explores methods and tools for making sound policy and strategy choices when the future is unpredictable and data are incomplete.

*The Four Tendencies* by Gretchen Rubin
Helps you understand how you respond to expectations and make decisions—a great resource for aligning goals with behavior.

*How We Decide* by Jonah Lehrer
Blends neuroscience and storytelling to explain how the brain makes decisions and how we can make better ones.

*Nudge: The Final Edition* by Richard H. Thaler and Cass R. Sunstein
Explains how subtle changes in choice architecture can steer better decisions in health, finance, and everyday life without restricting freedom.

*Thinking in Bets: Making Smarter Decisions When You Don't Have All the Facts* by Annie Duke
Written by a former professional poker player, this book shows how to embrace uncertainty and improve decision-making by thinking probabilistically.

## LinkedIn

*LinkedIn Unlocked: Unlock the Mystery of LinkedIn to Drive More Sales Through Social Selling* by Melonie Dodaro
For understanding how to present yourself online and make professional connections.

*Cracking the LinkedIn Code* by Dylan Boyd
Tactical advice on using LinkedIn for visibility, connections, and leads.

## Networking and Relationship Building

### BOOKS

*Give and Take* by Adam Grant
Explores how our interactions with others shape our success.

*The Doors You Can Open: A New Way to Network, Build Trust, and Use Your Influence to Create a More Inclusive Workplace* by Rosalind Chow
Introduces the power of sponsorship (beyond mentorship) as a more equitable and authentic approach to networking and accelerating career advancement.

*Your Invisible Network: How to Create, Maintain, and Leverage the Relationships That Will Transform Your Career* by Michael Urtuzuástegui Melcher

A practical guide to creating authentic connections for career transitions and personal evolution.

## Success Habits/Time Management

### BOOKS

*Atomic Habits* by James Clea
Practical, science-backed strategies for building good habits and breaking unhelpful ones.

*Four Thousand Weeks: Time Management for Mortals* by Oliver Burkeman
Challenges conventional productivity advice by reframing our limited time on earth—roughly four thousand weeks—as an opportunity to focus on what truly matters.

*Outliers* by Malcolm Gladwell
Popularized the ten thousand hours concept of mastery and how success is often built over time and under specific conditions.

*The Power of Your Subconscious Mind* by Joseph Murphy
Explores how belief and mental imagery can influence health, success, and personal transformation through the subconscious mind.

*The 7 Habits of Highly Effective People: 30th Anniversary Edition* by Stephen R. Covey
A classic guide to personal and professional effectiveness, this enduring bestseller outlines timeless habits for success and fulfillment.

## Job Search

*Job Moves: 9 Steps for Making Progress in Your Career* by Ethan Bernstein, Michael B. Horn, and Bob Moesta
Encourages you to think of each job as a platform for progress. Learn to interview the job instead of just being interviewed.

*3-D Negotiation: Powerful Tools to Change the Game in Your Most Important Deals* by David Lax and James Sebenius
Harvard experts introduce a strategic approach that goes beyond tactics, emphasizing setup and deal design, especially useful for complex job offers and career moves.

*Never Split the Difference: Negotiating as if Your Life Depended on It* by Chris Voss
A former FBI negotiator shares powerful empathy and communication techniques that work exceptionally well in job interviews and for negotiations.

*Knock 'em Dead Job Interview: How to Turn Job Interviews into Job Offers* by Martin Yate
A perennial Amazon bestseller, packed with advice to turn interviews into job offers.

*Interviewology: The New Science of Interviewing* by Anna Papalia
Based on data-driven research, this book categorizes interview styles and teaches how to adapt your approach effectively.

*Getting More* by Stuart Diamond
A *New York Times* bestseller used to train Google employees, focusing on perceptions, emotional intelligence, and value-based negotiation.

*You Can Negotiate Anything* by Herb Cohen

A longtime bestseller combining storytelling and actionable tactics for everyday negotiation.

### OTHER RESOURCES

Job search specialist Greg Langstaff's website. A practical, user-friendly source of advice, templates, and examples for resumes, cover letters, and LinkedIn profiles. Greg's content is clear, updated regularly, and tailored to real-world job search challenges. https://greglangstaff.com

## Leadership

*The First 90 Days: Proven Strategies for Getting Up to Speed Faster and Smarter* by Michael D. Watkins
A go-to guide for leaders in new roles, this book offers practical frameworks for building momentum and credibility in the critical early months of any transition.

*Leaders Eat Last* by Simon Sinek
Explores leadership from the perspective of building trust and motivation within teams and organizations.

*The Practice of Management* by Peter F. Drucker
A classic in the field (first published in 1954!), this groundbreaking work laid the foundation for modern management thinking. Drucker's principles for effective leadership and organizational focus continue to influence business leaders decades later.

*Principles* by Ray Dalio
Shares the renowned investor's life and work principles, offering a framework for decision-making, leadership, and building strong organizations.

## Critical Thinking

*The Art of Thinking Clearly* by Rolf Dobelli
A guide to common cognitive biases and logical fallacies that distort our judgment, with strategies to make clearer decisions.

*Lateral Thinking* by Edward de Bono
Provides practical techniques for breaking out of habitual thought patterns to spark creativity and generate innovative solutions.

*Thinking, Fast and Slow* by Daniel Kahneman
A Nobel Prize–winning psychologist explains the two systems that drive how we think—fast, intuitive responses and slow, deliberate reasoning—and how to use them more effectively.

*The Innovative Team: Unleashing Creative Potential for Breakthrough Results* by Chris Grivas and Gerard Puccio
Introduces a framework for understanding team members' creative problem-solving styles and how to harness them for innovation.

*Think Smarter: Critical Thinking to Improve Problem-Solving and Decision-Making Skills* by Michael Kallet
A practical guide with step-by-step tools to strengthen reasoning, clarify issues, and make sound decisions in business and life.

*Critical Thinking: Your Guide to Effective Argument, Successful Analysis and Independent Study* by Tom Chatfield
Offers accessible techniques for analyzing information, building arguments, and approaching problems with clarity and independence.

*Critical Thinking for Managers: Structured Decision-Making and Persuasion in Business* by Radu Atanasiu

Presents a manager-focused approach to dissecting problems, evaluating options, and influencing others through logic and evidence.

*Cracked It! How to Solve Big Problems and Sell Solutions Like Top Strategy Consultants* by Bernard Garrette, Corey Phelps, and Olivier Sibony
Breaks down a proven four-step method for structuring problems, generating solutions, and persuading stakeholders to act.

## Measuring and Celebrating Success

*How Will You Measure Your Life?* by Clayton Christensen, James Allworth, and Karen Dillon
A foundational text on using values, relationships, and purpose to define success.

*The Power of Regret: How Looking Backward Moves Us Forward* by Daniel H. Pink
Categorizes and explores the most common types of regret and how to use regret productively.

## Moo Pie Advisors

*Moo Pie Advisors*
Our site offers free resources and masterclasses designed to help you keep progressing toward what you really want.
https://www.moopie.com

# ABOUT THE AUTHOR

Julian Lighton is regarded as a leading expert on business decision-making, team building, and scaling companies. He has been a management consultant, an operational executive at Fortune 50 companies, a functional C-suite leader, a board director, and a business coach.

For thirty years, Julian has lived firsthand the pressures and possibilities that come with executive responsibilities. He leverages this experience by systematically turning confusion into pragmatic, practical insights and actions that drive better outcomes. His career experience includes being a chief strategy officer at four billion-dollar-revenue publicly listed technology companies; a general manager of Gamer Sensei, the world's largest esports coaching platform; an associate partner at McKinsey & Company; a business unit leader at Cambridge Technology Partners; and a senior global sales and marketing executive at Cisco and Hitachi Ltd. He has taken companies public and private and has led over thirty mergers and acquisitions.

Since 2014, Julian has worked independently through his firm Moo Pie Advisors, providing executive coaching and strategic consulting to boards, leaders, teams, and organizations.

Julian holds a BA and MA/BCL in law from Oxford University and a master diploma in negotiation from the Kennedy School of Government at Harvard University.

A graduate of the Hudson Institute of Coaching, Julian is one of only four hundred individual and team leadership coaches worldwide who holds PCC and ACTC certifications by the International Coaching Federation and is EIA senior practitioner– and ITCA senior practitioner–certified by the European Mentoring and Coaching Council. He was elected to the Forbes Coaches Council in 2023.He is a chartered company director by the Royal Institute of Directors in the UK. He is a fellow of the Royal Society of the Arts (FRSA).

He lives in Silicon Valley with his wife, daughter, and four very large, hairy dogs.